"*Everything about this biography is a delight.... Isak Dinesen has had the rare posthumous luck to have found the perfect biographer.*"

—*Ann Fremantle*, Boston Herald-Traveler

"*A magnificent book, well worthy of its aristocratic subject.*"

—*Joyce Carol Oates*, Detroit News

"*Perceptive and elegant.... An absorbing account of the places, people, and atmosphere around an exotic personality.*"

—Publishers Weekly

"*A truly extraordinary biography.*"

—*Cleveland Amory*, Cosmopolitan

"*Parmenia Migel has written a remarkably sensitive book that brings her subject to life and, while not shunning her small failings, never for one moment loses sight of her magic. Miss Migel has told Tania's own story as she would have wished it told, with accuracy and care, with wit and style.*"

—*William Jay Smith*, New York Times Book Review

"*Parmenia Migel achieves a rare feat: her writing and artistry approach that of her subject.*"

—Newsweek

"*The literary world has reason to be profoundly grateful to Parmenia Migel for this beautifully written account of a major literary phenomenon of this century.*"

—Virginia Quarterly Review

D1509982

Tania

A biography and memoir
of Isak Dinesen
by Parmenia Migel

—〜〜〜—

First published as Titania

McGRAW-HILL BOOK COMPANY

New York   St. Louis   San Francisco   Toronto
Hamburg   Mexico

1 2 3 4 5 6 7 8 9 S E M S E M 8 7

ISBN 0-07-041909-4

LIBRARY OF CONGRESS CATALOGING-IN-PUBLICATION DATA

Migel, Parmenia.
    Tania : the biography of Isak Dinesen.
    Rev. ed. of: Titania. 1967.
    Bibliography: p.
    Includes index.
        1. Dinesen, Isak, 1885–1962—Biography. 2. Authors,
Danish—20th century—Biography. I. Migel, Parmenia.
Titania. II. Title.
PT8175.B545Z76 1987   839.8'1372 [B]   87-1682
ISBN 0-07-041909-4

Originally published in New York by Random House, Inc. and in Toronto, Canada, by Random House of Canada Limited.

BOOK DESIGN BY BETTY ANDERSON

Acknowledgments

Permission to quote from the following work is gratefully acknowledged by the author:

Alfred A. Knopf, New York, for *African Hunter*, Copyright 1938, by
   Bror von Blixen-Finecke
Payson and Clark, New York, for *O City, Cities!*, Copyright 1929 by
   R. Ellsworth Larsson
Random House, Inc., New York, for *Gayety of Vision*, Copyright ©
   1964 by Robert Langbaum
University of Washington Press, Seattle, for *The World of Isak
   Dinesen*, Copyright © 1961, by Eric O. Johannesson
Harper's Magazine for "Isak Dinesen Conquers Rome" by Eugene
   Walter, Copyright © 1965 by Eugene Walter
Vogue Magazine for "Tale of Rungstedlund," Copyright © 1962 by
   Vogue Magazine
Alfred A. Knopf, New York, for *Freud, Goethe, Wagner*, Copyright
   1937 by Thomas Mann
Random House, Inc., New York, for *Isak Dinesen: A Memorial*, Copy-
   right © 1965 by Random House, Inc.
Random House, Inc., New York, for *Seven Gothic Tales* by Isak
   Dinesen, Copyright, 1934 by Harrison Smith and Robert Haas,
   Inc. Copyright renewed, 1961, by Isak Dinesen
Random House, Inc., for *Out of Africa* by Isak Dinesen, Copyright
   1937, 1952 by Random House, Inc.
Random House, Inc., for *Last Tales* by Isak Dinesen, © Copyright,
   1957 by Random House, Inc. Copyright, 1955, 1957, by The
   Curtis Publishing Company. © Copyright, 1957, by Atlantic
   Monthly, Inc.
Random House, Inc.. for *Shadows on the Grass* © 1960 by Isak Dinesen
The Paris Review for "The Art of Fiction XIV, An Interview with
   Isak Dinesen," Copyright © 1956 by Eugene Walter.

For Clara

For Arne and Niki

with gratitude

Preface, 1987

It is just twenty years since this, the first biography of Isak Dinesen, appeared and was enthusiastically received by the critics and reading public. During that interval a great store of new material has been explored and exploited in books, articles and films, much of it inaccurate or even deliberately falsified, some of it, alas, by writers who were vengeful or self-seeking.

In 1950 in Paris, when I took Tania to meet Pavel Tchelitchew, she asked me to write her biography. I demurred, but on seeing her pained surprise when Tchelitchew refused to paint her portrait for Denmark's Hall of Fame, I acquiesced. "You must do it," she insisted, "especially as we must make sure that it will not be undertaken by any Dane." Though Tania was by then an admired celebrity at home as well as abroad, she still harbored bitter resentment of what she felt was the ungenerous and unfair early reception of her books in her own country.

Nevertheless, she had sudden misgivings about not being immortalized by her compatriots and eventually encouraged too many of them to write about her, among them Viggo Kjaer Petersen, Aage Henriksen and even Thorkild Bjørnvig, who had fled her dominating influence. Finally she came to a decision and we then embarked on our many years of visits and interviews.

When Thorkild Bjørnvig's *Pacten* (Gyldendal, 1974; *The Pact*, Louisiana State University Press, 1983) and Aage Henriksen's essays appeared several years after Tania died, her friends and admirers were indignant. No doubt, Tania too would have been saddened and shocked by the one-sided and often sordid aspect they emphasized, and I myself was glad that Bjørnvig had hoarded the details for his own use and refused to be interviewed.

Tania mistrusted Freudian probing. "There are," she said, "in the nature and being of people many things, perhaps the most significant among them, that demand darkness and that need to go unobserved in order to grow soundly." This biography, therefore, besides an accurate account of her life and work, aimed to present a portrait of a Romantic and magical personality, not at all of the twentieth century. Rather than an effort at dissection, it opted for a more lyrical interpretation in keeping with Tania's spirit and intent. After all, should one attempt to perform Chopin in the style of Stravinsky?

Contents

Illustrations

Part I

Part II

following page 138

Part III

following page 170

Grateful acknowledgment is made to the Rungstedlund Foundation
for the use of early photographs of Isak Dinesen.

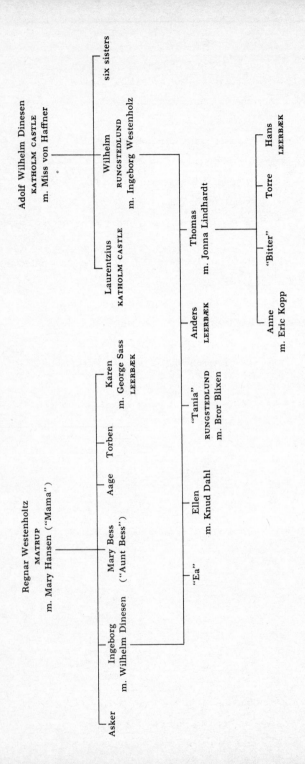

Maternal and Paternal family of "Tania," Baroness Karen Blixen
Isak Dinesen

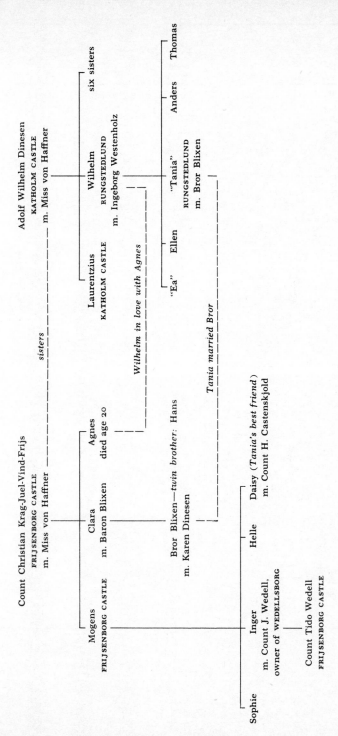

Relationship of families of Count Frijs and the Dinesens

Part One

Rungstedlund

I

Wilhelm

—◦◦◦◦—

For nearly four hundred years Rungstedlund has been standing by
the roadside, a halfway landmark for travelers faring along the
Sound between Copenhagen and Elsinore. No one knows who
lived there first. Its beginnings have vanished, as has the wilder-
ness which once stretched to its threshold—the moors and mist-
ridden fells, the sombre forest where wolves and boars prowled,
and the ghost of Grendel roamed.

In the sixteenth century, however, the house emerged from
legend to fact. The Strandvej was still only a rough, rutted track, in
winter blown too clear of snow for sleighs to pass and at other
seasons submerged in places by the sea. But Rungstedlund had
become a busy inn. The original simple structure had reached out
until it embraced the four sides of a large courtyard across from
the highway and the beach; the woods in back had been partly
cleared and the fen drained to make a pond for ducks. Many
people now stopped here for the night to break their cold, windy
journey—horsemen in plumed hats and capes, merchants muffled

in furs, sea captains, and even the hardy peasants who trudged across the ice floes from Sweden. And here the springtime wayfarer loitered to savor the sea breeze and profusion of wildflowers, to watch the first sailboats put out into the blue water, or to raise wondering eyes to the great northward migrations of geese.

Here, too, in the summer of 1773 came Johannes Ewald. Although he was only thirty, he was weary of a life of soldiering and adventures—dissipation had wrecked his health, a riding accident had crippled him, and he was embittered by the neglect of his family. At Rungstedlund the poet found a brief solace. Travelers provided the good talk he craved at times; the owner, Jacobsen, was a kind man whose daughter Anna Hedewig took care of Ewald with such concern and affection that he fell in love with her.

> *Fair one, in thy guileless breast*
> *Pure bliss suits best.*
> *Close thine ear to my lament,*
> *Turn thine eyes from woes unkenned.*
> *Thou whose never darkened eye*
> *Mirrors virtues Heaven clear,*
> *None but joyous tunes shall fly*
> *To nestle in thine ear.*

When he wanted to write he sat by his window, matching his moods to the changing ones of the sea, his rhythms to those of the soaring and swerving sea gulls. Or sometimes, limping painfully, he made his way behind the house and up to the wooded hilltop (today known as Ewald's Hill) and there composed one of his most beautiful poems, "Rungsteds Lyksaligheder" (Rungsted's Delights).

A century later Wilhelm Dinesen came to Rungstedlund, also

hoping to find peace of mind. Like Ewald he had spent most of his youth as a soldier and adventurer, and in a minor way he too aspired to become a man of letters. At eighteen he had distinguished himself at the Battle of Dybbøl in the Dano-Prussian War of 1864, and at twenty-five he fought in the Franco-Prussian War of 1870 as captain of infantry with the 18th Army Corps under General Billot. Having come unscathed through Esprels, Villersexel, Villargent and other engagements, he was finally captured and interned in Switzerland, but he escaped and joined a new regiment. At the end of the war he made his way to Paris. The Germans had already paraded down the Champs-Elysées and occupied the city, and at Versailles the King of Prussia had been proclaimed Emperor of all the Germanies. For the citizens who had endured months of bombardment, siege and famine, for the men who had fought the war, it was a terrible moment; but worse was yet to come. With the victorious, gloating Germans looking on, Frenchmen began to massacre their own countrymen.

Wilhelm had arrived in Paris on March 17, 1871—the day before the Commune. Observing the frenzied and senseless bloodshed, he felt his ideals, his very reason, tottering. Why had he fought, why had any of them fought, if it was all to end in chaos like this? To relieve his emotions he started to write a book describing the events he had witnessed. Then he received news that broke his heart. A young Danish girl with whom he was deeply in love had died suddenly while traveling with her family in Italy.

Wilhelm went home to Denmark at summer's end. The coveted Cross of the Legion of Honor was in his pocket, but it now seemed a dry-as-dust award. He had fought for nothing; he had nothing to look forward to. For a year he made a vague effort to find some purpose in living. Then he gave up altogether and escaped to the United States.

As soon as he set foot on American soil he started west. Stopping only briefly in Chicago, he continued as far as Columbus, Nebraska, where he worked at various jobs until he had set aside enough money to feel independent. Next he roamed the prairies for some months with the Pawnee Indians. Eventually he reached Wisconsin, where he met a congenial American doctor with whom he went hunting and sturgeon fishing. But Wilhelm was restless and also curious to know the Indians who had remained untouched by white civilization. So he set off alone again, this time journeying north up the Wolf River into Oconto County. On the riverbank, at the edge of the virgin forest, he came upon a hermit named Johnson, living in a rough two-room shack built of hewn firwood. He persuaded the man to sell his house, and there Wilhelm himself became a hermit. During two long years he saw no human being other than the Chippeway Indians, who appeared each spring and then migrated south in October.

Compared with huge, historic Katholm Castle, where Wilhelm grew up, the cabin was an oddly primitive place to live. He made no attempt to enlarge or improve it, though he did give it a new name. In remembrance of his beloved, he called the place Frydenlund, after one of the estates of her family. His grief over her death had not abated and his sleep was still troubled by recurring images of the Paris Commune. He would waken in a sickening sweat of fear and horror, and rush out into the night, and walk and walk in the forest until the morning light calmed and reassured him. But gradually the tranquil cycle of changing seasons, the serene beauty of the remote wild country, the example of the artless, contented Indians, all worked a cure. One day he suddenly felt ready to resume his life in Denmark.

At home Wilhelm was faced with the problem of finding a house of his own. When Kragerup, on western Sjælland, which had belonged to his grandfather Jens Kraft Dinesen went to the eldest son, Wilhelm's father had purchased Katholm, in Jutland, but this great castle would in turn pass to Wilhelm's older brother, Laurentzius. Rungstedlund, by Dinesen standards, was small and modest, but it had much to recommend it. Age had given a gentle harmony to the irregular roof line sheltering the accumulation of rooms on different levels. It was so near the sea that a boy might toss a pebble into the courtyard from the beach. It had farmland and woods, and the rough highway was so improved that the city was now no more than an hour away by carriage. Certainly it was an added attraction to know that Ewald had lived there, for the poet, having suffered the traditional indifference and lack of comprehension during his lifetime, had become a national idol. Finally, it was a good investment. A railway was certain to be built along the coast of the Øresund, and the land would then increase in value. At all events, Rungstedlund was for sale; Wilhelm Dinesen acquired it in 1879, and one of his sisters bought the adjoining property of Rungstedgaard.

Two years later, in May, he brought his wife there. Wilhelm had met Ingeborg Westenholz during a weekend party at Matrup, the picturesque old country estate of her family. At first sight she had not impressed him. She was eleven years younger than he and not a great beauty, but his interest was aroused when he began to talk with her. Ingeborg had been brought up in the ambiance of the intellectual bourgeoisie and had very advanced notions for the times. She seemed eagerly receptive to new ideas in politics, literature and religion, and in spite of the almost legendary riches of her grandfather, she struck Wilhelm as simple and unspoiled, almost overly conscientious. Wilhelm, who had sympathized with the Communards and had leftist leanings, who despised the narrow thinking of the aristocracy, was charmed by the serious girl. All this, he thought, was the basis for a sound marriage and a sure, safe haven for his wanderlust and sadness. The romantic atmosphere of Matrup did the rest. Like many another confused young man, he had been betrayed into believing that a woman's virtues would solve his problems.

At the birth of their first daughter, Inger (always called Ea), his mother-in-law moved from Folehave for a long stay at Rungstedlund. The good lady sailed in with innumerable other females in her wake—servants, friends and relatives, relatives, relatives. There were forty-four cousins of Ingeborg's generation, all close, affectionate friends, and Ea was the first child to be born to any of them. In all that commotion of petticoats, Wilhelm suddenly felt useless and shunted aside. He complained bitterly that the excited womenfolk crowded so constantly around the cradle that he could hardly get a glimpse of the new child, but his remarks passed quite unheeded. He had learned to assert himself, however, by the time a second daughter was born. This one he simply appropriated. She was to be particularly his own, he announced, his favorite.

Karen Christentze (always called Tanne) made her appearance in 1885. The day, to the general dismay, was April 17, a Tycho Brahe Day. For Danes, this was one of the thirty-two unpropitious days of the year when the stars are in evil conjunction. It was indeed the most unlucky day of all. But however her parents may have bemoaned the fact, whatever the stars may or may not have portended, Tanne's childhood at least began serenely.

"My very first memory is of being helped up a steep hill in order to see a spectacular view. That was when I was about three years old. By the following spring I had learned to read, as sooner or later everyone does, but I was particularly excited about it."

Her father was less impressed by this accomplishment than by the realization that the child was suddenly old enough to share his country walks. It soon became a habit for the two of them to set off together each afternoon, hand in hand, the tall bearded man adjusting his stride to the steps of the absurdly small girl, and stopping to explain to her carefully, patiently, everything they saw.

At the back door of Rungstedlund "the oldest lilac tree in Denmark" raised thick, gnarled branches to a profusion of purple and green. Wilhelm shook a branch and a marvelously cool and fragrant shower fell on their upturned faces. From there the path led across level lawn to a footbridge where the brook slid between reeds and rushes, elephant-ears and lily pads, into the pond. For Tanne it was a great temptation to linger there to see what freight the stream would bring—swirling leaves and blossoms, duck feathers, water beetles skittering vainly against the current.

But Wilhelm was always impatient to get to the woods, and his big dog, in a frenzy of barking, raced ahead of them under the trees. At this season the huge beeches were still grey and naked, creaking and clattering in the sharp spring wind, but beneath were such drifts of mayflowers that it seemed as if all the stars in the sky had floated down during the night to twinkle in the grass. The saplings had pale foliage, sticky to touch. Ferns were unfurling fronds patterned like lace. On old tree stumps hung with moss and lichen, jet-black snails added a shimmering embroidery. Why did some snails carry shells on their backs and others not?

"Stand still and listen," said her father.

The fallen brown leaves rustled and quivered where wood mice, ground birds and insects were stirring, and green things were pushing up toward the light. Each bird had a shape and color and song of its own, Wilhelm explained, as every plant had its own leaf form and blossom and seed. He named them patiently again and again, and expected Tanne to remember them.

At the top of Ewald's Hill was a wooden bench. While they

rested there he told her about Rungstedlund, and the poet, and about her family. The tales went back to Tanne's maternal great-grandfather Hansen, a shipowner, the richest man in Copenhagen, and a very romantic figure. He had brought a beautiful young wife from Guernsey whom he adored but who languished with homesickness like a wilting, transplanted flower. All his efforts to distract her were in vain until he thought of sending one of his ships back to the island for a cargo of gravel so that Emma Eliza could still walk on Guernsey soil in her new country. Who could resist such a gesture? Not Emma Eliza, and the story ended happily. Grandmother Westenholz was one of her eleven children. Tanne's grandfather Dinesen was also a favorite subject. He had gone to Algeria to fight for the French and had traveled to Rome with Hans Christian Andersen.

Nor is it every child that has the excitement of hearing Indian stories at firsthand. Wilhelm's supply was inexhaustible and he never tired of repeating them over and over again. They were wild and stirring narratives which always ended with a little lecture. "The Indians are better than our civilized people of Europe," he would conclude, "closer to nature, more honest. Their eyes see more than ours, and they are wiser. We should learn from them."

It pleased him to tell her these things because he was writing *Boganis* just then. It was as if he were thinking aloud, trying out his ideas and the sound of his prose on his small listener, who all too often failed to understand him at all. As he talked he fondled Osceola, the big dog who was always with him. "The Indians called me Boganis," he liked to remember. "Osceola's name is Indian, too."

Even Tanne noticed the tinge of longing in his voice when he spoke of his solitary years in the shack in Wisconsin. It had two small rooms, he told her, with a rough attic where he had impro-

Wilhelm Dinesen (above)/Katholm—country estate of the Dinesen family (below)

Tanne, Ea, governess, Ellen/Aunt Christentze Dinesen—Tanne's godmother

Matrup—country estate of the Westenholz family/Wilhelm and Ingeborg Dinesen at Rungstedlund (Tanne on the doorstep)

Family picnic (left to right: Ea, Ellen, Aunt Bess, Aunt Lidda, Malla, "Mama," Thomas, Tanne; center front: Mrs. Dinesen with Anders)/Ingeborg Dinesen

Hans Christian Andersen reading aloud (Agnes Frijs, center)/
Agnes Frijs—"Adelaide" in the tale "Copenhagen Season"

Tanne

Frijsenborg

Countess Mogens Frijs, Daisy, Helle, Inger and Sophie/Daisy Frijs (Countess Henrik Castenskjo

vised a bedstead and a mattress filled with dried ferns. The cooking stove stood in a lean-to, and he baked fresh bread there each day and prepared simple meals of the fish and game he had caught. He had neither books nor newspapers, and for distraction only his hunting forays, long walks in the forest and lonely treks upriver to the waterfalls. With spring weather the first Indians appeared and pitched their wigwams around his house, and one of the Indian girls might come to cook for him. In midsummer the whole tribe arrived, four hundred of them, to celebrate their yearly religious festival. He was busy for months then, entertaining them in his house, visiting them and learning their ways, selling or bartering the furs of the animals he had trapped and the produce of his small garden.

Tanne wanted to see Frydenlund and the Indians too. "And so you shall," said her father, "though probably it will all be quite changed by then."

Ellen, the third daughter, had been born a year after Tanne. The young mother, with Wilhelm in mind, had longed for a boy. For some time now, her husband had seemed to her sad in an indefinable sort of way, and even very depressed at moments. She could neither understand it nor cajole him out of his dark moods. He needed a son, she concluded rather naïvely, a boy who would tramp in the country and go fishing, hunting and riding with him. It was touching, though perhaps not quite appropriate, for him to disappear into the woods with Tanne each afternoon. Soon it would interfere with the child's schedule.

Ea and Tanne were, in fact, already launched on a serious program. They were being taught to sew, to speak English and French, to recite poems from memory. Their mother read aloud to them every evening, but they were also required to do a lot of reading on their own. Self-expression as such had not yet been heard of, and the little girls were expected to be industrious from morning until night. For amusement they rode in the carriage with their mother to Folehave, their grandmother's house in Hørsholm, or, more rarely, went to visit their father's family at Katholm Castle, or their uncle Asker Westenholz at Matrup.

For the parents as well as the children it was a placid routine. There were few distractions except for the *va-et-vient* of relatives making their continuous entrances and exits like a smiling corps de ballet. In marrying Ingeborg, Wilhelm had had to espouse the whole throng of Westenholz relations. Too often they frayed his oversensitive nerves with their unceasing chatter and gossip, their preoccupation with every minor detail of public and family affairs. In particular his patience was strained by his wife's crusading spinster sister, Bess, and by her militant mother, "Mama," for whom he felt real affection but whose activities and stern ethics and morals were hard to bear. To escape them all, and because he had a passion for hunting, Wilhelm accepted invitations to shoot on the great estates. He also went often to the city, where he was quite hopelessly involved in politics, and he sent hundreds of futile articles to the newspapers. At a time when Denmark was senti-mentally pro-Russian (the Danish Princess Dagmar had married Czar Alexander III), Wilhelm was convinced that the great threat to his country and to all western Europe was not Germany but Russia. He was opposed to the reactionary views of the nobility, was against the Army conservatives and the Ministry supported by the King. All of them lived, he said, in a world of antiquated customs, where everything was serene and pleasant for the privi-leged—but only for the privileged.

It was these considerations which kept Wilhelm from fully enjoying the success of *Boganis* when it finally appeared in 1890.

The reviewers drew attention to his individuality of style, which they felt would create a permanent niche for him in the history of Danish literature, and the critic Georg Brandes extolled him as "the perfect type of Danish country gentleman." But Wilhelm was neither flattered nor impressed. He was only interested in becoming a member of Parliament and making himself heard. A first attempt had failed, and when he did succeed in being elected from Grenaa, the nearest town to Katholm Castle, it only proved yet another disillusion. No one seemed interested in his ideals and proposed reforms.

As for his wife, she had shed none of her liberal ideas, but she was now too busy from morning till night with household cares and children to do more than listen absent-mindedly. Nor did the birth of the yearned-for sons, Thomas in 1892 and Anders in 1894, bring the joy she had anticipated for him. On the contrary, Wilhelm seemed, if anything, more remote and discouraged.

Wilhelm, of course, continued his excursions with Tanne, now nearly ten years old, and as if some premonition had come to him of his approaching death, his talks with her seemed to gather momentum. Allusions to people he had known, to an unnamed woman he had loved, reminiscences, warnings, advice, all poured out in a sort of accelerating monologue. Like a gardener trying to force a rose to premature bloom, he seemed to urge Tanne beyond her age and comprehension. She listened wide-eyed, at times almost frightened, and remembered what he told her without having understood it. One thing only was really clear: her father's thoughts on nature. Hardly a day passed without his coming back to the subject. There was nothing in life, he kept repeating like a credo, there was nothing of greater importance than learning to be observant of nature. To know nature, the earth, the forest and its creatures, he said, was to have a sort of magic key to the knowledge of everything—people, manners, even the arts, which, at first glance, might seem artificial. "The earth gave me peace," he said, "once when I was very confused about life."

This time, however, it could not give him the peace he needed.

Tanne never got over her father's death. It cast a shadow of sadness over her young years and left a permanent mark. He had abandoned her—deliberately. Why? When she was seventy, standing one day with a friend at the edge of Rungsted woods, which she was now too old and frail to explore, she spoke, as she still often did, of that bewildering early sorrow. "It was as if part of oneself had also died . . . the desolate feeling that there was no one to remember the talks on Ewald's Hill . . . suddenly one was pushed out into the foremost row of life, bereft of the joy and irresponsibility of childhood." She could never be sure whether she remembered or had simply dreamed of his pacing all night in his room like a fox in a cage during that last despairing week of his life. In winter she always thought of him, cold under a blanket of snow . . . and when it rained she thought of the water seeping slowly down through the earth to the place where he lay buried— the earth where, by his own hand, he had sought final peace.

After Wilhelm's death Tanne was absorbed back into a woman's world, a matriarchal atmosphere compounded of Victorian rules of conduct, the acquiring of domestic accomplishments, and earnest study, its drabness enlivened only by Mrs. Dinesen's eager intellect. Although dressed always in solemn black from the time of her widowhood, Tanne's mother concealed what bereavement she may have felt, and her days were, in any case, too full to allow of any real intimacy. House, gardens, farmland—the demands were many. There were servants to direct and a new coachman to be trained, Alfred Pedersen, who would remain at Rungstedlund for sixty-five years and become a family character.

Besides, the children were in the house most of the day. The nearest school was in the city, some twenty-five kilometers distant, so they were tutored at home by their grandmother and by a retired schoolteacher who lived in the village. "To which circumstances," Tanne used later to say, "I owe the fact that I am totally ignorant of many things that are common knowledge to other people." The two ladies were more ambitious for their pupils and more demanding than any professional. Although they passed over the sciences and mathematics with breezy unconcern, they thought it quite in order for a twelve-year-old girl to compose essays on Racine and Corneille, translate Scott's *Lady of the Lake* into Danish verse and unravel the intricacies of Latin classics.

The boys raced from their classes to the beach, where the business of men and boats was all-absorbing. But Ea, Tanne and Ellen went to Folehave in the afternoons for additional lessons with their grandmother "Mama," sessions rendered quite grim by the presence of Aunt Bess Westenholz.

This redoubtable female was the mainstay of the Unitarian Church in Denmark, no slight achievement in a country where Lutheranism is so firmly entrenched that every citizen is officially born into it, and she was always avid for converts. When the schoolbooks had been laid aside for embroidery, when the tea tray had made its appearance and "Mama" was in the middle of some enthralling story, then Aunt Bess would swoop down on them. She lived in the house and there was no getting away from her. Reproachfully, Tanne would raise grave eyes from her needlework to her aunt's determined, humorless face, and then toward the window. Her mind was engrossed in events that had happened outside there in Hørsholm a long time ago, which her grandmother had described and which she herself would one day work into the fabric of a tale called *"The Poet."* While Ea and Ellen, dismayed but docile, cringed under the spate of proselytizing, Tanne took refuge in images of Hørsholm's lake with its island castle subsiding slowly and inevitably beneath the water. But of what use was resistance? "She finally even took my sister and me to a Unitarian congress abroad, and one of my main reasons for going to Africa later was to escape from the tyranny of this aunt."

Meanwhile, Tanne had found another sort of escape. At the age of fourteen she had discovered Shakespeare. His plays beckoned her south to Italy to weep over the fate of a pair of romantic lovers. On a tide of resounding phrases they swept her north to Elsinore, where a brooding and undecided prince prepared his own tragic end. They led her imagination dancing and singing into the forest with sprites and woodland creatures. They ensnared her in sad, poetic dreams or betrayed her into delightful earthy laughter. They would instill in her a love of the sound of words, illumine her conversation, and eventually add a special flavor to the books she would write. The discovery, she always said, "was one of the really great events of my life."

II

Katholm

—〰〰—

As the old century slipped into the pages of history and a new century was being rung in, the Danes, in spite of political unrest and the strain of the recent Great Strike, hailed the New Year with song and celebration. On the Strandvej, automobiles were replacing the gleaming cabriolets, dogcarts and coaches, and Rungstedlund was now less than half an hour from town. Along the coast there were more and more lights to guide the night sailor as city and suburbs spread northward and nibbled away what remained of forest and field. Old people complained, as they always have, that the world was changing, but this time they were right. Soon the machine, the craving for speed, and modern manners (or the lack of any) would completely transform the gentler, slower customs they had known. It was also a moment of last reprieve before the leveling down of the aristocracy who had long ruled the land, often not too wisely.

For Tanne, now fifteen years old, 1900 was the fifth anniversary of her father's death, and he was constantly in her thoughts. Since he had died she had seldom seen his family. Her mother had never cared for them, nor they for her. Tanne herself shrank instinctively from any contacts that might renew a sorrow which, after five years, was still painful. But suddenly she became preoccupied with the notion that her father lived on in her, that only through her could his ideals survive, and that she should try to learn more about him. Perhaps she would find him again at Katholm, where he had spent his boyhood and happiest moments.

To arrive at Katholm was always a moving experience. Approaching along the narrow, twisting forest road between steep mossy banks and strangely contorted ancient trees, one came suddenly upon the clearing and the long rows of stables and barns which separated Katholm from the outside world. The foundations of the great castle had been laid in the year 1359, and succeeding generations had altered or added without ever marring its sombre beauty. In calm moments the castle was sharply mirrored in the wide moat, the reflection of the brick towers and battlements making it seem twice as huge and imposing. But Katholm was seldom quiet. The aqueous image was constantly breaking into rippling patterns of motion and color as riding parties trotted up to the door, hunts assembled, carriages came and went in flurries of waving and greeting. Beyond the park and farms, the moor stretched for miles and miles into the mist-obscured distance, rock-strewn and bristling with thickets of trees, untouched by the inhabitants of the castle. Although they rode on it often enough, they left no more trace of their passage there than did the flights of geese across the bleak Jutland sky.

It was perhaps the only thing upon which the Dinesens did not leave their mark, for they were, by all accounts, a dazzling family. For his debonair charm, his good looks and bearing the elder brother, Laurentzius, was the most outstanding. Because of this he had been chosen from among fellow officers of far greater rank and fortune to escort Princess Dagmar to St. Petersburg for her marriage to Czar Alexander III. After twenty years the romantic aura of that mission still clung to him. But all the Dinesen men were handsome, and their craving for adventure gave them added dash. Traditionally they began their careers in the Army, traveled to remote places and acquired sophistication in both Danish and foreign drawing rooms before they inevitably returned to the land. For, first and foremost, they were "country people," with a feudal attitude toward their estates, their servants and peasants.

Six sisters of Laurentzius and Wilhelm had grown up in the castle, had danced and flirted away the seasons, had broken a hundred hearts, had married and gone their various ways. Alvilde, Thyra, Anna, Emilie, Christentze (Tanne's godmother), Dagmar— they had been as good-looking as their brothers, as well as admired for their wit and elegance, and their intrepid horsemanship.

They all had, as Tanne would later write of them, "a great, wild happiness at being alive . . . *la joie de vivre.* Each single thing included in human daily existence—drawing breath, waking up or falling asleep, running, dancing and whistling, food and wine, animals and the four elements themselves—called forth in them a rapture like that of a very young animal, the ecstasy of a foal let loose in a paddock."

How, Tanne asked herself, had her father's life veered so far from all this to end in defeat and tragedy?

Only Laurentzius still lived at Katholm with his son, Wentzel, a charming boy of nineteen, destined by his father for the diplomatic service and by fate for an early death; but his daughter, Agnes, recently married to Count Gebhard Frederik Knuth, came often to visit, as did Laurentzius' sisters.

Laurentzius, now fifty-seven, had grown quite heavy but had

the stature to carry it well and was still remarkably handsome. His first wife had died a few days after the birth of a daughter, Christiane, and the child had not survived her mother by many months. Laurentzius eventually married again, but his second wife also died, soon after the birth of Wentzel. However, he seemed neither sad nor lonely. He was, Tanne observed, astonishingly like her father in many ways, but fair-haired and with clear, laughing eyes, whereas Wilhelm had been dark, with a brooding, earnest look. Like sunlight and shadow of the same day, she thought, but the resemblance was hard to define. Perhaps Katholm was the common denominator. Though the castle had belonged to the Dinesens only since 1839, it had shaped the characters of all the young people who grew up there, and made them feel different, set apart from other families whom they frequented during the winter season in Copenhagen.

Tanne rode out on the moor alone to ponder these ideas and to collect her thoughts in regard to her father. At night (not unlike one of those rather eerie young girls in *Seven Gothic Tales*) she wandered from room to room of the castle, examining the tapestries, the dark massive furnishings, the armor and weapons, which had been there since time out of mind. Or she sat up until late hours with visiting aunts and cousins, admiring and enjoying their insouciance and whimsical talk, so different, she decided, from the atmosphere of earnest endeavor she was used to at home.

Gradually her unasked questions answered themselves. The cherished image of her father, before which she had lighted the candles of her imagination and sacrificed too much of childhood happiness, began to smile at her through the laughing eyes of her uncle and his children. In all their gestures and habits, likes and dislikes, she rediscovered him but with added life and sparkle. They were so much of a piece, this family, so very Dinesen!

And, imperceptibly, she became one of them.

When Tanne returned to Rungstedlund a few weeks later, her mother found her quite changed. A child, and a wistful one at that, had left the house. Mrs. Dinesen had watched at the door while young Pedersen settled Tanne and her belongings in the carriage, and she had seen, as they turned out into the Strandvej, how Tanne's eyes had suddenly filled with tears.

Now a *jeune fille* had come home with all the implied turbulent changes of mood, the need to express herself—locked in her room composing verse!—and showing the first signs of a rather dreadful new spirit of independence. During the past year or so she had grown no taller, and perhaps never would, but she had learned at Katholm to coil her hair in a modish knot on top of her head. It added an inch to her height, and heaven only knew how many inches to her aplomb. She had grown critical too. "At my father's house . . ." she said, and she didn't mean Rungstedlund, which wounded her mother. From moment to moment she was gay in a hectic way or annoyingly absent-minded.

"Please shut the door behind you when you leave the room," her vexed mother called after her a dozen times a day.

Tanne didn't hear her. In her mind's eye she was still galloping over the bleached and brindled moors of Katholm. She was urging her horse over a stony ridge and down to the edge of one of the marsh lakes, where she slid from the saddle and stood transfixed as thousands of wild duck rose from the water with a fearful splashing and clatter. High overhead she could follow them as they circled and swerved away to settle again somewhere far out of sight, while silence ebbed slowly back to the lake. But was it silence? Couldn't she hear her father say, "Stand still and listen, Tanne . . ."? Less-than-sound became audible then: the acres of slaty water and hummocks of rustling sedge, the tremulous clouds of midges, the dragonflies flashing above the shallows where shoals of tiny fish needled their way through the reeds, the heron poised on one stilt among nodding plumes of swamp grass, all breathed forth an infinitesimal but distinguishable symphony of sound. Murmur and sibilance. Music and dissonance. She closed her eyes then to unravel the mingled threads of scents—salt tang blown in from the sea, fragrance of herbs and wildflowers, the mushroom odor of damp, decaying wood, the acrid smell of her pony. And suddenly she had known that this was her father's world.

"Tanne," the voice of her mother admonished, "you are like a sleepwalker. You still haven't arranged the dining-room flowers."

Jolted out of her daydreams, Tanne sighed, went mechanically about the task required of her, and escaped to her room to lose herself in another reverie. This one involved an ambitious plan to write a novel inspired by *The Sagas of the Norwegian Kings*. The best hours at Rungstedlund had always been at the end of the day when her mother gathered the five children around her to read aloud from this book. Mrs. Dinesen read well, and Snorri infused life and humor and pathos into his narrative of the ancient heroes and their acts of faith and revenge, but now Tanne wished to retell these tales in words of her own.

It was a fine project, no doubt, but the aspiring young novelist sat at her desk gnawing her pencil while her mind wandered in aimless confusion from one unrelated thought to another—the moor at Katholm, King Olaf, stories of Wilhelm which one of her aunts had related, details of the sagas . . . How clearly she envisioned her finished book! But somehow no line of it appeared on paper. The afternoon, every afternoon seemed to evaporate and Tanne presented herself at dinner, a dark and faraway look in her eyes, forgetting to speak, almost forgetting to eat.

What was to be done with the child? asked her mother. How was one to channel this scattered energy until she was old enough for parties, flirtations and marriage? Or for some useful role in life? suggested Aunt Bess. The usual petticoat council—Mother, "Mama" and Aunt Bess—had met to discuss the problem. After much talk they came up with a happy solution. There was a Professor Carlyle at Oxford, highly recommended, at whose house foreign students could stay while they perfected their English. He supervised their leisure as well as their studies, and chaperoned them on visits to places of interest. An ideal arrangement. Tanne and Ellen would go there together, and even if the professor found Tanne somewhat difficult to manage, he would at least be charmed by a Danish girl with such an impressive knowledge of Shakespeare. In any case, Tanne was likely to be less vague and moody if they made her feel responsible for her younger sister.

The summer at Oxford was a real success. Both girls loved it and they struck up a great friendship (it would last a lifetime) with Professor Carlyle's two daughters. Thanks to "Mama" their English had been fluent since childhood but now they spoke it with Oxonian assurance.

Over their teacups, the three ladies congratulated themselves on a wise decision. They were far less pleased when they met a few weeks later to discuss Tanne's latest whim. Art school! The mere idea of a girl of seventeen in Copenhagen and at such a place was preposterous, sniffed Aunt Bess, who still hoped to enlist her niece in work for the church. And why couldn't the child simply develop her talent for writing? asked "Mama," who had enjoyed her granddaughter's early attempts at verse, and particularly a play in which all the children had acted. The culprit was called to the drawing room, questioned and scolded.

"*A parti pris, point de conseil*" was Tanne's pert response. She had a fondness for foreign proverbs and mottoes, and she had made up her mind to be stubborn. She did not want to write, she insisted. She wanted a career as a painter. If Ea could have singing lessons, why couldn't she go to art school? The discussion lasted all afternoon. It was resumed often during the weeks that followed, but in the end, the Royal Academy of Fine Arts acquired another dilettante.

III

First Stories

—◌◌◌—

The next years sped by in a whirl of congenial work and good times. Tanne was making sufficient progress in painting to satisfy her instructors. The family council at first admitted rather reluctantly that she was not without talent, and then passed to open admiration and pride.

They had further reason for being proud when she began to make her appearance at balls, the opera and ballet. Unendowed with the striking beauty that had made her father's family almost legendary, Tanne nevertheless had great personal allure. Her erect, graceful bearing compensated for her lack of stature, and the projection of a positive inner quality attracted immediate interest. Smoldering dark eyes and an unusually low, vibrant voice completed the conquest. Years afterwards, even people who had met her only briefly would speak of the extraordinary and deeply moving effect of her eyes. A photograph made at this time shows a poised Tanne, her fine-spun chestnut hair puffed into the elaborate structure which was the fashion of the day, her shoulders framed in a romantic lace fichu, her eyes steady and penetrating. Most revealing, however, is the touching sensitivity of the mouth, a mouth that betrays past woes, a mouth destined for tragedy.

But for the moment, the Dinesen *joie de vivre* was in the ascendancy and it wafted the young girl on wings of excitement through the hours of absorbing work at the academy, out into Copenhagen's round of receptions and parties, and to gay country weekends, especially in the company of Daisy Frijs.

There were many reasons for the intense attachment between Tanne and Daisy, one of the daughers of Count Mogens Krag-Juel-Vind-Frijs. Mogens Frijs bore one of the proudest names in the country and was also lord of Frijsenborg Castle and the vastest estates in all Denmark—a feudal realm of farms and fields, forests teeming with deer and pheasant, thirty hamlets with their own churches. He had spent four years as attaché at the Danish Embassy in London, where he became a personal friend of King Edward VII before he assumed an active role in home politics. Tanne and the Frijs sisters had met as children, since their fathers were friends and Frijsenborg was not far distant from Katholm. The two men often hunted together, and though they had widely divergent ideas on national affairs, they discussed their differences amicably enough. They were also cousins, a relationship which Tanne, in her present frame of mind, was eager to exploit.

As she discovered the new, grownup world of Copenhagen, Tanne felt more and more intolerant of the bourgeois, puritanical atmosphere at Rungstedlund and Folehave. How unutterably boring were the constant family gatherings so dear to her mother and aunts: the inevitable heavy dinners, followed by the inevitable talk of church and social reforms, and all of the women, in their outmoded dresses, busy, busy with their inevitable squares of needlepoint. One glance at Daisy's well-cut frocks was enough to make her shudder disdainfully at the thought of the dowdy garments which her mother's relatives considered "Sunday best." And how narrow they all were, how strict and unrelenting! She still cringed over the humiliation of having been ordered to her room when Georg Brandes called. Why was it so shocking for a young girl to have sent a letter and flowers to an admired author who was sick in the hospital? Since he had been courteous enough to go out to Rungstedlund later to express his thanks, she herself, not her mother, should have received him. It was unbearable.

How alluring, on the other hand, was the fashionable, aristocratic *monde* to which Daisy was a sort of "open sesame"! There were, in addition to Daisy, three Frijs sisters; Sophie, who was a pretty child; Inger, who delighted everyone with her intelligence and gaiety but whose spirit of fun was tempered by good sense; and Helle, a reckless sportswoman who could outride any man and would soon progress to automobile racing and piloting airplanes. Daisy, equally reckless in her pursuit of sophisticated pleasures and capable of turning anybody around her finger if she decided to do so, was the one Tanne loved, envied and preferred. Daisy was flattered by the preference and enjoyed the effect on her country cousin of her daring escapades.

But Daisy had an added secret attraction for Tanne. Frequently Daisy would be surprised to notice that her cousin was staring at her, studying her with peculiar intensity.

Tanne was, in fact, searching Daisy's face for some resemblance to photographs of Agnes Frijs, sister of Daisy's father—Agnes, whose reign as the most beautiful girl in Denmark had ended with her death at the age of twenty—Agnes, whom Wilhelm Dinesen had loved so hopelessly. Tanne had finally learned that it was Agnes of whom her father had spoken during those last months at Rungstedlund before he died. She was his unnamed beloved! How disturbed and moved Tanne had been by even the few discreet allusions that had escaped him at that time. It was only long after, at Katholm, that she had wrested more details from her godmother, Aunt Christentze, who had also been Agnes' closest friend.

"She was," Aunt Christentze had said, *"une princesse de conte de fées"* whom everybody adored. Everyone was in love with her, your father most of all. When she died so suddenly, so young, all Denmark mourned." She went on to describe how Agnes, on a trip to Italy with her father and mother, caught typhoid fever in Naples and died a few days before her twentieth birthday. Her parents, who were almost insane with grief, had had another dreadful experience during the return voyage. Their ship ran into a violent storm in the Bay of Biscay and the terrified sailors had threatened to throw the coffin overboard. Count Frijs had only with great difficulty dissuaded them.

"Agnes' mother," Aunt Christentze continued, "never recovered from the shock of losing her daughter. As for your father, who had once been so gay, he was already profoundly saddened by the horrors he had witnessed during the Paris Commune. Agnes' death was the final blow."

Observing Daisy, Tanne's thoughts would often revert to those other two cousins of a previous generation, Agnes and Christentze. Perhaps they had sat in this very room which was now Daisy's, whispering and laughing together about the day's adventures, their frocks and their dancing partners. Had Agnes been cruel to Wilhelm, she wondered, and was it true that he had gone to war on her account? Had he really left for America because he found life unbearable in Denmark after she died? There were photographs of her all over the house—Agnes as a pretty child, listening to Hans Christian Andersen reading his tales aloud; Agnes as a charming young girl working at an embroidery frame with her rather plain sister, Clara; Agnes, slender and elegant on horseback; Agnes in clouds of filmy batiste, her luxuriant dark curls bound in a velvet ribbon. Yes, she had been beautiful. More than beautiful. And it was easy to understand that Wilhelm had loved her. The story troubled and haunted Tanne. It lingered on in her subconscious like an underground river, to emerge after fifty years as that poignant tale "Copenhagen Season."

In the meanwhile, the writing of other stories preoccupied her, for, in spite of the emphatic protests she had made at home, literature attracted her as much as painting. The Norwegian saga never became a novel, though it did reach near-completion before it was laid aside for "The Hermits" and "The Ploughman," short stories which appeared in print during 1907, with the young author hiding behind a curious nom de plume. A modern psychologist might have been interested to note that she chose "Osceola," the Indian name of her father's dog.

The stories were competently written and had individuality of style; in spirit and content they were "gothic" tales and, in every sense, forerunners of the famous Seven. "The Hermits," which appeared in the August issue of *Tilskueren* magazine, tells of a newly married couple who decide to live on a remote, uninhabited island so that the husband may devote himself without interruption to writing a book which he hopes will reform the world. So absorbed does he become in his task that he completely neglects his bride. But a visitor arrives to console her—a ghost, to be sure—who finally lures her away to the eerie realm of the spirits.

The tale, which was the kind that might have inspired the choreographers of *La Sylphide* and *Giselle,* is less well constructed and less mature than "The Ploughman," although it is quite successful in establishing the weird atmosphere which was to become the hallmark of Isak Dinesen. Mario Krohn, editor of *Tilskueren*, hastened to seek out the author.

"I have given my only other story to another journal" was all the satisfaction he got from Tanne. "I doubt very much that I shall write any more after that appears. I intend to become a painter, not a writer."

October readers of *Gads Danske Magasin* were as delighted as Krohn had been to discover the work of the new contributor. It tells of a frightened girl who, passing by a gallows at nightfall, encounters a young man who engages her in conversation. He tells her that he has arrived at an impasse in his life, that the wild witch-blood of his mother and the staid bourgeois heritage of his father are so at war within him that he can find no peace of mind, nor succeed in anything he attempts. As she cannot help him, the girl begs him to let her go on her way. But his plight continues to trouble her after she reaches home, so she sends her sister to fetch him and offers to hire him to plough her fields. The ploughman is finally healed of his frustration and despair by his contact with nature, as he plods back and forth turning the furrows. "The earth has spoken to me. It gave me peace," he says; and, of course, he is speaking for Tanne's father.

"The Ploughman" was well received by the critics, and deservedly so. Mario Krohn, who was not a man to be easily discouraged, returned to the assault. Tanne had a fine and original talent, he insisted. She must give up painting because one cannot serve two masters properly. He offered to publish anything she might write. He did more—he offered to marry her. Both propositions were politely but firmly refused, although he did succeed in extracting one more story.

"The de Cats Family," in *Tilskueren*, January 1909, is very different in mood from the previous efforts. With sly humor and an almost O. Henry twist, it describes the respectable de Cats family of Amsterdam, who bribe one of their relatives to be their "black sheep." They have a curious notion that if all their innate wickedness can be shifted onto the shoulders of one member of the family, the rest of them will somehow be able to escape temptation and retain their respectability. The victim, of course, gets the best of the deal. With a natural preference for a reckless life and his relatives' money jingling in his pockets, he is only too pleased to comply with their schemes.

This tale and some unpublished poems—"Wings" (longing for wings to fly far from here), "Cradle Song" (for a son dead in battle), "Moonlight" (trees in pools of black shadow), "To Artemis" and "Tailwind"—brought the first phase of Tanne's literary production to an end. Except for a poem entitled "Ex Africa" (1925) and *Sandhedens Hævn* (The Revenge of Truth), a revised, marionette version (1926) of a playlet in which she and her brothers, sisters and friends had acted as children, she would publish nothing further for twenty-five years. To Mario Krohn, when he made a last attempt to change her mind, she protested, "I want all things in life more than to be a writer—travel, dancing, living, the freedom to paint." She would have been quite surprised had she known that within a year she would be saying as much against the artist's career for which she had so stubbornly defied her family.

Mario was alone in encouraging Tanne to write at this time— and she always remembered him for it with gratitude—but he was far from the only one to fall in love with her. Although her connections with the Danish aristocracy were tenuous (her grandfather Adolph Vilhelm Dinesen and Count Christian Frijs of Frijsenborg had married two sisters of a non-noble family, the Haffners), her own family, paternal and maternal, were well known and highly respected. They were intellectuals and people of considerable property, with as many friends among the nobility as among other groups, and Tanne was certainly considered a very desirable match. A many-faceted personality made her more so: daring horsemanship and a passion for dogs and the out-of-doors made her especially appealing to sportsmen; the more seriously inclined were impressed by her interest in art and her successes in print. And her charm was undeniable. So it was hardly astonishing that a number of acceptable young men declared themselves heartbroken by her persistent indifference. Exceedingly feminine, she flirted with all but felt nothing like love for any of them. Perhaps the explanation lay in the fact that her inner eye was still focused upon what Freudians would later call "the father image."

Tanne's mother and "Mama" began to view the situation with some concern. Aunt Bess, never one to let pass an opportunity for sarcastic comment, reminded them that of the three unmarried girls in the house, the oldest was nearing the fatal age of thirty, and Tanne was all of twenty-five. If they couldn't find husbands, let them work for the church, she advised as usual.

Since her moment of triumph in Parliament, Aunt Bess was more outspoken than ever. People listened to her with awed deference. Danish women did not yet have the right to vote and presumably took no part in politics, but they had strong opinions about the affairs of their country and at this time were especially incensed by the endless dispute over the Danish Defense Plan. They were working to get the vote for themselves, but Aunt Bess couldn't wait. One day she simply stalked into the great hall of Parliament while the debate was in full swing. Seizing the Chairman's bell, she rang it loudly while the poor man, too stunned to prevent her, sat there moaning, "She has taken my bell! She has taken my bell!" In a voice as clear and ringing as the bell Aunt

Bess announced, "Here you sit, men of Denmark, with all the authority in your hands, and all you do is betray the honor of your country. But this you shall hear: all the women of Denmark despise you." There was a shocked silence, and then she turned her back on them and strode out.

Ea was too engrossed in her singing lessons to give any thought to marriage or to her aunt's opinions. The younger children, however, were deeply impressed. Ellen, a shy, insecure girl, regarded the activities of her Aunt Bess with admiration. But rather than devoting herself to the Unitarian Church or local politics, she chose to think herself a Russian nihilist. Thomas, in particular, respected and loved his crusading aunt, and much of his thinking developed under her direct influence. Only Tanne seethed and raged inwardly. Never, she told herself, would she let them push her into a career of good works or a dreary marriage. Rungstedlund, Folehave, the whole of conventional Denmark which regarded the slightest fantasy as eccentricity, were stifling her. She must get away before she succumbed to a creeping paralysis of the spirit. The fact that she was beginning to feel much too attracted to a man who remained oblivious of her existence made escape all the more desirable. She asked for permission to spend a year in Paris to study painting at a more important academy, and felt both surprised and relieved when permission was given. It seems quite possible that the sense of relief was shared by her family.

IV
Bror

—◊◊◊◊—

Enrolled at the Académie de Simon et Ménard, Tanne had difficulty in concentrating on art. That could come later, she told herself, and anyway, how could she absorb what the Paris artists were
to teach her before she had felt the atmosphere of their city? So
she made excuses for not working and set out to explore her surroundings.

The young and inexperienced traveler is always preoccupied
with comparisons. Tanne concluded that Copenhagen might be a
lively, delightful city, but Paris had grandeur. Here tragedy did
not hide behind doors but walked the streets as visibly etched on
the sallow, hawk-nosed faces of people as on the façades of the
beautiful, crumbling houses. The French had a particular humor
too, wry and sarcastic as her own would become when more unhappiness and physical suffering had whittled away her illusions.
At home she had felt only impatience at her mother's interest in
political events and in such questions as church reform and the
vote for women. Now she was astonished and amused at the pas-

sion with which everyone discussed politics—greybeards and students, fiacre drivers, waiters, and all those idlers who seemed to
spend their entire lives at terrace cafés. The Balkans were already
in the ferment that would lead to the Great War, and it was
impossible not to be caught up and excited by the endless arguments about what it all portended. French cuisine was another
discovery. In Denmark she had seen that many of the great houses
prided themselves on lavish entertainment and a good table. Here,
for the first time, she heard even simple people discuss cooking as
a fine art, worthy of study and veneration. This would become one
of her absorbing interests and later she would take cooking lessons
with Perrochet, chef of a celebrated Paris restaurant.

Conscientiously she spent hours at the Louvre, admiring the
classic painters. The year was 1910, and it was the time when
Gertrude Stein was a pioneer in sponsoring Picasso and other
avant-garde painters; when Matisse was shivering in an unheated
studio while his economical wife flavored her soups with the leaves
of a giant laurel wreath that the painter had received from a lone
American admirer; the Cubists were producing their masterworks;
the Italian Futurists had published their manifesto and were preparing to launch a frontal attack led by Severini; a new art, a new
vision, was being forged by all of these groups and by such individuals as Juan Gris, Modigliani, Braque, Derain, Marcel Du-
champ, Léger, Rouault. The initiated haunted the gallery of gloomy
Vollard rather than the Louvre, but nothing, nothing of all this
impinged on Tanne's consciousness. Simon et Ménard was an unfortunate and bourgeois choice for a young person of her rebellious
nature, who might have enjoyed defending the New Art. As it was,
the Académie neither stimulated her imagination nor did anything
for her talent except to further somewhat the conventional technique she had begun to acquire in Copenhagen.

In the afternoons she went for drives in the Bois with respectable friends of the family. Chaperoned by them, she also went to the opera and to the Diaghilev Ballet, which was having its second Paris season and making a sensational success with the critics, the fashionable *monde* and bohemia. But she never ventured as far afield as the châteaux of the Loire, nor even made the traditional pilgrimage to Chartres. Actually, she was busy just "living," as she had told Mario Krohn she would be. And to banish thoughts of her unsuccessful flirtation in Copenhagen, she encouraged a trio of admirers, one of whom would make a dramatic reappearance twenty years later. She was also savoring her first real independence, away from the constraint of the older women who habitually had influenced and directed her. More and more, too, she was divesting herself of her father's ghost. She was becoming, rather late perhaps, a complete person, ready to fulfill her role as a woman—ready to love.

Indeed, when she returned to Copenhagen she fell in love. "For the first time and really forever," she used to say. The months spent away in Paris had only intensified her feeling for the man she had hoped to forget. With what sly and vicarious pleasure she later described this reluctant lover, disguised as a dozen different heroes in her *Tales!*

Who was he?

"No one would remember after all these years, so let him remain nameless."

What was he like?

Well, he was a splendid horseman—was she not also?—but when they were both guests at the same country weekends, he chose other riding companions. He was a graceful dancer and she adored dancing . . . but he preferred other partners. He talked brilliantly . . . but with anyone else. He had fine eyes . . . but they were not for her, and never would be.

Which, she now asked herself, was the greater torment? To continue visiting friends and going to parties in the hope of seeing her beloved, to see him and suffer, or to lock herself up at home and not see him at all? To stay at home and be harried by Aunt Bess and treated by her mother as if she were still a child of fifteen, that was not good either. Oh, those inescapable and maddening Sunday lunches! And the endless advice and supervision!

To make matters worse, she was clearheaded enough to have realized by this time that talented though she might be, she was not of the stuff of which great painters are made. "They talk about the tragic unhappiness of great artists" said Gertrude Stein, "a little artist has all the tragic unhappiness and the sorrows of a great artist and he is not a great artist." Instinctively Tanne felt that this would be her lot if she persisted at the Danish or any other academy, and she was far too proud and self-demanding to accept such a compromise. It left her, however, with her home life, her social life and her career, all equally thwarted, and she concluded miserably she had arrived at a total impasse.

Her cousin and best friend, Daisy Frijs, offered a temporary solution. Daisy had been married for over a year to Henrik Castenskjold, who had been Danish Minister in Oslo and was now appointed to the double post of Rome and Vienna. Daisy invited Tanne to spend three months with them in Rome.

"We rode in the Borghese Gardens then, every day. There were carriages with all the great beauties of the day in them, and one stopped and chatted. It was delightful—" was Tanne's most pleasurable memory. But she also accompanied the Castenskjolds on their round of embassy obligations—the daily luncheons, teas, formal calls, dinners and receptions—with as much sightseeing as could be crammed into whatever hours remained. And finally, after midnight, there had been the tête-à-tête talks with Daisy. Inevitably Tanne had met Rome's eligible bachelors and a host of suave young diplomats, and Daisy looked on eagerly, hopefully, for some sentimental response in Tanne. But she had been "stungen unto the herte," said Tanne ruefully, by someone in Denmark, whom she refused to name and who did not reciprocate her feelings, and there was no cure for the poison of that shaft.

Nevertheless, toward the end of her stay she confided to Daisy that before leaving Copenhagen, she had half promised to marry her Swedish cousin, Baron Bror Blixen-Finecke. Perhaps it was better to marry a person one didn't love than to eat one's heart out for a love that was unattainable. Bror had asked her again and again to be his wife, she told Daisy, and she had refused each time not only because her affections were elsewhere engaged but because she could not imagine herself leading the constraining life of Stjärneholm, the tenant farm which Bror had as a sort of dependency on his father's estate of Näsbyholm in Skåne. Then Tanne's uncle Aage Westenholz offered Bror a job on his rubber plantation in Malaya. That seemed interesting enough, until Bror happened one day to talk to Daisy's father. Count Mogens Frijs had just returned from big-game hunting in Africa with such tales of the safari, the landscape, the climate and especially the extraordinary farming possibilities of the almost virgin terrain, that Bror was fired with hope and excitement. Once more he asked Tanne to reconsider and to start a new life with him in East Africa.

Could she learn to love him? asked Daisy with misgivings, since she knew her cousin Bror so well.

Never, thought Tanne. But he had a real feeling for the out-of-doors and was as keen a hunter as her father had been. He had verve and could be a gay companion. Since he belonged to her "set" and spoke Danish as readily as Swedish, she was used to him. Besides, she sensed that he needed her and was perhaps the only human being who did. His father treated him cavalierly as an unimportant younger son who was merely the secretary and manager of the estate, and Bror chafed under such tactless handling and longed to get away and be someone on his own. She was, it was true, a year older than Bror, and he had formed a sort of habit of relying on her because he felt she had a spirit of independence which he couldn't quite muster up alone.

Perhaps he was somewhat insensitive, Tanne admitted to Daisy's questioning, and unlettered . . . After rebellious years at school he had taken courses in agriculture instead of going to the university. She couldn't, she added wistfully, imagine his sharing her deep feeling for Shakespeare.

The return journey decided her. As her train neared Copenhagen she saw clearly how impossible it would be for her to remain there. Sooner or later she would betray her wretchedness over a man who cared nothing for her, and it would be written on her face for all to see: unloved.

But never could she have imagined what a storm her decision would touch off. Bror might be a cousin with the best connections and he had always been a welcome visitor at Rungstedlund, but he was not acceptable as a husband. Mrs. Dinesen's intuition told her that Tanne did not love him, and that there was also something unreliable about him. He had no money of his own and the African project was nebulous, to say the least. She was prepared to resist anything that would remove her daughter to a place so remote and little known. Aunt Bess added her bit of sarcasm. Of all the seven children in his family, Bror was the only one, she remarked acidly, who had a moody, unsteady character—even his twin brother, Hans, though he rode races and was generally a daredevil, was a more settled and serious person. Why marry a cousin anyway?. . . . and her eye glittered with the remembrance of Wilhelm's fatal attachment to Agnes Frijs, although even she dared not allude to it in front of Tanne's mother.

Opposition only served to strengthen Tanne's resolve. Having decided to make the dreary compromise of a loveless marriage, she would be uncompromising about carrying it out, and she had the added pleasure of feeling that she was defending an underdog. All of them had wanted her to marry. Well, she would, and whom she would, and when she would! What she kept to herself was her secret elation at marrying a first cousin of the Frijs sisters, the consequent closer ties with Danish and Swedish aristocracy and the satisfaction of being addressed as "Baroness." She knew only too well that her mother's family would have considered such notions contemptible.

Bror, who professed to have no use for books, nevertheless wrote one twenty years later, perhaps as a rather vengeful retort to Tanne's success with *Seven Gothic Tales*, perhaps out of some sort of nostalgia for Africa. In describing the long years in Kenya, he speaks only twice of his wife but he does give Tanne her due for having the courage to implement the escape they both longed for.

"The human imagination is a curious thing. If it is properly fertilized it can shoot up like a fakir's tree in the twinkling of an eye. Tanne knew the trick, and between us we built up in our imagination a future in which everything but the impossible had a place. The promised land which hovered before our eyes was called Africa, and our golden dreams included a large farm, teeming with fine fat cattle . . . We would milk cows and grow coffee . . . and the only anxiety was how I should be able to put all the money in the bank.

"Our optimism was shared by relations and friends, who asked nothing better than to get a corner for themselves and share the ample gains, and after a voluminous correspondence with Africa a farm of seven hundred acres was bought. The gold mine was ours. All we had to do now was to extract the rich ore."

Bror busied himself with arranging the loans, mostly from Tanne's relatives but some from his family too, and then left for East Africa to prepare for Tanne's arrival. It was a long journey in those days: by ship and train to Marseille, by steamer to Port Said, through the Red Sea and Indian Ocean to Mombasa, and finally eighteen hours from there by train to Nairobi. For an unbookish person, what Bror writes of this in *Nyama* is surprisingly vivid and colorful. His hunter's eye made him a sharp observer of other things than game, and in his rough way he was not without imagination.

When he learned in Nairobi that there was no money to be made in cattle raising, he lost no time in trading the farm for a coffee plantation and set out to find the seven hundred native laborers needed to clear the ground and plant the young trees. It was hard work, but after a few months he was able to survey his land with pride and write to Tanne that all was ready. Even a small new house had been built for her. Pending her arrival he went out on his first safaris to learn something about hunting lion, elephant and buffalo.

All her life Tanne hated hurry. When she had come to know the Kenya natives, one aspect of them that she understood particularly was their ability to live entirely in the moment, with no thought at all of the morrow or of anything that might need to be done. ". . . if you commission a Kikuyu to hold your horse while you make a visit, you can see by his face that he hopes you will be a long time about it. He does not try to pass the time then, but sits down and lives." Every letter that Bror sent home now filled her with mounting excitement about the new existence awaiting her, but she took her time over the preparations for the journey, lingering over each detail of a curious trousseau, supervising with care the packing of the fine china and glass which she refused to leave behind, the books, the guns. At last all the leave-taking calls had been made. There had been quiet talks with her mother, for whom she suddenly felt an unbearable tenderness. There had been a solitary hour on Ewald's Hill. Farewell, Rungstedlund, farewell!

Part Two

—ⱱⱱⱱ—

Africa

I

Tycho Brahe Days

—ⅷⅷⅷ—

When Tanne embarked on the long journey to Nairobi, in 1913, it was none too soon. By the following August the whole of Europe was embroiled in the Great War and the voyage would then have been difficult, if not impossible. As it was, the ship sailed serenely down through the Mediterranean, the Red Sea and Indian Ocean, and the British and pro-British passengers innocently made friends of those persons who ten months later became the enemy—the eminent German doctor, for instance, who was on his way out to Africa for the twenty-third time, hoping to find a cure for sleeping sickness. There was, most particularly, General von Lettow-Vorbeck.

Between the forty-three-year-old German officer and the young Danish woman who was going out to so much that was new and strange—the Dark Continent, marriage and all the unforeseeable future—a friendship grew which would survive more than one war. When the ship docked they had dinner ashore and talked of the safari they would one day make together. On parting the general gave Tanne his photograph, inscribed in German, and Tanne promised to buy him some horses he wanted but which he would not have time to choose before going on to German East Africa. These horses were never delivered, but the efforts Tanne made to obtain them were to cast a disagreeable cloud of suspicion upon her during the first months of the war. In private life the general was a courtly and attractive man; in military affairs, harsh but just. "No one had a greater admiration for von Lettow-Vorbeck than the Englishmen who fought against him," said Bror, who later served in the British Army. After the Armistice the general and Tanne would resume their friendship, and at ninety he would still be penning gallant letters to her.

Bror did not go to meet Tanne at Aden. Instead, he sent Farah, the Somali servant, to organize the baggage and details of the final landing at Mombasa. What must Farah have thought of this new mistress, so young and frail for the rigors of African life, and what of the deerhound, Dusk, who never left her side and was the most precious of the many wedding presents she had brought from Denmark? Farah, like all Somalis, was a fanatical Mohammedan. He was therefore prepared to treat women with reverence, but he held the belief that dogs were vile and unclean and sinful to touch. As for Tanne, her artist's eye took immediate delight in Farah's appearance. Lithe and fine-boned, he was dressed, with the vanity and natural elegance of the Somalis, in a long robe, gold-embroidered vest and brightly colored turban. She could hardly have imagined, however, the respect and devotion he would inspire in her and which would prompt her to say twenty-five years later, when she wrote of events in Kenya: ". . . one figure, straight, candid, and very fine to look at, stands as doorkeeper to all of them: my Somali servant, Farah Aden. Were any reader to object that I might choose a character of greater importance, I should answer him that that would not be possible."

If she had any last misgivings about the life she was choosing, Tanne put them resolutely out of her mind when Bror appeared in Mombasa, armed with the marriage contract, capable and sure of himself, already sunburnt and stamped with the unmistakable look of a Kenya colonist. The ceremony was performed on January 14, 1914. Tanne was twenty-eight, and the first of the three sisters to marry. No member of her family was present to witness the ill-starred event, but Prince Wilhelm of Sweden as best man lent a touch of resplendence to the occasion. Looking at her husband, Tanne saw, for an instant, another man standing in his place, but she shut her eyes to the intruding vision.

The wedding formalities over, Tanne was immediately absorbed in her first contact with Africa: the coral reef of the port rose from the blue, blue Indian Ocean, encrusted with the crumbling ruins of old Portuguese fortifications and even more ancient banyan trees. It was the mooring place of the German East Africa Line ships, which arrived each fortnight from Hamburg, the steamers which plied between Africa and India, and all those smaller picturesque vessels which traded up and down the coast. On the mainland the town had its wide avenue with giant mango trees, a stately Government Square, a residential suburb, and Roman Catholic and Anglican churches, but mostly it was a labyrinth of crooked streets and alleys seething with Europeans, Arabs, Indians and blacks, in every sort of fantastic garb. Only ten years before, the great Uganda Railroad had been completed, which now was pouring ivory, furs, coffee, grain and tropical fruits into this feverish city, but for hundreds, even thousands of years Mombasa had been supplying the outer world with all these wares, as well as a more fearful, bloodstained merchandise—the slaves for the Arabian market. The Sabeans had been there in the first millennium B.C., the Phoenicians too, when they circumnavigated the continent of Africa two thousand years before anyone else, and Roman traders had also come this far.

It was a pity not to linger and learn more of Mombasa, but Farah with gentle efficiency put Tanne and Bror and their belongings on the Nairobi train, and she waved what she thought would be only a brief good-bye to her general. Eighteen more hours of travel, three hundred and fifty miles across the bleak coastal strip and then up, up, six thousand feet up, into the green highland which was to be her home. Elspeth Huxley, returning to Nairobi at the end of World War I, described this journey vividly, as did Bror von Blixen, although his hunter's heart was more stirred by the game he saw from the train windows than by the scenery. It is curious that Tanne, who was so impressed, should never have troubled to write of it. At the time she hardly knew whether she was more impatient to reach their destination or whether she wanted the panorama to go on unfolding before her astonished gaze forever—the strange arid plains, the equatorial night engulfing the jungle and its fabulous beasts, the fiery dawn igniting the snow-capped spires of Kilimanjaro.

If Tanne had pictured romantic beginnings as a bride, as co-owner of the upland plantation, as mistress of hundreds of native servants and laborers, with occasional exciting ventures into the bush to hunt for big game, then a rude shock awaited her. The minute Bror was through with his farm work he always wanted to be off on safari, and Tanne, with a longing backward glance at her new house, was obliged to follow him like a humble novice. When she unpacked her precious china and fragile glass goblets, Bror simply laughed at her. She would never use them, he said. But when war was declared a few months later, she was grateful for the rapidly acquired experience of trekking and camping, of learning to cope with the natives and the animals. Bror and his Swedish friend Erik von Otter, and the two Swedish assistants at the farm, immediately reported to the Allied Recruiting Office in Nairobi. Erick joined the King's African Rifles; Bror was put in charge of liaison between Nairobi and Lord Delamere's headquarters and was sent south to the border of German East Africa; Tanne was to run the farm as best she could with such help as Bror might give when he came home on leave.

Tanne sat out the first weeks of the war in great distress over the turn of events, and feeling rather an outcast because of the people who mistrusted her loyalty to the Allies. The rumors about von Lettow-Vorbeck's horses were taking some time to live down. She stopped moping when she learned that there was a project to put all the white women of the colony into sort of concentration camp for the duration in order to protect them from the Germans and the natives. What irony it would be to have come all the way to Africa only to be cooped up with a nondescript mob of European women! To escape such a fate, she volunteered for a war job at one of the communications centers in nearby Kijabe, and had hardly settled when she received an urgent message from Bror. He "wrote and instructed me to load up four ox-wagons (with provisions and ammunition for the border forces) and to send them down as soon as possible. But I must not, he wrote, let them go without a white man in charge of them, for nobody knew where the Germans were, and the Masai (the fiercest tribe of Kenya) were in a state of high excitement at the idea of war, and on the move all over the reserve."

No white man was to be found to head the expedition, so Tanne undertook to locate the supplies and the sixty-nine oxen needed to draw the wagons, and then, with twenty-one Kikuyu natives and three Somali, with Dusk the deerhound beside her and the faithful Farah following behind, she set forth on an adventure that was to last three months.

During this lone wartime trek, Tanne's love and understanding of the Africans was born. "The introduction into my life of another race, essentially different from mine, in Africa became to me a mysterious expansion of my world. My own voice and song in life there had a second set to it, and grew fuller and richer in the duet." She was amused to learn that Farah, on his own initiative, had brought along her signed photograph of General von Lettow-Vorbeck, who was now commander in chief in German East Africa. They would show it to the Germans in case they were taken as prisoners of war, he explained. But greater hazards than capture were in store. The expeditions's first mishap not only established her prestige with the natives but elicited the only real tribute to her in Bror's book, *Nyama* (*African Hunter*).

"On the third evening, just as they were preparing to pitch camp, there was a fearful disturbance among the oxen, which had been left quite alone for a few moments. Tanne hurried up and saw two lions, each of which had jumped on an ox's back." She had been warned against marauding lions but had relaxed her vigil for a few minutes in order to hold a lamp while the natives tried to pry loose a large stone which was blocking one of the rear wagon wheels. "It need not be said that the teamsters had disappeared like phantoms, and my wife faced the two lions alone and unarmed, for, through an oversight, the rifles had been carefully stowed away among the baggage. But she had the heavy stockwhip, and with it she literally whipped the lions away from the oxen." And he added admiringly: "My wife made light of the incident."

Where did such courage come from in a young woman who had led a sheltered life and to whom lions were still too savage and unpredictable? Stendhal underwent his baptism of fire when Napoleon's army crossed the St. Bernard Pass. Astride a horse for the first time in his life, he rode along the icy, slippery edge of the ravine, with cannon balls falling all around, and concluded that courage was "the fear of being ridiculous or cowardly in others' eyes." It was not so with Tanne. Courage was an integral part of her nature, a reliable weapon against dangerous emergencies, or worse, for it is perhaps not so difficult to be brave in the face of a sudden crisis. Years of unremitting physical or spiritual suffering require a special and greater courage. Tanne had it, and would soon have further need of it.

With the expedition successfully concluded, Tanne went back to her volunteer job and the farm. The two managers were still at the front, and Bror, though he often came home on leave, never seemed to stay for more than a hurried visit. Alone, inexperienced, and still far from fluent in Swahili, Tanne struggled to keep the coffee plantation going. The war had disrupted shipping, and it grew more and more difficult to find needed farm supplies and machine parts. Prices fluctuated erratically, and she was at a loss as to how she should market the first coffee crops. Perhaps all their cherished plans and calculations would end in ruin. As the war dragged on, the news from Europe was disheartening, and British East Africa, though the European and American public were never aware of it, was having a hard time. Battles raged along the Tanganyika border and many men lost their lives; bridges were blown up and most of the colonists suffered in one way or another. But farm and war problems were no more shattering than the personal ones which began to unsettle Tanne's life.

For the first year or so she had been content with Bror. If he had felt like an underdog in Sweden, frustrated and angered by the limitations of his daily existence and his father's tyranny, here, she thought, he reached his full stature. Running Stjärneholm had given him the assurance he needed for directing the African farm, and a fund of practical knowledge which could be applied even to coffee growing. And he was in his element, gun in hand, tracking and slaughtering the jungle animals and piling up hunting statistics. It also suited his temperament and gave him a sense of accomplishment to be an officer in the British Army.

In spite of her first protests at leaving the house too often, it had been a great joy to go with him on safari. Each time, even when they revisited an old site, she had an exhilarating sense of discovery. Every subtle change of light brought out new beauty in the plains of shimmering, spice-scented grass, the groves of tremulous jungle bamboo, the forests and crags of the hill country. Even the air had a special, rarefied quality. One might almost rise and float in it like the eagles drifting above the Ngong peaks. As for the inhabitants of this *paradis terrestre*, surely the memory of her father's admiration and sympathy for the Indians made her particularly receptive to the natives.

She extended the same love to the animals. "Out on the safaris, I had seen a herd of buffalo, one hundred and twenty-nine of them, come out of the morning mist under a copper sky, one by one, as if the dark and massive, iron-like animals with the mighty, horizontally swung horns were not approaching, but were being created before my eyes and sent out as they were finished. I had seen a herd of elephants traveling through the dense native forest, where the sunlight is strewn between the thick creepers in small spots and patches, pacing along as if they had an appointment at the end of the world . . . I had time after time watched the progression across the plain of the giraffe, in their queer, inimitable, vegetative gracefulness, as if it were not a herd of animals but a family of rare, long-stemmed, speckled gigantic flowers slowly advancing. I had followed two rhinos on their morning promenade, when they were sniffing and snorting in the air of the dawn . . . and looked like two very big angular stones rollicking in the long valley and enjoying life together. I had seen the royal lion, before sunrise, below a waning moon, crossing the grey plain on his way home from the kill, drawing a dark wake in the silvery grass, his face still red up to the ears, or during the midday siesta, when he reposed contentedly in the midst of his family . . ."

In this old-new primitive world Tanne was happy as she had never been before. Bror had seemed pleased with her companionship and proud of her progress as a hunter. And hadn't it been, for both of them, a particular happiness to come back from safaris to the large old-fashioned house they had purchased in place of the small temporary one that Bror had built? Designed by one of the early Swedish colonists, Åke Sjögren, it had a sweeping view of the Ngong Hills, the forest and their own acres of precious coffee. Sjögren had wisely left groves of native olive and croton trees when he laid out the lawn, and he had devised a house of stone and timber which seemed to rise harmoniously right out of the landscape. Always awaiting her homecoming was Farah, attentive, resourceful, anticipating her every whim. Tanne had grown more dependent on him than she realized.

Then one day at the farm she suddenly caught her husband in a lie. It was a small, unimportant lie but it shook her profoundly. Why had he lied? She was half prepared for it when it happened a second time, but as she listened she felt such shame for him that her face burned. Soon everything he said seemed a deviation from the truth and she felt she was walking on quicksand. Why, why? Anyone in Nairobi could have told her, since Bror was neither

subtle nor clever enough to behave with discretion. He was having
an affair. Several affairs, in fact. And they went on and on, one
after the other. This sort of thing has happened to countless thousands of women, Tanne philosophized, but he made matters em-
barrassing and impossible by lying so clumsily. Fearful of sordid
scenes, she would walk out of the house into the chilly African
night; she exploded only once, when he invented too lame an
excuse for not coming home after a club dinner. The car broke
down, he said naïvely, but it happened that she knew where and
with whom he had spent the evening. She not only resented his
making a fool of her but was more indignant over this particular
affair than she had been about any of the others. The woman's
husband was one of Bror's close friends who trusted him and who
had even lent him a large sum of money to buoy up the shaky
finances of the farm.

At the same time Tanne's health began to suffer. At first she
attributed the illness to her state of mind and imagined it would
pass if she could learn to control her emotions. She put off seeing
a doctor but soon felt so much worse that it seemed she could
never cope with the day's work and then sit with pretended calm
opposite her husband at night. She was shocked, but no more so
than the doctor, to discover how serious her condition had become.
She must go home immediately to begin a long cure, he warned
her. But Tanne would not, could not go to Denmark. Surely he
could understand that. Well then, Paris had specialists, he said
wryly, and he would make the arrangements for her. It would not
be easy, he added, to get passage on any sort of ship in wartime,
but he could help her with that too.

She did a minimum of packing and spent the remaining days
locked in her room; Bror would assume that she was leaving him
and Africa in a fit of jealousy, and she did not enlighten him. At

the end she sought him out only to tell him that she would take Farah with her, since she felt too ill to travel alone. When Bror protested that he himself needed Farah, Tanne informed him bluntly, in a cold white rage, why she had to go and how grave her illness was. Bror stared at her incredulously for a moment, struck silent by her unaccustomed outburst, and then he turned and left the room.

Farah, who had been so resourceful, so adaptable to any and every situation in Africa, seemed too much out of his natural environment by the time they reached the Mediterranean. It was surprising because he had once been cabin boy on a French ship and still spoke fairly fluent French and excellent English too. He might easily, Tanne decided, become a burden rather than a help during the trip. He would want to serve her and be with her constantly, and might suffer if left to his own devices. So when they reached Marseille, she sent him back—a sad parting for both of them but it was a wise decision. Farah could perhaps have become adjusted to Paris, but alone in Denmark he would surely have felt quite lost.

The French doctor had been too discouraging, holding out no hope of a permanent cure for Tanne unless she were to submit to tedious treatment that might last for nearly a year. Tanne had never written to her mother about her troubles and hoped to conceal them from her, but in her misery she suddenly longed for home. She would throw herself on the mercy of kind Professor Rasch, whom she had known since childhood. The sobering three-day train journey to Copenhagen made her change her mind again. She went straight to a small private hospital, the discreet haven she needed, where the head doctor gallantly kept her secret until he pronounced her well enough to go back to Africa.

It had never occurred to Tanne that she would not return to the farm. Africa was already in her blood. Her place was there, and her responsibilities. The natives trusted and depended on her and she could not let them down. Nor could she abandon the coffee plantation while Bror was still in the Army. Several of her relatives had invested in it, and she owed it to them to make it as productive as possible and to see to their interests. But she returned to a year of sorrow and her first experience of being terribly alone, and she always recalled 1917 with bitterness.

The first distressing news that reached the farm concerned Katholm Castle. Uncle Laurentzius Dinesen had died the previous April, at the age of seventy-three. His life, which had begun with the brilliance and excitement of fireworks, had flickered out in loneliness and disappointment. At twenty-three he had returned from his Russian mission to find himself the most sought-after young man in Copenhagen, an Adonis with great allure and dash, resplendent in his uniform. For a while he had been a princely host at Katholm, but he had allowed the estate to become run-down; and when Wentzel, his heir, died in Paris a few years before Tanne went there to study painting, the place began to suffer from total neglect. To compensate for the dreariness of it all, Laurentzius had become a teller of tall tales, magnifying the remembered adventures of his youth. "When I was in Russia they served us whole sturgeon three meters long . . ." "How did they ever carry them to the table, Uncle Lars?" "Five big blackamoors carried them in . . ."

"When I was in Rome I was greatly honored; I was placed on the right of the Pope's wife at a banquet," the children invented to go him one better. Lars the Liar they called him behind his back. Fate had not even permitted Laurentzius to keep his good looks. Years of illness ending in apoplexy had caused his death. Only his daughter, Countess Agnes Knuth, was left, and now the slow post from Europe (always awaited with mingled anticipation and dread) brought the news that she had sold Katholm to strangers.

Bror was away, so Tanne sat alone by the fire (after dark there was always a fire against the night chill of the African upland), letting her thoughts run sadly over the past. No doubt she would never see Katholm again. All the Dinesen children had gone there, off and on, during their summer holidays, and they shared countless memories of great weekend parties (Thomas later remembered eight-course dinners with two bottles of wine for each man), duck shoots and fishing, and wild rides across the moors. How they had laughed, remembering the beach cabin where a flag was run up as a signal forbidding any man to approach within three hundred yards while the ladies changed into the bathing attire of the day—black garments with sleeves and ample skirts, black shoes and stockings, and kerchiefs on their heads.

Thomas had preferred Matrup, but Tanne and Anders had always had a deep possessive feeling about Katholm. They had been very bitter after Laurentzius' death when Thomas refused the inheritance of the estate because its farm could no longer be run profitably. Katholm, to be sure, had been in the family for less than a hundred years, but the particular atmosphere of the house and its moors and marshes had indelibly stamped three generations of Dinesens. Her father had been born there, and it was there that Tanne first began to understand his complex nature—and her own too. Perhaps it was just as well that the place was sold. She herself would never have a child to take there, of that she now felt certain.

Her thoughts drifted on to her mother's family, where there were also great changes, equally sad. "Mama" had died and with her a whole era of family life had passed away. Ea's silvery voice would be heard no more in the concert halls and drawing rooms of Copenhagen. After ten years of unremitting work, minor successes and great disappointments, she had abandoned all idea of a career.

She had married Viggo de Neergaard and had moved to his estate among the great forests. Ellen had taken her modern ideas to Russia, a silly venture, and had tried unsuccessfully to join the British Nursing Service when the war broke out, and at last she had married Knud Dahl, a man whom Tanne disliked and whom Ellen herself didn't love. What dismal compromises! What a miserable end to so many aspirations! But had she done any better in marrying Bror?

Outside, the relentless cicadas were shrilling and from time to time the short, coughing roar of a lion, hunting in the hills, reverberated in an otherwise silent night. Too silent, she thought, and to create a diversion she called to Farah to bring her a glass of wine.

"Champagne?" asked the intuitive Farah, sensing that all was not well.

"No thank you. Just a glass of white wine."

The next post brought far worse news. Tanne's hands shook as she opened the black-bordered envelope. Thomas was at the front, somewhere in France, no doubt in constant danger, and at home anything might have happened. It took her several minutes, and she had to reread the letter before her mind could take in the fact that Daisy Frijs had died. For the rest of the day while she went about her work, dispensing medicine to the natives, settling their petty disputes, attending to details of the crops, farm animals, marketing, she put the letter out of her mind, as if by ignoring it she could render it nonexistent. After dinner she read it for the third time, and suddenly the house was too small to contain all her sorrow.

Out in the chilly night, heedless of the lions or leopards which might be prowling nearby, she ran down the driveway. To left and right the rows of whitewashed stones reflected the moonlight and unconsciously she let herself be guided by them, for she had little notion of where she was going. Overhead, bats skittered back and forth, and falling stars ran over the sky "like tears over a cheek." She had reached the place where the road turned off toward Nairobi when, without warning, a figure materialized out of the darkness. It was Farah. Without a word he handed her a warm coat and was reabsorbed into the night. The suddenness of it startled her, but a moment later the thought of his watchful presence, somewhere close by in the shadows, gave her a sense of gratitude and comfort. She walked slowly back to the house and went to bed and slept.

During one of Bror's brief visits to the farm Tanne tried to talk to him. It did not matter, she said, that he was indifferent to her happiness and well-being; she was learning to take care of herself and there were other things than marriage to fill a life, but she could not, would not tolerate the whole structure of petty deceptions and lies which were an insult to her intelligence and dignity. But how tell a man that you consider him devoid of moral values, even a menace to society? Because what he had done to her he would do, was doing, to others. It had been reported that he even beat the natives. Would he beat her if she angered him sufficiently? Bror heard her out, staring at her with a look of malevolent incomprehension, and without answering at all. A little later she heard him close the front door behind him too carefully, and then the rattle of his car as he drove off to Nairobi. A Tycho Brahe day, she reflected bitterly. An endless series of Tycho Brahe days, made worse by constant anxiety about Thomas at the front. She wondered to what place of violent fighting in France the Canadian Army had sent him. Had he even received the poem she had written for him?

Bror's angry departure coincided with the arrival of his friend

Baron Erik von Otter, who burst into the house with an obviously trumped-up excuse, and then lost no time in bringing the conversation around to the subject on his mind. That was like him. It was not without reason the natives, who had descriptive epithets for all the white settlers, called him Resase Modja ("One Cartridge"), a tribute not only to his accurate marksmanship but also to his unhesitating approach to any problem in hand. Out on safari Tanne herself had witnessed this singleness of purpose when a rhinoceros charged out of a papyrus swamp, a stone's throw away from the campsite. The natives scattered like dry brown leaves before a gale, but Erik confronted the irate beast without a qualm—one shot and no fuss.

Now, too, he came straight to the point. He knew all about Bror. He knew all about the miserable life Tanne was leading. He loved her. She was to get a divorce and marry him!

Having once declared himself, he came back to the farm whenever he could escape from military or other duties, and though Tanne was not in love with him, gradually his presence became a sort of necessity. His devotion did much to restore her faltering self-esteem, and flirting with him gave her a sense of being womanly again. He had sound advice for the plantation, and laughed her out of her morbid fear of opening letters from Europe.

"You see! What did I tell you?" he crowed when the exhilarating news came that Thomas had been awarded the V.C., and again when a letter from Ea announced the birth of a niece and namesake for Tanne, Karen Christence de Neergaard.

During the long pleasant evenings they spent together by the fire, Tanne's affection and admiration grew for this "ideal soldier and hunter" who was full of kindliness and virtue. When conversation languished, as it often did because he was a man of deeds rather than words, she would fix her very-seeing eyes upon him, trying to adapt him to her personal image of love or trying to alter her idea of love to fit the man that he was. The emptiness in her heart was such that she might easily have made another compromise and married Erik without love. But at this point Denys came on the scene and her whole existence regained its proper focus.

II

Happiness in Africa

—◠◠◠—

In 1919 Tanne met Denys Finch-Hatton, who was to play the most meaningful role in her life—more than the father whom she had lost too soon; more than the "really forever" love of her girlhood; more than Bror, who had briefly been the good companion but had left her a legacy of illness, humiliation and bitterness.

Denys, the younger son of the Earl of Winchilsea and Nottingham, had been subjected to every effort to give him the traditional education for the role he was expected to fill, but none of this had he found acceptable on his own terms. From the beginning Denys went his own way and did as he pleased. Not that he ever antagonized anyone; rather, he disarmed them. At Eton, although always involved in some sort of escapade, Denys "was a great figure, not only to the Masters and boys, but to the Eton population at large, human and animal . . . Autocrat and democrat, an adored tyrant . . . his real life was his friends." He was an ardent and discriminating student of poetry and music, and had talents and qualities of every kind. "How else could he have dominated the school as few boys can ever have dominated it before or since?"

Even his stint in the war had been marked by an idealistic inability to conform; on Christmas Day, when grenades were being hurled into the enemy lines, Denys had flung Christmas puddings and got demoted for his trouble. Afterwards, to evade the routine career in England which he felt lay in wait for him like a devouring beast, he left for Africa, where he at once, and for the first time in his life, was *en rapport* with himself and his surroundings.

"Denys could indeed have been placed harmoniously in any period of our civilization, *tout comme chez soi,* all up to the opening of the nineteenth century," wrote Tanne in *Out of Africa.* "He would have cut a figure in any age, for he was an athlete, a musician, a lover of art and a fine sportsman. He did cut a figure in his own age, but it did not quite fit in anywhere. His friends in England always wanted him to come back; they wrote out plans and schemes for a career for him there, but Africa was keeping him."

Based in Nairobi, he made his own career as a safari expert. Either he led the safaris, or alone in his small airplane, he flew over vast areas of Kenya, locating herds of elephant and buffalo. He was not, however, a professional killer and was, in fact, more interested in conserving the game than destroying it. He shot lion ruthlessly when their marauding raids on cattle became a problem; otherwise he worked to help the government establish a census of the wild animals and formulate the hunting regulations needed to protect them. The natives were abjectly devoted to him, and the Kenya colonists fell equally under his spell.

When Tanne first saw Denys she was, like everyone else, dazzled by his appearance. The "superb good looks" mentioned in the

Eton Chronicle consisted in a lean, lithe physique of pantherine grace, curly blond hair bleached lighter by the tropical sun, the keenest of eyes, a sensual mouth and an astonishingly Greek profile. Many years later Tanne enjoyed bringing out photographs of Denys and one of a Hermes statue to point out the extraordinary similarities—the long straight nose and almost too short upper lip, the classic proportions and sculptural curls.

In Africa, Denys had no proper home of his own. He possessed a few acres of land on which he built a small house, but it was remotely situated on the Indian Ocean near Takaungu, north of Mombasa. When he was not on safari he lived, rather drearily, in a room at the club in Nairobi. Lacking in quiet and privacy, with nothing personal in it to come home to, it was simply a place to lay his head between jobs. All this changed when he met Tanne. From then on he "had no other home in Africa than the farm, he lived at my house between his safaris, and kept his books and gramophone there. When he came back to the farm, it gave out what was in it; it spoke—as the coffee plantations speak when with the first showers of the rainy season they flower, dripping wet, a cloud of chalk. When I was expecting Denys back, and heard his car coming up the drive, I heard, at the same time, the things of the farm all telling me what they really were."

Sometimes Denys showed up after an absence of two or three months. Sometimes he remained at the farm for a few days only, or occasionally he stayed for many weeks. He came in from his long treks or his lonely flights to faraway places, hungry for everything that he knew the house would provide; European food, chilled wine in Tanne's fragile glasses, the visual delight of the flowers which she arranged with such skill, a hundred things to charm a discerning taste, but, above all, good talk. At the farm he could air his thoughts, discuss the books he had been reading and the ideas that had preoccupied him while he was alone in the jungle. "We sat over the dinner table into the small hours of the morning, talking of all the things we could think of, and mastering them all, and laughing at them."

He was a teacher as well as a talker. In knowledge of Shakespeare, Tanne was a match for him, but in Bible lore, the classics and poetry Denys far surpassed her, and he never wearied of explaining the details of his preferred passages or the merits of this or that author. He went to infinite trouble to instruct her, sending home to England for books to add to the considerable library he had kept at the club and which he now installed at the farm.

So Tanne's intellectual horizons widened, and her spiritual horizons reached out too. Having finally broached with Bror the distressing features of their eventual divorce, the resentment in her seemed to melt away. It was settled that Bror would liquidate his interest in the plantation (Tanne's family had after all been the largest investors) and that he would purchase some other property which, in any event, he would hardly use, since he was now a professional hunter and constantly on safari. At last Tanne could walk out on the farm, her farm, with serenity in her heart. Six thousand feet high under the African sky, six thousand acres of land, six hundred acres of it planted in coffee, with six hundred coffee trees to the acre. Wasn't there a sort of magic in these numbers?

There was, in any case, magic in what went on between Tanne and the natives. When she first arrived in Kenya she had set up a clinic on the terrace next to the house. "I knew very little of doctoring, just what you learn in a first-aid course. But my renown as a doctor had been spread by a few chance lucky cures, and had not been decreased by the catastrophic mistakes I had made." Her patients came each morning, and when medicine was lacking she improvised. The power of her imagination and the extent to which the natives trusted her are nowhere more beautifully illustrated than in the story, "Letter from a King," in which she tells how, after a terrible accident, one of the farm hands was actually relieved of pain by her placing a letter from the King of Denmark in his hands and convincing him that it was really a talisman.

She also started an evening school on the farm to teach the natives reading and writing. Old and young attended faithfully, even, to her great pride, when lions were known to be prowling near the schoolhouse. It was Tanne the natives sent for when these lions raided their herds. They knew she would go out to shoot them more fearlessly than any of the farm managers. Their chiefs conferred with her and she presided at the *kyamas* (native trials) where her word was final. Such prestige was not lightly come by. She put her heart into learning native lore, and in order to pass judgment on disputes among the Somalis she had even studied the manual of Mohammedan law. The Somali women were educated, led very protected lives and were extremely coy and shy, but even they invited Tanne to visit them, and she in turn took them to call on the priests at the French mission or to have tea at the houses of friends, treating them with all the consideration she would have bestowed upon her neighbors at Rungstedlund.

Totos (small native boys) were underfoot all day, doing odd jobs or playing games, and always watching with astounded joy the hourly performance of the cuckoo clock. In particular there was Kamante, a little Kikuyu boy whom she had found herding goats on the plain. Undersized for his age, emaciated, his legs raw with running sores, Kamante had been a pathetic, even a horrifying sight. Tanne's remedies had failed to make him well. She took him to be cured at the Scotch Mission Hospital, and then adopted him into the house. First he was dog *toto,* proud of his responsibility for the deerhounds, who were bigger and stronger than he was; then he became medical helper, cook's assistant and finally an inspired chef.

A motley assemblage of animals had been added by degrees to Tanne's great family of dark-skinned humans. Lulu, the antelope, became a spoiled and petted tyrant, and even after she had gone back to the jungle in search of a mate she returned for visits. Standing at the far edge of the lawn with her buck and fawn, who were too timid to venture nearer, she would stare wistfully at the house and the people she had known and trusted. A tall stork also had the run of the house, and there were always cubs of one kind or another, and of course Dusk the deerhound and later his son, Pania, as well as horses and ponies, much beloved. Contemplating them all with tenderness and sometimes, it must be admitted, with exasperation, Tanne's thoughts would revert to her father, from whom she had inherited her joy in simple people and animals; he would have been pleased with her now, she concluded.

As time went by, there were many visitors too from the colony of white settlers: Hugh Martin, a brilliant talker; Ingrid Lindstrom, wife of a Swedish farmer, who loved her land and her animals more than her life; Gustav Mohr, a Norwegian colonist who was famished to the point of frenzy for serious conversation; "Uncle Charles" Bulpett, a delightful Victorian Englishman; and many others who became devoted friends. The reader must seek them out in the pages of *Out of Africa*, where they have acquired their particular immortality. Beyond all, there was Berkeley Cole, who was Denys' friend to begin with and who, in the end, became an intimate of the house. He too must be sought out in Tanne's book, and known, and inevitably loved.

It was to please Berkeley Cole that Tanne had brought back from her second visit to Copenhagen a pair of old ship lanterns to hang at the main door of the house. Berkeley, who was English and a brother-in-law of Lord Delamere, the *éminence grise* of Kenya, "had a great, ever unsatisfied love of the sea"—a longing shared by Tanne. Coming as she did from a seafaring nation where it is never possible to be more than fifty miles distant from the shore, it was the one thing she missed in the African highlands. After dark, when the lanterns were lighted, the house took on the look of a ship riding at anchor, and a further trick of the imagination could transmute the night-shadowed lawn into a wide expanse of blue-black sea. The lanterns were a final touch to crown the perfections of the house. Denys, left to his own devices, would have "modernized" and hung paintings by Picasso and Matisse, but Tanne and Berkeley reveled in every old-fashioned detail. The sitting room had a high ceiling with hewn beams, sombre paneled walls and a stone fireplace, all of which reminded Berkeley of English manor houses as much as it reminded Tanne of country places she had known around Elsinore. In the paneled dining room were prints which Wilhelm Dinesen had owned and loved, and all of her childhood was evoked by the white-painted eighteenth-century furniture that had been sent out for her bedroom.

The coffee trees planted four years ago were now beginning to flower and fruit. Many had been killed by drought or pests but they were being replaced. Tanne supervised while the farm hands carried the trays of new young trees out to the fields in the downpour of the rainy season and set them carefully in the ground with the taproots straight. Soon these trees too would flower. Like everything else in nature, it was a mysterious and poetic cycle, she thought, and as she was profoundly religious, she prayed often that she also would fulfill God's destiny for her "in a manner worthy of His intention." At the end of a day of exhausting activity

it restored her calm and contentment to gaze out over the plantation and see, according to the seasons, the patterned rows of bright-
green foliage, the drifts of white, bittersweet-scented blossoms, or
the gay red berries of the harvest.

The days were full, but too often the solitary nights were hard
to bear. They brought a frantic need for the sound of a civilized
human voice to offset the heavy silence indoors with its incessant
obbligato of cicadas shrilling outside the house. Denys' absences
seemed long, too long. The natives, with their fine intuition, knew
what was wrong. Their acute extrasensory perception also con-
veyed information to them before it could be substantiated by the
sober facts the white man relied on. "Bedar will be here in three
days," they would announce. How did they know? And in three
days, it was true, Denys would be sitting beside her, describing his
own adventures and listening to her account of all things, good or
bad, that had happened at the farm during his safari—talking,
laughing, until the neglected fire had dwindled to blue-grey ash on
the hearth and dawn showed blue-white at the windows.

"There is such magic in the people and the land here," she
said to him on one such evening.

Denys smiled at her with affectionate condescension. "The
magic is not in the people and the land," he replied, "but in the eye
of the beholder. Imagine how many people would find this place
insufferably dull! You bring your own magic to it, Tania." And
after a moment he added with tenderness, "Titania."

"Tania" he called her, for Denys had not only transformed her
life but had changed her name as well. She was Tania to Denys,
and it was the name she chose to use to the end of her days.

III

Denmark Revisited

—⁓⁓⁓—

She had not admitted it to anyone, not even to the Nairobi doctor, but by 1920 the state of her health was causing Tania great anxiety. Too often she suffered from fatigue that accorded ill with her soaring spirits. From time to time, pain made her catch her breath and stop whatever she was doing, waiting helplessly for the spasm to pass. It happened more and more often. Soon it would no longer be possible to hide it from Denys or anyone else, and she finally had to concede that she couldn't postpone another visit to Denmark. Anyway, it would make her mother happy. She would see her sisters, and Thomas, home from the war. Anders had been in Jutland for a year managing Leerbæk, the estate of George Sass, husband of "Mama's" youngest daughter, Aunt Lidda, but of course he would come back to Rungstedlund when he heard that Tania was there. And the question of her illness could perhaps be settled for good.

This time she was sure that she couldn't be away from Africa without having at least one native with her. Farah could not be spared from the farm, and all her Kikuyus were far too wild and ignorant. Her choice finally fell on Abdullai, a Somali boy about twelve years old who had all the alert intelligence and gentle manners of his tribe. The first step was a ceremonious visit to Abdullai's mother to obtain her permission, and then an equally solemn call on the priest, who demanded a promise that the boy would never eat pork during the trip.

When they eventually set sail from Mombasa, it was not direct for Europe as usual, but via Bombay. From there a ship would take them to England. Tania was too sick to enjoy much sightseeing, but she was glad of a ten-day delay in India that gave her some glimpses of another and very different civilization. Her main amusement, however, was observing the reactions of her Somali boy. His first ride in the elevator at the Hotel Taj Mahal left him gasping. His eyes bulged in amazed disbelief. But after that initial surprise he was never caught off guard again. It was as though he had made up his mind that he had, once and for all, entered a world where everything impossible was possible.

In London, the Hotel Carlton was crowded and no accommodations could be had for Abdullai. Tania felt too responsible for him not to keep him close by, so she ended by installing him in her bathroom and had to remove him from the tub whenever she wanted to bathe. For the first few days he clung to her, but then he became fast friends with an elevator boy named Hopkins. He rode up and down in the lift for hours at a time and Hopkins' word became law. In any subsequent discussion with Tania (and there were many), Abdullai would say firmly, "No, msabu, it cannot be so because 'Opikins says . . ." One day he announced that Hopkins would have an evening off and had invited Abdullai to spend it with him. Tania thought it prudent to inquire into the plans for the outing. The Russian Ballet! Could Karsavina and Sokolova ever have danced for an odder pair of spectators? "I saw several mem-sahibs who could fly," reported Abdullai gravely.

But neither this sortie nor exciting shopping tours (Tania couldn't resist seeing her boy in trim little London suits with his vivid turbans) seemed to equal Abdullai's joy in visits to the zoo. Each day he insisted on going there and Tania was at a loss to understand it. Was the child perhaps unconsciously homesick for Africa and its animals? Abdullai enlightened her: one of his sisters, he said, had been carried off and eaten by a crocodile, so he derived a special satisfaction from seeing the captive crocodiles, harmless and humiliated behind the bars.

All this was pleasant, but Tania was impatient to get to Copenhagen. Shipping hadn't yet gone back to the normal efficiency of prewar days, so weeks went by and still no passage could be obtained. Denys, who had taken advantage of Tania's absence from the farm to visit his own family in England, finally located a small ship which was to sail to Bergen from Newcastle and he drove her there in his car. "Don't forget to come home" was all he said as they stood on the pier, but it was enough. The African farm was really home. They both knew it.

On the back of the ship's menu Tania drew a map. "See, Abdullai, how far we have traveled to reach my other home!" Even the wanderer Odysseus, whose story she often told to the native children, had not gone nearly so far: from Mombasa to India, England, Norway and finally Copenhagen.

Alfred Pedersen, the old coachman, now in his twenty-fifth year of service with the family, was there to meet them, this time driving an automobile.

Oh, the happiness of once more walking under the great beech trees up to the top of Ewald's Hill, and from there to feast the eyes on all the lovingly remembered details of the landscape! The sloping cow pastures were now silvery with rime, and snow lay on the boughs of the great lilac tree at the back door. Beyond the house and beach, out in the Sound, Hveen Island was adrift in its veils of winter fog.

Soon after the homecoming the pond froze over. Tania explained the phenomenon to Abdullai with a warning. "The ice is still too thin to walk on," she said. But what twelve-year-old boy could wait to make the experiment? While Tania sat talking to her mother and Thomas, Abdullai fell through the ice. He was lucky enough to struggle ashore, and sneaked up to his room hoping not to be seen but, alas, a telltale wet trail betrayed him. White with rage and fright, Tania raced upstairs. He had escaped drowning, but he might have caught pneumonia.

"Will you tell your family about this?" she asked when peace was restored between them.

"Of course not, msabu! How would they ever believe that I walked on water?"

It was difficult for Tania to tear herself away from Rungstedland, but there was the doctor to face. He was far from reassuring. The treatment during her previous stay at the hospital, too drastic and too curtailed, had done permanent damage. She must face the fact that she would never be really well again, would always have to endure pain, would always have to be careful not to tax her strength. There was, however, nothing immediately dangerous. Having dreaded much worse, Tania's spirits lifted. She faced her treatments bravely and she was able to enjoy the remaining weeks in Denmark.

Abdullai followed her wherever she went, waiting outside for her during the trying sessions at the doctor's office, carrying packages when she felt well enough to shop. With his eager brown face and flashing smile, his colorful turbans and new London clothes, he seemed a bright flame against the early winter darkness, the grey mist and snow flurries of the Copenhagen streets. The stolid citizens turned around to stare at him and whisper among themselves. And who is to say that Tania (who all her life loved to *faire de l'effet*) had not had all this very much in mind when she had chosen to travel, like an eighteenth-century *grande dame*, with her own exotic blackamoor?

Abdullai was unimpressed by the commotion he created. In fact, he adapted himself to his surroundings with ease, and before it was time to return to Africa he was speaking Danish with the exact inflection of Alfred Pedersen, who had become his boon companion.

IV

Thomas in Kenya

—⁓⁓—

For several years after the war, life in Kenya was very hard. Prices had dropped suddenly from the wartime high, and farmers found no market for African products except at rates that could only bring on bankruptcy. In consequence, land values also fell—a personal disappointment to Tania, who had hoped to lure her older brother to Africa. While Thomas was serving in the Canadian Army, she had taken advantage of a land privilege available to British officers and had secured for him the right to buy a fairly large farm at a special price. He traveled back with her when she returned from Denmark, in December 1920, but by the time they arrived in Kenya the purchase privilege was no longer worthwhile and he did not avail himself of it, although he did stay on for a long visit.

In 1921 formal divorce proceedings were begun between Bror and Tania. Depressing, she thought—like having to put a period at the end of a badly written sentence. At least it was a comfort to have Thomas there to advise and help her with the sordid aspects of it, as he also did with the ever more complicated business details of the farm.

It was good to be able to cling to him too when they learned that Ea had died. Tania's religious acceptance had helped her through many troubles but now it was shaken, and for weeks she could think of nothing but her gifted sister who had died so young. It was futile, she knew, to wrestle with the unanswerable question of death, but there had been too many deaths in the family since she had come out to Kenya. She couldn't cope with so much without trying to understand something of it. Had Ea's life reached some sort of fulfillment which the rest of them couldn't perceive? Having given up the singing career she had longed for, had she resigned herself to domestic happiness during her six brief years of marriage? Who would ever know? As who would ever know the misery which she herself had endured with Bror?

Thomas lingered on for two more years. Like Bror, like Denys, like every man, it would seem, who found himself in Africa, he must needs go big-game hunting, and again there were lonely hours at the farm. Tania spent them painting and produced a number of interesting portraits. Farah's young brother Abdullahi, a Kikuyu girl, a Masai warrior, these were colorful subjects and she enjoyed the work which she had so long neglected. But her pictures became a matter of controversy with both Denys and Thomas. Denys, with no intended unkindness, was critical because he preferred modern art; Thomas erred for want of a more exacting opinion.

"Now, what do you think of it?" Tania demanded of her brother when he returned after a few weeks' absence.

"Splendid," poor Thomas replied. "The hands of the old man are just right now."

"Oh, you are hopeless! I haven't worked on the hands at all. No, it's impossible to do any good work when no one in Africa takes any real interest in it!"

There were heated debates with Denys, whose tastes in art she refused to understand, and a violent quarrel with Thomas about the laws of perspective. In the end, she laid away her brushes and paints.

Thomas departed, but the following year, 1924, he returned, bringing their mother. Mrs. Dinesen was still grieving so much over Ea's death that her alarmed doctor had insisted on a change of scene. She was coming to visit Tania for several months.

There were storms of tears when she arrived, and then, as the doctor had foreseen, she became engrossed in her new surroundings. The scenery, wild animals, unfamiliar trees and flowers, it all delighted her. Tania's hard-working day on the farm astonished her more than anything else, and she wanted to be shown everything, from the morning first-aid clinic to the outspanning of the oxen at night. The natives, who called her "the old memsahib," were deeply impressed by her. The only white women they had seen until then were young, lithe, suntanned, with close-cropped hair like Tania's. Mrs. Dinesen, imposing in her voluminous, long black dresses, also had a remarkable head of hair. It still retained its warm color, in spite of her sixty-six years, and was so long that she could sit on it.

"Take down your hair, Mother," Tania begged her time and again. "Let the native girls see it."

One day Tania simply pulled out the pins and the great coils of hair came tumbling down. "*Un succès fou*, Mother! Lady Godiva could not have done better!"

The native girls stood around, gasping like fish out of water. And for a long time afterwards they kept coming back to the house at the hour when Mrs. Dinesen came downstairs for tea. They would wait for her on the terrace and ask to see her hair again.

. . .

This time Thomas had discussions with Tania which reached the point of anger. He had lent her money and helped her in every possible way, but conditions did not improve. He advised her to sell the farm and return to Europe before the whole venture collapsed. All the money their mother and uncle and he himself had invested would be lost if she persisted. It was better to save what they could.

Tania listened, her heart contracted with panic and despair. She believed in the farm and her ability to run it successfully. She loved Africa and wished to live nowhere else. She did not speak of Denys. But how could she leave him?

Mrs. Dinesen went home, and at the end of a seven-month stay Thomas abandoned any plan of settling in Kenya himself. He departed for Denmark, stopping off for a safari in British Somaliland. Tania knew he would never return when, after less than a year's interval, he married Jonna Maria Lindhardt and eventually bought a house not far from Rungsted. Tania would not have liked what he had to say in later years when he recalled his last visit to Kenya: ". . . in contrast with my sister I never had any faith in the future of the farm, and before I left Africa for good I had almost given up hope for its success. Such a view necessarily gave my whole stay a dreary aspect. The genius of my sister as an author apart, she was perhaps the greatest woman I have known, but as a farm manager she was totally incompetent."

The troubles of the farm were so numerous by now as to be insoluble. In all their discouraging details, Elspeth Huxley has described similar difficulties at the plantation in Thika. Tania's farm was two thousand feet higher in the uplands and all the difficulties were multiplied. When coffee prices had fallen so low that it meant bankruptcy to sell at the going rate, she attempted to ward off the final catastrophe by producing charcoal, by starting a dairy business, by raising flax, by any expedient to prevent selling her land, which the Danish investors now urged her to do as they saw the revenue on their money dwindling more and more. But how could she live away from the Ngong Hills and her own beloved acres? How abandon her family of natives?

And that great family had grown. By 1927 a whole village of thatched *manyattas* spread out from the edge of the tilled land toward the plain, and natives of every kind, feeling welcome and understood, kept arriving from faraway places, singly or in groups. Once there had been two thousand of them to attend a *ngoma* (native dance festival). The staff too had changed and grown with Nichols, the new South African manager; Belknap, the American manager of the coffee mill; and Pooran Singh, the Indian carpenter. Farah had brought a wife, and a son was born to them at the farm. Esa, the old head cook, after a lifetime of yearning to be a gardener, died with his hand in Tania's and was replaced by Kamante, now a young man and, amazingly, a genius in the kitchen. His reputation in the colony was legendary and he cooked at least one immortal dinner when the Prince of Wales came to the farm. And "sometimes visitors from Europe drifted into the farm like wrecked timber into still waters, turned and rotated, until in the end they were washed out again, or dissolved and sank. Old Knudsen, the Dane, had come to the farm, sick and blind, and stayed there for the time it took him to die . . ."

"These are my people, this is my world" was now constantly in Tania's mind, and when Denys next came home from safari, she told him that she felt sure she would live out her life and die in Africa, and had chosen her burial ground in the Ngong Hills. They rode out there to look at the place, and Denys said that he too would be buried there. A solemn moment.

But Denys was as likely to tease as to respond with sympathy. He always insisted that he had inherited his character from an ancestor, the seventeenth-century poetess Anne Finch; but the poet in him was constantly being jilted for the imp who still loved schoolboy pranks. He would spend a whole evening soberly propounding to Tania the significance of a Bible passage, and the next morning he would deliberately terrify the townspeople by doing "loop the loops" above their houses in his rickety plane, rolling about in the sky like a playful dolphin. His family went on imploring him to return to England and make use of his brilliant gifts in some serious career. When he did go to London it was on a whimsical impulse to hear a concert, and he came back to Africa the same day without even calling them on the telephone.

What he loved most at the farm was his absolute freedom to come and go. Alas, each time he went it seemed to Tania harder to bear. It "was very lonely, and in the stillness of the evenings when the minutes dripped from the clock, life seemed to be dripping out of you with them." Sensing all this and feeling too much alone himself, Berkeley Cole came often to dine and Tania felt needed by him and appreciated, but it was not enough.

It was even difficult, at such times, to concentrate on reading. "In Africa when you pick up a book worth reading, out of the deadly consignments which good ships are being made to carry out all the way from Europe, you read it as an author would like his book to be read, praying to God that he may have it in him to go on as beautifully as he has begun. Your mind runs transported, upon a fresh deep green track." Books like this were rare, but chance brought her Ernest Hemingway's *The Sun Also Rises*. In one of those letters which, conscientiously, she wrote every Sunday she told her mother, "You will hear of this talented writer again," and later was proud of having been so discerning. Hemingway never knew of the letter, of course, but he returned the compliment when he received the Nobel Prize and told the press that he felt unworthy of the honor, which, in his opinion, should have been bestowed on Isak Dinesen.

As a last resort against worry and loneliness Tania began to write. A long time had passed since she handed "The de Cats Family" to Mario Krohn—eighteen years—and in the interval nothing had appeared in print except for a poem in 1925, and the following year the marionette comedy, a grown-up version of the little play she had written when still a child. Now, threatened with the loss of her farm, exile from the land she loved, she began to record her impressions of Africa and to set down first drafts of the stories which she invented and told to Denys to amuse him on rainy evenings.

Soon her nights passed all too swiftly and she began to steal time from farm work, writing far into the day and thanking God for the excuse it gave her to avert her eyes from the ravages out-of-doors. During the cold season, frost had browned and withered the coffee berries. Now there was drought, shriveling the trees and the hearts of those who watched the disaster. In 1927, Mrs. Dinesen came for another visit, with a further loan for the farm; she had hoped to bring comfort with her presence, but she returned to Denmark as convinced as Thomas had been that the situation was hopeless.

It was more than anyone could bear, said Denys, viewing the ruined crop. He had also noticed that Tania had seemed distressed when she learned that Bror had remarried. She must get away from it all, if only briefly; and brushing aside her protests, he shipped her to England to stay with his family.

V

Farewell

—⁓⁓⁓—

Two years before, Denys' father had died and his older brother, Viscount Maidstone, became the Earl of Winchilsea. "Maisie" and his American wife, Margaretta, and their children had lived since then at Buckfield, the family estate, and it was there that Tania went for her holiday in 1929. One may wonder what her impression was on first seeing the place where Denys stayed. She never wrote or spoke of it. Perhaps it was too closely linked in her mind with the sad events that followed. But thirty years later "Maisie's" daughter Diana described the scene. She had been a small girl when Tania arrived; now she was a grandmother and all the main players of the drama had disappeared—"Maisie" was no longer alive; Denys lay buried on a high peak of the Ngong Hills he had loved; and Tania herself had found final repose beneath one of the great beech trees on Ewald's Hill.

"It was a large ugly red brick house," Diana remembered, "redeemed by being almost completely disguised by wonderful creepers—magnolia, wisteria, clematis—which grew right up to the roof. Inside, it was spacious and comfortable and friendly. I think that its real charm lay in the atmosphere of unity and love which my devoted parents created.

"After my American grandfather gave us one of the first automatic gramophones we always had music every night, gradually collecting a huge record library from which we all selected what we wanted to listen to—except for *Petrouchka*. This was strictly *verboten*, because it had been Denys' favorite. The garden was glorious—sweeping lawns, old beautiful trees, a lake, a swimming pool surrounded by flower-beds and yew hedges, a wood full of rhododendrons and lilies.

"Now that it is a girls' school, all the creepers except the magnolia have been torn off, so that it looks rather as Queen Mary might have had someone wrenched the pearls from her neck and knocked the toque off her head.

"We rarely asked anyone to stay at Buckfield twice; after the first occasion they invited themselves."

To Buckfield, Denys had brought the woman he loved, and "Maisie" and Margaretta were prepared to love her on his account. Tania, however, enjoyed being loved for her own sake. She put herself out to be charming, which was very charming indeed. She was that rare guest who could walk in the gardens and name each flower, who could discourse knowingly on the pleasures of wine and the table, who could beguile the children with tales of African *totos* and animals, whose low-voiced talk was warm, wise, humorous, who seemed to have *le mot juste* for everything.

They found her delightful. But did they notice a strained, sad look in her eyes when conversation lapsed? Alone in her room, she cried helplessly or sat staring at emptiness as she wrestled with the questions that would have to be settled the day she returned to Kenya. If she had to give up the farm, what would become of her?

What dreary new life would she have to begin again away from Africa, Denys and everything she cared for? And what would become of her natives if she abandoned them? Denys had offered the small house on his property in Takaungu. He had even suggested building something larger and more modern for her, but white people could not live long in the climate there. How would her damaged health withstand the heat and humidity of the equator at sea level, where even the nights were feverish? Neither would she ever permit herself to think of a more permanent future with Denys. He was a wild bird, not to be tied like a falcon at the wrist, nor caged in a conventional marriage. He must be free to come and go or he would fly away forever, as he had fled responsibilities in England and the mild restraints of Nairobi. No! She must go back to Kenya as quickly as possible and face what had to be faced.

"Farah came to meet me in Mombasa, and I dared not ask him about the coffee crop straight away; for some time we talked of other news of the farm. But in the evening as I was going to bed, I could not put it off any longer and I asked how many tons of coffee they had picked on the farm in all. The Somalis are generally pleased to announce a disaster. But here Farah was not happy, he was extremely grave himself, standing by the door, and he half closed his eyes and laid back his head, swallowing his sorrow, when he said: 'Forty tons, memsahib.' At that I knew we could not carry on. All colour and life had faded out of the world around me; the bleak and stifling Mombasa hotel room, with the cemented floor, old iron bedstead and worn mosquito net, took on a tremendous significance as the symbol of the world, without any single ornament or article of embellishment of human life in it. I did not say anything more to Farah, and he did not speak again, but went away, the last friendly object in the world."

"At destruction and famine thou shalt laugh," said the Book, but even Job had complained. And as with Job, there would be further trials to bear. Grasshoppers came to the farm, the terrible Biblical scourge of locusts. There were such hordes of them that for days they darkened the sky. They broke the branches of trees by the sheer weight of their numbers. They devastated the land. Flowers and vegetable gardens, shrubbery, grainfields, everything that was Tania's or belonged to the pathetic native huts was reduced to tattered leaves and stripped, bare stalks. Nothing was spared. It was the end.

In 1931 the farm was sold to a real estate development. The furniture was dispersed, here, there. The horses were sold, and Dinah and David, grandchildren of Dusk the deerhound were given away. Denys gave all of his books to Tania and moved, with the rest of his belongings, back to Nairobi, but he drove out each evening to dine with her, both of them sitting on the packing cases that contained his books and hers.

" 'He shall lean upon his house, but it shall not stand; he shall hold it fast, but it shall not endure,' " she quoted for him. Denys could not tolerate tears, and she could at least spare him that. She could please him, rather, by showing how apt a Bible student she had been.

One more thing had to be attended to before she could turn her back on Africa. Her natives wished to remain together and a place had to be found for them. Many meetings with government officials would be needed to accomplish this, and while Tania was busy with the project Denys flew to Takaungu to see to some repairs on his property. On the sixth day, when he was expected back, Tania went into town in the morning. Panic seized her when everyone she met seemed deliberately to avoid her, but at last someone had the courage to tell her that there had been an accident: as Denys was taking off for the homeward flight to Nairobi his plane crashed.

Denys was buried on the Ngong mountaintop which he and Tania had chosen together. Afterwards Farah helped Tania raise a white banner there so that during the time that remained to her on the farm she could look up toward the hills and see the exact place of the grave.

Berkeley Cole had died too, while Tania was in England, but Gustav Mohr drove over from his farm to help her. That great talker was now silenced by the sorrow he shared with Tania. The natives were silent too. For several days Denys' safari boys and Tania's servants lingered outside the house. There was nothing for them to do. They simply sat on the ground, huddled in speechless grief. Then one by one they went away. Pooran Singh returned to India. Farah's family moved to Nairobi's Somali village. The others drifted away, leaves fallen from the parent tree, leaves which the wind scatters to their separate dusty destinies.

Farah, as he had always done, would travel with her as far as Mombasa, and Gustav Mohr drove both of them to Nairobi station. Farewell, Nairobi! Farewell, farm and jungle and plain and sky of Africa! Farewell, Denys!

Part Three

—◦◦◦◦—

Rungstedlund Again

I
Seven Gothic Tales

—〰〰—

Almost unconsciously Tania sought out the old bench on Ewald's Hill and sat there each day, unaware of surroundings she had once loved. The beech trees now seemed meaningless to one who ached for the flame-trees, the coffee trees and bamboos of Kenya and a world without Denys' voice and face was empty. Inevitably she thought of her father, pacing back and forth in his room, asking himself whether it was possible to prolong an existence that had no reality at all. Ah, she understood him now!

"*Quant à moi*," she reflected bitterly, "I have come home alone and a failure. A sort of prodigal daughter; though it's not the fatted calf that's being served up, but the ill-disguised pity of everybody who comes to the house."

Only one person regarded her return as a triumph—the artist with whom she had flirted during her student days in Paris. At that time they had laughed over the curious fact that for three generations, relatives of his, one after the other, had been in love with women of Tania's family. And here was Tania now, divorced and free! Why shouldn't they begin where they had left off in Paris and make a new life together? After all, he pleaded, he had proved himself by loving her faithfully, doggedly, for twenty-one years. But soon it was obvious even to him that he was in love with a phantom—that this was not the Tanne he had known. This was a mature woman, numb with private sorrows which he could neither share nor alleviate, a stranger who only wanted to be alone. Even her name had changed! When he finally realized the hopelessness of trying to recapture what was past and gone, the unfortunate man killed himself. To Tania, in her overwrought state, it seemed a sign: for her, too, it was the only thing that remained to do.

After this, Ewald's Hill became a place to avoid. Her father's ghost still lingered there; he had taken his own life too, and now she became unsure that Denys' death was an accident. She fled to the beach and people shook their heads when they saw her there, walking, walking, desperately walking, her long wool cloak billowing behind her like the sails of the fishing boats out on the sea. Sometimes the magnified sound of voices from the boats came echoing toward her over the water, and always it seemed a sound of laughter. Empty laughter.

If gradually she was restored to some sort of calm, it was due to Thomas, who realized her depths of despair and the difficulties of her readjustment. Although he was now a married man with two children, he arranged to see her often. Wise and kind, he understood her nervous compulsion to tear at her wounds, and he let her talk on and on about Africa, consoling her for all the mistakes that had brought on the debacle. He foresaw, too, how impossible it would be for Tania, after so many years of independence, to adapt herself to living with her mother at Rungstedlund, especially with no money of her own.

"If you get desperate," he said, "come to me and I'll help you."

Tania had not imagined that there would be any vexations at all. She was to share a large house with her mother, and had assumed that it would provide more than enough privacy for both of them. But the problem was Tania's role in the house. Because she was back in her girlhood room, her mother instinctively reverted to treating her like a child. She was constantly saying "Do this" or "Don't do that." Tania, saddened and matured beyond Mrs. Dinesen's understanding, and accustomed to being her own *maîtresse de maison,* found it unbearable. Aunt Bess came to cackle over her humbled return to the fold, and even Alfred Pedersen was patronizing. His stolid, simple mind retained the image of Tanne, a small tearful girl crouched in the back of his carriage, and refused to take in the idea that she could drive a car. He himself had become a willing if erratic chauffeur and now when Tania wanted to drive, he insisted on sitting beside her, giving maddening instructions at every turn. It gave Tania a sense of futility, as if she had somehow gone backwards in time and would have to live everything over again. Most irksome of all was having to beg for trivial sums of money.

"You smoke too much" was her mother's usual reply when she asked for a few kroner to buy cigarettes. One day she also remarked that Tania had become very spoiled in Africa.

"You don't even close doors behind you," she complained, as if this were the sum total of all grievances.

"Of course not!" snapped Tania, suddenly furious. "In Kenya my boys did it for me."

When she was next alone with Thomas, she was very contrite about losing her temper. "But it has made me realize that I can't go on like this. If you could lend me the money," she pleaded, "perhaps I could prepare for some sort of career and free myself of being dependent on Mother. It might even give me an interest in living." And she averted her face to hide a rush of tears.

When Thomas asked what sort of career she had in mind, Tania pointed out rather defensively that she had always displayed patience and imagination in handling children and simple or backward people. "I believe I'd also succeed with the mentally deficient. Couldn't I train to be matron of an asylum?"

Thomas' expression of horrified disbelief gave way to a shout of laughter, but Tania was unabashed. The farm, she suggested next, had had a great reputation for its cuisine, and though it had begun with the mere desire of pleasing Denys and Berkeley Cole, she had, after all, studied with a famous Paris chef. She could learn to supervise the kitchens of some restaurant or hotel.

"Impossible, Tanne." And Thomas explained that such jobs, if they were worth having, were always reserved for men. Women got only the second-rate places, which would be sordid, and besides, it was hard to imagine her spending the rest of her life among pots and pans.

"Perhaps I could write," she proposed tentatively, and was surprised at her brother's sudden enthusiasm. Indeed she wrote splendid letters, he said. He had also been quite impressed by three stories she had read to him in her hotel room in Marseille, where he had gone to meet her when she returned from Africa. Considering her early successes with *Tilskueren* magazine, she might do quite well if she really devoted herself to it. Besides, it was a decent profession for a woman.

"Would you write about Africa?"

Tania couldn't say.

She could not write about Africa. Not yet. She was still too deeply affected by all that had happened there. But other stories were only waiting to be told—countless stories. They might make a book, many books even, and in a mood of excitement and optimism she began to write them.

The enforced idleness of the first few months at Rungstedlund had been the restorative Tania needed after too much anxiety and emotion, and as her creative energies took wing, the petty daily vexations evaporated. Her relationship with her mother, though it was never one of real understanding and sympathy, became pleasant and easy. And she no longer viewed the scene around her with the hostility of a person who yearns to be somewhere else. Her love of Denmark and its old traditions revived. She walked up Ewald's Hill now, not to rail and weep, but to find inspiration; and surveying the countryside, she wondered how she could have been even momentarily blind to its particular beauty and legend. If these feelings only took final shape in Adam's homecoming, in a much later story called "Sorrow-acre," they at least set the stage for many of the *Gothic Tales*.

Nevertheless, Tania began her literary career writing in English rather than in her own language. Her adult exploration of literature had been in Kenya with Denys, in English; and English had been her spoken language for seventeen years. Another equally valid reason was Tania's need for "escape."

She took refuge not only in a language which was not her own, but in another age. She had always been hostile to modern trends: as an art student in Paris she had ignored them; her mother's interests in reforms and women's rights bored her. Her rare quarrels with Denys had been about modern music and painting. Her delight in flying over Africa in his airplane was an exception to her general attitude toward modern contraptions; and it was typical that to the end of her days she preferred horses to automobiles.

In a sense, too, she was really a stranger to the contemporary scene. She had been isolated in Africa during most of the war and the ensuing years when Europe was becoming modernized.

Tania's spirit roamed at ease in her father's nineteenth century. His personal tragedies and searing war experiences had saved him from the vapid sentimentality which was the heritage of his times, the hangover from the Romantic era with its weeping willows and tender violets, its fainting women, its men in transports over ethereal ballet sylphs, sunsets and mawkish verse. Tania, too, dispensed with the silly aspect of the period, extracting from it whatever was most austere, replacing the sentimentality with sentiment and with "what was most profound and exquisite in true Romanticism, the transfiguration of ordinary things, the clothing of common reality with a mantle of splendour."

"My characters begin to speak to me," she confided to a neighbor who inquired how the work was progressing. And they were destined, although their author would hardly have dared imagine it, to speak to multitudes of readers. Count Augustus von Schimmelmann, who could well have been one of Wilhelm Dinesen's melancholy friends; the visionary old maids of Elsinore; Fransine and the Poet from Hørsholm, the town where "Mama" had lived; the witty and gallant Contessa di Gampocorta and her Nordic counterpart, Miss Malin Nat-og-Dag—prophetic portraits, in a sense, of the old lady that Tania herself would become; Athena; Pellegrina . . . they did not come into being without a struggle. The hours of doubt and despair which every writer experiences were worsened for Tania by constant attacks of illness and pain and by anxiety about the eventual results of her efforts. As once she had thought that her very life depended on saving the African farm, so now she felt that she must succeed with her first book or face a hopeless future.

Nearly two years later she set out for England. Her manuscript, in the meanwhile, had been mailed back with rejection slips from several English publishers, but Tania was determined to try her personal powers of persuasion. Her London hostess was a close friend of Constant Huntington's, head of the publishing house of Putnam, and had arranged a luncheon meeting.

Although she was very nervous about the interview and also impatient to see "Maisie" and Margaretta, she went first to the crocodile pen at the London Zoo, a sentimental gesture. Her Somali boy Abdullai would by now be a tall young man of twenty-five, as vain of his robes and embroidered vests as he had once been of the London suits she had bought for him; and she wondered if he even remembered her. Standing there, prey to nostalgic thoughts of Kenya, Tania could hear a familiar short, coughlike roar from the lion house, but she had no heart to visit those great caged beasts. She had loved them too much in the freedom of the African plains. Sighing, she left the zoo for the luncheon at Lady Islington's, where Mr. Huntington would decide the fate of her book.

As the meal began Tania described her morning's adventure and her reluctance to see the lions. She had hunted them, she said, when she first went to Africa, but after a few years had lost all desire to kill. Like her friend Denys Finch-Hatton, she had then shot them only when they raided the cattle pens. Mr. Huntington, she could see, found her talk entertaining and seemed well disposed toward her, so she went on to tell of her amusement at receiving a letter from Ismail, her Somali gunbearer, addressed to "Lioness Blixen" and which began: "Honourable Lioness." She was proud, she admitted, of having the natives associate her with the noblest of Africa's animals, and she was pleased, too, when people in Kenya began to call her "the Lioness."

At last, over the coffee, she dared to broach the subject of her book. "What sort of book is it?" asked Mr. Huntington encouragingly. But on learning that it was a collection of short stories, his attitude changed abruptly. There was no chance at all of seeing it in print, he told her firmly.

"But, please, at least look at it. Read it," Tania pleaded.

"I'm afraid I must refuse," said Mr. Huntington. Short stories were always difficult to sell, he explained, and if written by an unknown author—it would be quite out of the question. He preferred to tell her so without reading her book, otherwise she would remain convinced that he had disliked her work. "No, no, no! Go home and write a full-length novel," he exhorted. "Then come and see me again."

The refusal was so categoric that it left her speechless. As soon as she could withdraw politely, she fled to seek comfort from "Maisie" and Margaretta, as she often did when she was in London. She relied on them as she had once relied on Denys. This time they simply laughed at her distress. Of course someone else would publish her book, they insisted, when she began to bewail her two wasted years, her indebtedness to Thomas and her dwindling hopes of an independent future. It was merely a matter of trying again.

A few weeks later Thomas handed the precious manuscript to Dorothy Canfield, a family friend, who was visiting in Denmark. When she returned to her home in Arlington, Vermont, she passed it on to her neighbor, the publisher Robert Haas. "I am so much under its spell (it feels exactly like a spell) . . ." she wrote after reading it over a second time. Robert Haas also succumbed. And it was a spell which did not diminish.

"Some five years ago a friend handed me the manuscript of *Seven Gothic Tales,* by a writer whose pseudonym was Isak Dinesen. It took but little discernment to recognize its extraordinary quality, but to tell the truth, I published it without very high hopes of anything but a *succès d'estime*. Short stories, and written in English by a Danish author unknown even in Denmark! I was frankly apprehensive . . . and completely mistaken, for the public as well as the critics took the book to their hearts and made a best seller of it . . . A very great artist," he concluded.

"Over a quarter of a century ago," Haas was to say later, "I had the privilege, as a publisher, of presenting to American readers Isak Dinesen's first book, *Seven Gothic Tales*. Its strange and wild beauty arched meteorlike across our literary skies. Thousands of us kept eager watch for more wonders and were not disappointed."

In the meanwhile, Tania was not going to miss a chance for a dramatic effect. Thomas and his wife, Jonna, were invited to dine at Rungstedlund, a rather unusual event. No guests had been allowed there for a long time so that Tania could have the quiet she needed for writing. During a lull in the conversation she glanced around the table. "You may congratulate me," she announced in a tone of gentle triumph. "I had a cable today to say that my book has been selected as Book-of-the-Month!"

For a while she also enjoyed the mystifying effect of the nom de plume she had chosen: Isak Dinesen—Isak, which in Hebrew means "laughter." Like Sarah, who in middle age at last gave birth to the child whom she called Isaac, Tania, who was nearing fifty, had finally found fulfillment and happiness as a writer. She had found laughter again. The critics and public naturally assumed at first that the author of the new best seller was a man, but of what nationality no one could guess. Before she gave up her anonymity Tania had the satisfaction of being really "he who laughs." Mr. Huntington, she was told, had written a letter to Robert Haas full of praise for the author of *Seven Gothic Tales* and asking for *his* address because he wanted the book for England.

"Isn't it wonderfully funny," said Tania, "to think that he met me in London as Baroness Blixen and caused me the greatest despair by refusing even to look at my book." She enjoyed the joke and harbored no resentment against Huntington, who became her publisher and good friend.

It is difficult to analyze the phenomenal success of *Seven Gothic Tales*, a success which had in no way been foreseen by experienced British and American editors. Certainly there was no single explanation. People fell in love with the book for many different reasons. They were seduced by its marvelous and very sensuous imagery, by its storytelling quality, which carried the reader impatiently from page to page, and by a style which could pass, glissando, from the very florid to the succinct essentials. In this latter respect, one has only to consider the beginning of the fourth story, "The Roads Round Pisa," where in a single, compact paragraph, the whole atmosphere of the tale is set up—the period, the place, the character, and condition, mood and appearance of the central figure—all with no sacrifice of poetic detail. Professional writers were admiring and perhaps not a little envious of a fellow author who dared to be "old-fashioned" and "romantic" and to quote in a friendly, familiar way from the Bible and classics at a time when the ideal was harsh realism and the stripped-down, suggestive style of a Hemingway, and who dared to state that the "story" was more important than any amount of psychological probing. A cosmopolitan savoir-vivre untainted by brittle sophistication enlivened the dialogue, with its alternate wit and slow, deep wisdom. And finally, there was the prose itself. The fact that for Tania, English was an acquired language, that most of her reading had been classical and that most of her literary discussions had been with a scholarly British mind such as Denys Finch-Hatton's, gave her writing a special flavor. American readers often felt that it was Anglicisms which set the tone, while to the British these same turns of speech just as often seemed slightly foreign, quaint or outmoded. In any case, the result was extremely personal and evoked an immediate response in even hard-bitten modernists; Hemingway himself was no exception.

In a long article Dorothy Canfield introduced the new author to the members of the Book-of-the-Month Club:

" . . . there is a great deal more to an author than the spirit that animates him, let that be as curious and rare as it will. There is his style. And I don't know how to tell you what the style of the book is any more definitely than what the spirit of it is, because the style, too, is very new to me, and will be to you, I think.

"You will probably read it as I did, laying it down from time to time, to look up at the ceiling, pondering. Is it of Cervantes' leisurely, by-path-following style, that it reminds me? Or perhaps just R. L. Stevenson's more mannered—no, no, it is more like a Romantic School German narrator's way of telling a story. Or is that only because the grotesque and occasionally gruesome touches remind me of Hoffman? Perhaps it is because a foreigner, writing in English, often falls as it were by accident on inimitably fresh ways of using our battered old words. Perhaps, quite simply, the style seems so original and strange because the personality using it is original and strange. And having come to no conclusion at all, you will turn back to read until you are again stopped by some passage for which you cannot find a comparison in the writing you know . . . 'Where,' you will ask yourself, puzzled, 'have I ever encountered such strange slanting beauty of phrase, clothing such arresting but controlled fantasy?' As for me, I don't know where."

In view of such enthusiasm, it is surprising that Tania's book was so little appreciated in her own country. Denmark, however, was still under the influence of lingering Victorianism, and in literature, had come to a sort of dead end in sociological realism. Neither the critics nor the reading public was ready for the strangeness and sophistication of *Seven Gothic Tales*, and Tania found herself in much the same situation as Edith Wharton thirty years earlier, who had been warned that "no great work of the imagination has ever been based on illicit passion" and to whom a reader had written: "Dear Madam, have you never known a respectable woman? If you have, in the name of decency, write about her." Furthermore, though Tania had foreseen a hostile reception, it had no doubt been a tactical error to delay publication at home until after her work was well received in America and England. Those successes had not been sufficient to lessen the shock and anger over her opinions and the subjects she had dared to broach. Some of the reviewers seemed very annoyed that a Danish author should have made a great stir abroad before they themselves bestowed their approbation, and one of them, Frederick Schyberg, also attacked the book as decadent and snobbish, the worst possible condemnation in a country as predominantly democratic as Denmark.

Tania made a great effort to ignore the slights and accusations. In any case, the practical response in the United States, the sale (for short stories) of an unprecedented number of copies, fired her imagination, as had the first talks with Bror about the El Dorado possibilities of a farm in Kenya. With her mind's eye she saw herself spending the American dollars which she knew would pour in—in an endless stream. And with her heart always yearning for Africa, her immediate thought was to return to set up and run a children's hospital on the Masai Reserve.

"There was much disease among the Masai, mostly such as we had brought upon them; on my safaris I had seen many blind children. But the Masai refused to take their sick to hospital.

"The Masai did not like us and had no reason to do so. For we had put an end to their bird-of-prey raids on the agricultural tribes, we had taken their spears and their big almond-shaped shields from them, and had splashed a bucket of water upon the halo of a warrior nation hardened through a thousand years into a personification of that ideal of Nietzsche: 'Man for war, and woman for the warrior's delight, all else is foolishness . . . '

"Neither did the white settlers in general like the Masai, who refused to work for them and kept up a sullen and arrogant manner in their dealings with them. But I myself had always been on friendly terms with my neighbours of the Masai Reserve, and they might, I felt, consent to bring their sick children to a nursing home of mine. I traveled to London to see Dr. Albert Schweitzer on one of his visits to England and to learn about conditions from him. He kindly gave me the information I wanted. But I soon realized that the expenses of the undertaking would by a long way exceed my means—you do not make as much money on writing books as is generally believed. The images of an existence nine thousand feet up, under the long hill of Bardamat, among the Masai children, dissolved like other mirages above the grass."

II

Geneva Interlude

—⁓⁓—

A quite different opportunity to serve Africa presented itself before the end of 1935. "Though words are beautiful things, rifles, machine guns, planes and cannon are still more beautiful," Mussolini had proclaimed to an enthusiastic audience in 1930. The significance of his remarks eluded the world at large, and four years later he was ready to invade Abyssinia. "Unprovoked aggression" was the trumped-up explanation he gave out as a cover for his real motives. By involving Italy in a war, Mussolini was hoping to divert the attention of the malcontents at home from the effects of the economic depression, and to blot out, once and for all, the memory of Italy's rankling defeat by the Ethiopians in 1896, when in a single day General Baratieri lost the whole Italian expeditionary force at Adowa. This time Mussolini planned to stage something bellicose, dramatic and effective, at a minimal cost to the nation (the Abyssinians surely would not put up more than a token resistance to the modern war machine of the Italians). The world looked on helplessly or cynically while the destruction of the

Ethiopians was set in motion, in October 1935, and people were hardly shocked when, three months later, the Hoare-Laval plan failed.

Tania had followed the developments leading up to the war with more than ordinary interest and sympathy. It was *her* Africa which was to be invaded, *her* natives who were going to be sacrificed. For generations every man in her family had fought in aid of some foreign cause and she could hardly wait to do her part. The quickest way of getting to Africa would be as a war correspondent, and to this end she went once more to London. Armed with impressive letters of introduction, she besieged the various War Offices and all the newspapers, only to come up everywhere against regulations which forbade employment of women for this kind of work. In vain she insisted that an exception should be made in her case, considering her long experience in Africa; she set forth her intimate knowledge of the natives; she described how during the World War she had, as the sole white leader of a three-month expedition, delivered arms and supplies for the British Army at the Tanganyika border. The authorities turned deaf ears to all her pleas.

To compensate for her great disappointment, Moura Budberg suggested a trip to Geneva. Tania had met Baroness Budberg at Mr. Huntington's house in Hyde Park during a previous visit to England, and they liked and admired each other immediately. Moura, Russian-born, had taken refuge in London in the late 1920's, and had begun her career there as a translator of Russian and French. In short order she progressed to script adviser for a number of film makers, and was friends with everyone of importance in the milieu of books and the theatre. She was a tall, imposing woman, with great vitality and the special warmth peculiar to Russians in exile. Tania found her stimulating. As for Moura, she said she was attracted by the "being" of Tania. They had corresponded, and were delighted to meet again.

In September 1935, with their cards as delegates to the League of Nations, which Moura had miraculously obtained, they were off to Geneva. To Tania, after the years of seclusion in Africa, followed by her almost cloistered life with her mother at Rungsted, it seemed as if she were suddenly at the throbbing center of world affairs. During the three-week stay she was in a state of almost delirious excitement. She listened to speeches by Sir Samuel Hoare, Salvador de Madariaga and Geneviève Tabouis, and lost no time in making friends with Wolde-Marian, the Abyssinian delegate, who derived much comfort and pleasure from talking with her. She was not (like so many others) merely voicing banal emotions about his country's hopeless cause. She really loved and understood Africa. "We have no tanks, no airplanes. . . ." he said to her, but when she expressed her concern and sympathy over the seemingly desperate situation, his reply was: "Madame, we trust in God."

"We stayed at a hotel that had a cabaret," Baroness Budberg later recalled, "and Tania, though she was in despair about the pending invasion, was avid to see and do everything. We listened to speeches all day and got intoxicated with dance music all evening." But on leaving Geneva after those weeks, every moment of which had seemed vital and stimulating, Tania suddenly had the strange sensation that it was all nothing. It was like coming down from the magic mountain into a real world in which Geneva, its brilliant statesmen and journalists meant nothing at all. When they returned to London, Tania and Moura sat up and talked, night after night, until dawn.

Since actual participation in the war had proved impossible, talk, talk, talk at least relieved one's feelings. The endless talk of statesmen did not accomplish much more, nor did the League's imposition of economic sanctions. In October, relentlessly, the invasion rolled forward, implemented by experienced generals, half a million men, heavy artillery and an air force. Mussolini was not going to risk another Adowa.

It was a wonder that against such odds, the Abyssinians were able to hold out for six months before Addis Ababa surrendered. Tania, back in the calm harbor of Rungstedlund, wept over every setback, every mile of lost ground, and raged over the bombing of unprotected villages and the slaughter of children and women. It seemed impossible that the world could call itself civilized and yet permit such things to happen. Ordinary people could not conceive of such depravity. But Vittorio, Mussolini's son, had boasted to the war correspondents about his air raids. "When the bombs fall on the native huts," he said, "the explosions are like fiery roses bursting into bloom." They gave him pleasure! How admirable by comparison were the quiet dignity of Haile Selassie and the heroism of Ras Desta Demptu.

III

Out of Africa

—◠◠◠◠—

Somehow or other the war had to be driven from Tania's mind, and so she resorted to writing again. It was five years since she had left Africa, and it was good to find that at long last she could think of her life there with some sort of equanimity. Doubtless the greater tragedy of Abyssinia had given her a sense of perspective about her personal sorrows. She began to sort out the notebooks which she had filled with impressions and sketches at the farm. Once again she sat daydreaming on the old wooden bench at the top of Ewald's Hill. She had a notion that the poet's ghost was wandering there and would bring her inspiration. By degrees the book began to take shape, a sort of *mémoire* of all that was most dearly remembered of the seventeen years in Africa. Of all that was saddest too.

She wrote with no sense of anxiety this time, being confident that Robert Haas would want her book, and with no sense of tension because she was beginning to feel assurance in her métier.

The book was well started when the publishing house of Holger Schildt in Stockholm brought out *Nyama*, by Bror Blixen.

Tania was astounded that Bror, who had always claimed to hate literature, had written a book. She wondered if he recognized an unflattering portrait of himself in Baron Guildenstern and had now, as an act of bravado, written a retort to her *Seven Gothic Tales*. Perhaps he had guessed that sooner or later she would write about Africa and therefore, in one more vengeful act, had tried to forestall her by publishing his own version first. Perhaps she was being unjust. It might be that he needed money or that friends had urged him to write an account of his life in Kenya. Perhaps, distressed over the failure of his second marriage and recent divorce, he was trying to recapture happier moments. She was determined not to read his book and permit it to influence what she herself was writing; and yet, she was equally sure that she *must* read it to make certain of neither repeating nor contradicting anything Bror had written. The confusing pros and cons aggravated her chronic illness and she stopped writing.

She was fretting needlessly because, as it turned out, Bror's book was no threat to hers. "I cannot say how old I was when I had a gun in my hand for the first time, but that my fingers itched to hold a weapon rather than a book is beyond question. I do not think I can be charged with being afraid of hardships—these pages should rather prove the contrary—but I have always stood somewhat in awe of bookwork." So begins Bror's book. It is less a book which reveals the Africa of that period than the handbook of a hunter who happened to pursue his calling in Africa rather than elsewhere. That he was a fine hunter is certain and he was much sought after as a safari leader during his twenty-three years in Kenya. In temperament he much resembled Hemingway, who was his personal friend, but he was no writer. And though a keen observer of natives, animals and terrain, as all good hunters must be, the descriptions of even his most exciting adventures remain somehow inanimate. *Nyama* was brought out in translation by Alfred A. Knopf the following year, 1937, and met with little success.

The publication of Bror's book had been a shock to Tania but she knew she must not allow herself to give in to despondency. "Go to another country," she had once advised a forlorn and anxious friend; now Tania, too, searched for a place of escape. Skagen, the northernmost point of Jutland, was of course part of Denmark, but it was somehow another world, remote and mysterious. Considering the rugged midwinter journey to reach it (across the whole of Sjælland, the long ferry crossing to Aarhus, and another two hundred kilometers of icy roads), she could feel quite certain of working there undisturbed by intruders.

When she arrived at Bronnums, the main hotel, she felt ill at ease and wondered if it had been a mistake to choose this lonely refuge. But after a few days she found the ambiance she needed at Skagen's Hotel. The owner, Mrs. Østergaard, was a gentle, intelligent woman who was descended from generations of local seafaring folk. She was much loved by the people of the village, and she enticed Tania into the life of the community without ever disrupting her regular hours of writing.

Very quickly Tania established a routine of work to which she adhered, except at Christmas when Thomas came to stay with her. During the few hours of winter daylight she was out exploring, driving her small blue car past the port with its square ship basin; past the harbor, where more than a thousand fishing boats lay moored side by side, a forest of masts with furled sails which were invariably brown or seaweed green; past the piers where other boats were racked up in dry dock and where fishing nets, also brown and green, hung in windblown festoons. Not far from Skagen huddled the little group of houses known as Old Skagen, surrounded by miles and miles of barren, shifting sands. In summer, the villagers told her, the dunes would be overgrown with bluebells, pink scabiosa, and tiny wild pansies no larger than violets, but now the dunes were a lifeless sort of lunar landscape, with not a tree in sight except where a house gave it shelter from the tearing wind. Often she left her car and went down onto the beach, defying the freezing gale and sea spray for the ageless pleasure of picking up pebbles, red porphyry, rose granite, white and amber-colored quartz. And one day she walked out to the point of land's end. There was something awesome about standing on that last flat spit of solid earth, facing the sea, where waves from both directions met and clashed. She was glad of the friendly presence of one of the small boys from the village whom she had brought along.

It was a curious contrast to come in from the wind, the cold, and early darkness, to sit down at her desk and conjure up the heat and color and light of Kenya. She wrote, hour after hour, until it was time to go down to the lounge for tea. There, from her table by the window, she could nod to her friend the postman, whose flamboyant mustaches exactly repeated the curves of his bicycle's handlebars, or she could wave to the small boys of the village who would rush in and beg for a ride in her blue car. Neighbors came to share her tea and hear tales about Africa, and all of them would laugh when the cross-tempered schoolteacher passed by on his way home. It was a standing joke that Tania would turn her back to the window or even move from her table in order not to see his sulky face. After an hour she would go back upstairs to write for the rest of the evening and far into the night.

As work on her book gathered momentum again, Tania was able to become oblivious of everything around her, and the face of Africa which had been slumbering in her subconscious rose up, visible, tangible, as she evoked it. She had only to close her eyes, it seemed, and the sound and sight of Nairobi, its particular smell of drooping eucalyptus trees, dust and squalor, and the pungent spices of McKinnon's grocery shop, all pervaded her senses as if she had just dismounted there and handed the reins to Farah. She remembered how ugly she had thought Nairobi when she first saw the place. "Like an empty old anchovy tin," Bror had said, which wasn't bad at all, but she had grown to love it more than any shining city. "There is no world without Nairobi's streets." Almost in tears she decided: "I must write it all down quickly—Nairobi, the farm and its people, Africa, because soon it will all change and no one will ever see or know what I have seen and known." Civilization, or what passed for it, would reach out from Nairobi toward the farm and engulf it, as in her father's time the city of Copenhagen had stretched forth its tentacles toward Rungsted. She wondered whether she would already feel quite lost and strange if she could now revisit Kenya.

Sometimes, as she wrote, she also came close to laughing aloud. There was a memory, for instance, of an overheard conversation between Kamante and a group of native boys. Msabu had convinced him, he was telling them, that all those odd sheets of paper which lay strewn on her desk and which the wind often scattered across the floor, all those loose pages could truly be made into a book. It would hold together, he told them, and be heavy and solid, with a firm cover, just like *The Odyssey* from which she read aloud to them. Though perhaps, he added, not even Msabu would be able to make it blue.

In 1937 some of those scattered pages which had caused

Kamante such concern appeared in Danish as *Den Afrikanske Farm,* and shortly after in English as *Out of Africa.* The indifference, the hostility even, which Tania had felt in her own country after the appearance of *Seven Gothic Tales,* had rankled more than she realized, especially compared with the ecstatic reception of her book in America. The venom had lingered, but now she could shrug off the "mosquito critics with a poisonous sting."

The Danes could not object to any aspect of the book about Africa, and their critics joined the American and British reviewers in unanimous praise. The response of readers was so intense and personal that many of them felt impelled to write to the author. Hundreds of letters arrived at Rungstedlund and at the publishers' offices. One that Tania preferred and always remembered came from a cigar vendor in Copenhagen, but there were also treasured ones from celebrated writers—Louis Bromfield, Aldous Huxley, Rebecca West, and many others. "I have just finished the African book this evening," said Bromfield's letter, "and before sleeping I feel I must write you to say how much I was moved by it—Not only by the beauty of the writing and the descriptions but by the spirit behind it. I read a great deal but splendid books are few and far between and when I find one it is like discovering a new world and a new friend. The chapter on the death of Finch-Hatton is of extraordinary moving beauty, and the 'farewell' is simple and heartbreaking."

If she could come to any conclusion about her readers, said Tania when questioned about the deluge of letters, it was that the little man, the simple man, seemed in great need of magic and fantasy, much as her simple natives in Africa, who could never get enough of her telling of fanciful tales.

Out of Africa was chosen for the Book-of-the-Month Club by the same panel of judges who had bestowed the honor on *Seven*

Gothic Tales—Heywood Broun, Henry Seidel Canby, Dorothy Canfield, Christopher Morley, and William Allen White.

Fourteen years later Bernardine Kielty would write the introduction to the Modern Library edition. A first reading had given her the urge to go out and see Kenya herself. When she returned, she reread *Out of Africa* and was even more deeply moved. She could not find enough superlatives to convey her admiration. "Her memories, born of passion and tenderness, re-create that distant scene for all time."

There was, however, one dissident voice. Old Pedersen had now been in the family for forty-three years, which gave him the right to speak out. It behooved him, he said, to tell Tania that it was highly improper for a "young lady" in her situation to make money by writing books.

Tania spent most of that April thanking reviewers for their kind words, acknowledging letters of congratulation and receiving visitors. She laid aside these pleasant obligations in order to go to England once more, this time for the wedding of Denys' niece Diana. Tania was included in the family dinner which preceded the event—a touching attention that filled her with gratitude. It was natural that she should feel a profound attachment for Denys' niece—to anyone who had belonged to him—but she did not really expect this feeling to be reciprocated. In the warm glow of that acceptance she attended the wedding. Diana in a silver gown; her mother, Margaretta, madonna-like in a flower-strewn hat—Tania remembered every detail when, later, Diana's daughter married.

She came home to Rungstedlund in time for that recurring miracle, the Danish spring, with its blue sea foaming over the white beaches and a white froth of mayflowers on all the wooded green slopes. "One has to have seen it with one's own eyes to understand how incredibly beautiful it is," mused Tania, and though it was nearly evening she ran out-of-doors.

As she started to walk up Ewald's Hill she stopped for a minute, lost in twilight thoughts, on the little footbridge which straddled the stream. Across the pond, the water's edge was already in shadow, but on the near side the tall reeds were spear-points impaling the last rays of light. Among them she could distinguish quite clearly a water bird, motionless as if cast in bronze. She had often been aware of Denys' presence while she was writing *Out of Africa,* and the visit to England with his family had fortified the impression. Tonight again, at this moment, she felt him very near. She suddenly realized that she could now think of him without a sense of bitter loss. The minutes became an hour and it was finally too dark to walk to the top of the hill. Overhead in the deep-blue field of sky, stars began to appear. Night vapors were swirling up from the surface of the pond. The water bird had not stirred.

> *. . . and herons stand*
> *forever poised*
> *upon the margin of the*
> *lake*
> *as images of you*
> *forever poised*
> *upon the margin*
> *of my thoughts.*

Images of Denys . . . they were now forever poised upon the pages she had written. She hardly dared hope that her book was as good as the critics had said. Perhaps . . . And a great happiness swept over her as it had once before, when she felt her father's presence by the marsh lake at Katholm—a sense of happiness and fulfillment.

IV

More Tycho Brahe Days

—∿∿∿—

Happiness was ephemeral; it slipped through Tania's fingers, and the following year, 1939, seemed a never-ending procession of Tycho Brahe days. " 'One woe doth tread upon another's heels,' " commented Tania, addicted as ever to quotations from Shakespeare. The one joy to cling to was the birth, in February, of Diana's daughter, who was christened Tania and afterwards always spoken of as "Little Tania."

A week after this child was born, "Maisie" died unexpectedly. He had seemed, after a six-month illness, so much stronger that he went out to see his new grandchild. His death was a heartache to Tania, who had grown to love him and for whom he had been the closest remaining link with Denys.

The sorrow of losing so dear a friend followed close on the more painful wrench of losing a parent. Mrs. Dinesen had died on January 27, and Tania's mourning was embittered with remorse and self-reproach. Her mother had been a remarkable woman. Being married to the gifted but moody Wilhelm must often have been an ordeal, and by taking his own life he had left her, while she was still in her thirties, with the double burden of forever asking herself what she might have done to prevent his death, and the task of raising five small children alone. She bore her responsibilities with dignity, uncomplaining. In fact, she belittled whatever she did, deferring to the splendid example of her own dear "Mama," who had become a widow at thirty-four with no less than seven children to bring up. Mrs. Dinesen had been not only a conscientious mother but also a credit to the community. By 1915 her tireless efforts to help get the franchise for women met with success and then she was the first woman in Denmark to be elected chairman of the parish adminstration.

And what had she not done for Tania? Twice she made the arduous journey to Kenya to offer both moral and financial support. And when Tania came back from Africa she turned the whole house over to her—her other children and all her personal friends were literally banished from Rungstedlund over a period of years so that Tania might work undisturbed.

And Tania thought of how she had repaid her mother. She had groaned audibly over the Sunday lunches at "Mama's." She had derided her mother's political activities and lack of social ambition. She had drawn unfavorable comparisons between the simple pleasures her mother enjoyed and the more aristocratic *train de vie* at Katholm and Frijsenborg. She had taken all of mother's sacrifices for granted.

It would have relieved Tania to unburden her sense of guilt to Thomas—she had shared other troubles with him in the past—but she was denied this comfort now. Thomas was profoundly shaken by his mother's death and a wave of resentment rose in him against his sister. Her pride would brook no criticism, he thought, and it was shocking that she had not done more for their mother's happiness. Whenever Thomas met Tania now, they got into futile arguments. The inheritance of Rungstedlund was a prickly question—he and Anders and Tania had received equal shares in it, but Tania was determined to go on living there alone. Rankling details about the African farm were also dragged up for discussion. Thomas defended their uncle Aage Westenholz, with whom Tania had quarreled over the Kenya investments. Thomas also defended their brother-in-law Knud Dahl—Tania's dislike for her sister's husband had turned to such antagonism that she was even estranging Ellen. The bickering between Tania and Thomas, as had happened in Africa, often flared into angry scenes and left a smoldering residue.

Any personal grievances of the Dinesens were put aside when the Germans marched into Poland, and England and France declared war. As hackles rise on a dog's back at the smell and sight of a loathsome intruder, so every Dane bristled with instinctive hatred of the Germans. It was the old enemy. Thomas himself had the V.C., testimony of his heroism when he fought the Germans in the World War; Wilhelm Dinesen had fought them in two wars; and as far back as 1848 *his* father had engaged in the battle. Confronted with Germany's latest acts of aggression, Tania's family was ready to fight again, but not one of them could imagine the humiliation, anguish and defeat that the enemy would soon bring down on them.

In the meanwhile, the changed international situation forced Tania to abandon a cherished plan. With the help of a travel grant she had received, she had hoped to meet Farah for a pilgrimage to Mecca. In Africa they had often talked about this project, and the prospect of realizing it at last was very exciting—something new, strange and solemn to explore, with Farah and his mother, devout Mohammedans, at hand to make the experience more vivid. Now she would stay at home, alone and fretting, while the vacuum winter of the Maginot Line dragged on and on. There was nothing to do but wait.

Another wish, unfulfilled at the time of the Abyssinian war, did, however, become a reality. In March 1940 she got a job as a reporter. Three Scandinavian newspapers commissioned a series of twelve articles on wartime Berlin, Paris and London, and Tania was to spend a month in each city. It was not an easy assignment. In Berlin she wrestled with the Propaganda Office for weeks without obtaining much more than permission to visit the UFA studios and observe the filming of *The Jew Suss*. In spare moments she dashed to the theatre for the new experience of Shakespeare in German.

It was the Nazi attitude toward women that made the deepest impression on her. Woman—the whole world of woman—was so emphatically subjugated, said her first dispatch, that she might have been walking about in a one-sexed community. Considering that Tania had never been concerned with the plight of women, it is curious that this should have struck her in particular.

In Africa, at the beginning of World War I, she had experienced a moment of panic over a rumor that all the white women of the colony were to be placed in a camp for the duration as protection from the Germans and the Masai. Even temporarily, a world without men was unthinkable. Tania had deeply loved Daisy Frijs; in Kenya she also became a devoted friend of Joanie Grigg, the Governor's wife, and of Ingrid Lindstrom; and she even condescended to occasional ladies' tea parties. Nevertheless, she always preferred the company of men, and said so quite frankly. In their eternal losing battle with the not-so-frail sex, she ranged herself on the side of the men. To her they were ". . . all the young men who had been, through the ages, perfect in beauty and vigor . . . who had been changed, against their wishes, into supporters of society, fathers-in-law, authorities on food and morals. All this was sad." Lined up against them were the intransigent mothers, the matchmaking aunts, the joyless wives, and the eternal Madam Knudsen: "She was the woman who ruins the pleasure of man, and therein is always right. She was the wife of the curtain-lectures, and the housewife of the big cleaning-days, she stopped all enterprises, she washed the faces of boys, and snatched away the man's glass of gin from the table before him, she was law and order embodied. [She] did not dream of enslaving by love, she ruled by reasoning and righteousness."

When Tania had accomplished as much of her reporting assignment as seemed possible in Berlin she went on to Bremen, completely forgetting that there might be formalities about traveling from one city to another. On returning to Berlin, she was summoned to police headquarters.

"You informed us you only intended to visit Berlin."

"So I do."

"But you have been to Bremen."

"Oh, of course. So I have."

The Nazi official worked up such a rage that Tania couldn't help laughing. She had no idea how dangerous it all really was, but perhaps to be on the safe side it would be better to be conciliatory.

"I apologize," she kept saying. "I apologize, and here I am back again, so what does it matter?"

Actually, she had gone to Bremen because she wanted to conclude her work in Germany by learning the opinions on Nazism of the "old school" officers and she had made an appointment to call on General von Lettow-Vorbeck.

She had not seen the general since her first crossing to Africa in 1913, though they had exchanged letters. As gallant, as courtly as ever, he seemed nevertheless, after twenty-seven years, inexpressibly older and sadder. He had recently lost two sons in the war but displayed no bitterness before Tania, whom he remembered with affection and admiration. She had been a brave young woman in those days and apparently she still was, he said, when she recounted some of her exploits. They talked for hours about the old Africa, their Africa, which they knew would soon exist only in the memories of people like themselves, and Tania was very reluctant to leave, little realizing the risk she was running by staying on even a few more days in Germany. She barely reached home in time. On April 9 the nightmare invasion of Denmark began, and her reporting assignments in Paris and London were never carried out.

V

Winter's Tales

—ᴡᴡᴡ—

"The next two or three years stand out by nothing but their nothingness" was Tania's comment about this period of her life when she wrote of it later in *Shadows on the Grass,* and yet, for her, those first years of the German occupation were crowded with impressions, events and accomplishments.

The King, who had always inspired respect and reverence in Tania, had asked the people of Denmark to maintain a dignified calm, so it was necessary to accept the degrading identity cards in silence, and Tania had to swallow her sense of outrage when the Germans set up camp in her very backyard, on the slopes of Ewald's Hill. She also had to keep her temper when they came to the house with the twofold insolence of the conqueror condescending to the defeated and the arrogant male bullying the despised female. She had to keep her temper, patch up old clothes, walk instead of ride, live with a minimum of light and forget the existence of luxuries and pleasures. Like the rest of Denmark, she had to learn to live without visits or news of any faraway relatives or friends.

The occupation lasted for years—longer than anyone could have imagined. On the hillside where the Germans held their drills in gas masks, the mayflowers bloomed and faded, and the green leaves of summer browned and fell to earth. Winter came and the wind blew silvery swirls of snow across the Strandvej and Rungstedlund's dormant gardens. Then the cycle began again. Nature was oblivious of man's ugly pursuits. The seasons changed, but with the enemy desecrating all the beloved places, there was no joy in going out-of-doors, and Tania's only incentive for a walk was the hope of picking up the scraps of war news that trickled in, somehow, through underground channels—the Nazis in Paris . . . in Athens . . . on Russian soil . . . Pearl Harbor.

Winters were hardest to bear. Cold seemed to penetrate every corner of Rungstedlund, inadequately heated with fires and old-fashioned iron stoves, and silence followed her doggedly from room to room. Tania, ill and miserable, sat huddled in woolens at the window and stared angrily out at the sea for hours and hours. In normal times she loved the sea—it was the one thing she had missed at the farm. "There is nothing for which you feel such a great longing as for the sea. The passion of man for the sea . . . is unselfish. He cannot cultivate it; its water he cannot drink; in it he dies. Still, far from the sea you feel part of your own soul dying, disappearing, like a jellyfish thrown on dry land." Now the sea seemed the vast divider that held Denmark apart from the rest of the world, that kept out news from Africa and friends elsewhere. Every year since leaving Kenya, Tania had sent a sum of money at Christmas time for Farah to hand out to all her old servants, and each of them, after his fashion, had written, or had dictated to the

Indian scribes at the post office, messages for her filled with warmth and gratitude and awkward devotion. Abdullahi had written from far Somaliland on the typewriter she had sent out to him. She hoped they would understand why they no longer received gifts from her. Here, from the wall of the study, Abdullahi looked down at her. It was, she felt sure, one of the best portraits she had painted, but now its level gaze only made her feel more exiled and more aware of the constricting loneliness in the house. Outside were German soldiers, not native boys whom she loved.

She began another book almost in an instinct of self-preservation—twice before, writing had saved her from nearly going mad. The *Winter's Tales* which, one by one, evolved out of her present misery were not, however, a reflection of what she was enduring; rather, they were a withdrawal into a world of fantasy where pain was transformed or forgotten and creatures of the imagination replaced unwanted realities, a world which, on rare occasions, her brother was invited to enter.

Thomas, trusting that his sister would be well enough to see him, and hoping to dispel her loneliness and his own anxieties about the war, bicycled from Hillerød to Rungstedlund whenever possible. "I felt, in a way, a weight lifted for a little while from my shoulders when, during my visits to her, she showed me a glimpse of an entirely different universe, a world of visions and dreams, above space and time and this absurd, inhuman war. We certainly did not always agree in our opinions, but after every talk with her I rode back, generally late at night, to our strange war duties with fresh inspiration."

In 1942 the book was ready and went off to Gyldendal, her publisher in Copenhagen. Tania herself tells how she delivered other copies to Putnam and Random House. It had been "out of the question to get the manuscript to England or America from

Denmark. By rare good luck and with the aid of mighty friends, I managed to get it with me to Stockholm and to make the British Embassy there forward it by their daily plane. I wrote to my publishers in London and New York: 'I can sign no contract and I can read no proofs. I leave the fate of my book in your hands.' For three years I lived in the ignorance of that irresponsible person who shot an arrow into the air and left it to fall to earth he knew not where. Now, in the fair month of May, 1945, by one of the very first overseas mails, I received my book in the Armed Services Edition and shortly after, through the Red Cross, a number of moving and cheering letters from American officers and soldiers who had happened to read *Winter's Tales* just before or after some attack in Italy or the Philippines. I gave one of my two copies to the King, who was pleased to know that from his dumb country one voice at least had been heard in far places."

Not only soldiers responded to that "one voice"; thousands of American civilians at home were transported by it. *Winter's Tales* did, in fact, include some of the finest stories Tania would ever write. "Sorrow-acre," which derives from a seventeenth-century South Jutland folk tale, and in which dark tragedy is emphasized by visual effects of brilliant sunlight and touches of frivolity, may well be considered her chef-d'œuvre. The story demonstrates not only the technical mastery which she had achieved as a writer but also the ideas which a difficult life had welded into Tania's personal philosophy: the proud man finds his happiness in the fulfillment of his destiny. The manner of that acceptance was to Tania as important as the acceptance itself—the bad was to be taken with the good, debonairly, not groveling and complaining: ". . . the very same fatality, which, in striking the burgher or peasant, will become tragedy, with the aristocrat is exalted to the comic. By the grace and wit of our acceptance hereof our aristocracy is known."

A great deal of nonsense has been written about Isak Dinesen as "the Baroness," "the Aristocrat" who lived in "ancient Rungstedlund"; but Tania was not born into the Danish aristocracy, and Rungstedlund, though spacious and beautiful, was no more than a country residence, a manor house rather than a castle. There was, however, no greater aristocrat in spirit than Tania. This spirit was evident in her bearing and speech, in the very personal way she dressed, in her dealings with people, in what Moura Budberg referred to as her "being." If she wrote sympathetically of the aristocrat, it was because she understood and respected the dignity and grand manner, the grace and wit which a long tradition had distilled into the quintessence of *le parfait gentilhomme*. She made a careful distinction between great lord and peasant, master and servant, individualist and mere imitator. Even in the animal world the distinction was apparent. There were the respectable pigs and poultry "who behaved as was expected of them," and the proud, wild creatures whose "course was drawn up by the finger of God."

If in "Sorrow-acre" she invests the old lord with such admirable and credible aristocracy that the reader, who sides at first with Adam's modern, democratic ideas, is gradually swayed toward the older man, it is not at all because she undervalues Adam or the peasants. She called her Somali servant Farah "the greatest gentleman I have ever met" because Farah fulfilled his role in life proudly and according to a high personal code of honor. What she did despise was that no man's land of humanity—those dull bourgeois who, with no pride in their separate destinies, live in slavish imitation of their millions of neighbors, the ones whom Saint-Exupéry called "the docile, passive, unprotesting cattle."

Her attitude had been much misunderstood in Denmark when *Seven Gothic Tales* was published. The critic who described the book as decadent and snobbish (and there were even some who called it frankly blasphemous) was as far from the truth as the sentimental American enthusiasts who thought Tania was making a valiant last stand for a class which was disappearing from the contemporary scene. Neither was Robert Langbaum altogether right when he simplified the question by saying, "Isak Dinesen treats her aristocrats ironically." Certainly her approach was tinged with irony, as indeed it had become in regard to everything and everyone, herself included; but the ironic was more often than not a decorative veneer for the more serious substance she had in mind. In "The Deluge at Norderney," for example, the dialogue becomes a wonderfully witty game, reminiscent of the art of conversation practiced in the French salons of the eighteenth century, but beneath the surface of the most flippant remarks is a core of deeply felt truth. And always, intermingled with the entertainment, there are the solemn statements which may be taken as stepping stones to a final understanding of her real attitude toward life:

"Madame," said the Cardinal, "you speak frivolously. Pray do not talk or think in that way. Nothing sanctifies, nothing, indeed, is sanctified, except by the play of the Lord, which is alone divine. You speak like a person who would pronounce half of the notes of the scale—say, *do, re* and *mi*—to be sacred, but *fa, sol, la* and *si* to be only profane, while, Madame, no one of the notes is sacred in itself, and it is the music, which can be made out of them, which is alone divine . . . The lion lies in wait for the antelope at the ford, and the antelope is sanctified by the lion, as is the lion by the antelope, for the play of the Lord is divine. Not the bishop, or the knight, or the powerful castle is sacred in itself, but the game of chess is a noble game, and therein the knight is sanctified by the bishop, as the bishop by the queen. Neither would it be an advantage if the bishop were ambitious to acquire the higher virtues of the queen, or the castle those of the bishop. So are we sanctified when the hand of the Lord moves us to where He wants us to be."

Winter's Tales was the third work by Tania selected for the Book-of-the-Month Club, and rarely had any writer received such ecstatic reviews. "A serene and frosty genius, she is an artist of précieux and impeccable talent who scorns the conventional, the direct and the clearly understandable. A writer, she forsook her native Danish tongue and has written her books in an English of such coldly glittering beauty she has hardly a living rival as a literary stylist." The review appeared in the *New York Times*, May 1943, but it would be a long time before Tania, in encircled Denmark, would hear of it.

VI

The Angelic Avengers

—◠◡◠—

There were, at this time, about eight thousand Jews in Denmark. Because of the King's resolute stand in regard to them, and the Nazis' leniency toward the Danes in general, they did not suffer the persecutions inflicted on Jews in other Hitler-dominated nations. The King personally visited the synagogue of Copenhagen the day after some Germans had tried to burn it down, and he deterred the occupation authorities from enforcing the decree which obliged the Jews of other countries to wear armbands with the Star of David. "If this decree is enforced," he proclaimed, "my family and I will be the first to wear armbands as a mark of distinction." Toward the end of the summer of 1943, however, the Germans altered their policy. Suddenly fearful because of Italy's September 8 surrender, they began to take sterner measures in Denmark. The King was forbidden any freedom of action, Parliament was dissolved, and there were harsh reprisals for acts of sabotage by the Resistance.

That the Nazi authorities finally decided to deport all Jews to the Theresienstadt concentration camp in Czechoslovakia was an indication of their having no understanding of the Danish people, who by an extraordinary chance learned in advance of their intentions. On September 27 a German Embassy employee, G.F. Duckwitz, informed a few Danes of a secret order to raid all Jewish homes on the night of October 1. Such deportation could only mean death for the victims—or something infinitely worse—and at once the Danes decided that they could not permit this to happen to their fellow citizens. Until this time the Resistance, in obedience to the King's request for calm and order, had functioned in a rather limited way, but now, literally overnight, an intricate underground network came into existence. By October 1 the Jews had vanished.

Two days later from every pulpit in Denmark came an announcement: "The persecution of Jews conflicts with the humanitarian concept of neighborly love and the message which Christ's Church set out to preach. We shall fight to preserve for our Jewish brothers and sisters the same freedom which we ourselves value more than life." It was remarkable in itself that the Lutheran bishops, on three days' notice and hampered as they were by inadequate means of communications, had been able to have the announcement made simultaneously in every church. The congregations, however, did not need any such exhortation. For them it was merely an official confirmation of what they believed to be their duty.

Later that day Tania was scheduled to speak at a librarians' meeting in Hørsholm. "It was on that Sunday, October 3rd, that I first met Tania Blixen," noted Birthe Andrup, one of the librarians (they soon became good friends and exchanged many letters), "but that meeting was to me not only a matter of facts and dates. It was much, much more—We were deeply involved in the war.

For Tania it had an added dimension which concerned her father and the battle he had fought at the age of eighteen against the Germans at Dybbøl. The same fight was now ours."

The first objective was to continue hiding the Jews until, under cover of darkness, they could be moved in small groups to the beaches. They were then to be ferried to neutral Sweden in fishing boats, rowboats—in anything that would float. It was fifteen miles across the Sound, and German patrol boats with powerful searchlights ranged back and forth all night. Danish sailors and fishermen who were caught helping the refugees knew they would be deported to Theresienstadt along with the captured Jews.

Many of the houses on the Strandvej became way stations on the escape route, among them Rungstedlund, where a door was always left open for Jews in case they were afraid to ring. "There were Jews in the kitchen and Nazis in the garden," said Tania. "The hair-raising problem was to keep them from meeting."

Often when the German officers arrived to inspect the house, Tania held them at bay at one door, assailing them with sarcasm and rude taunts while their intended victims were being smuggled out by another door to a new hiding place. Her heart pounded with anxiety for the people she was sheltering, but she had no more actual fear of the Germans than of the lions she had faced in Africa. It was a pleasure and satisfaction to insult them and there was, if anything, too little risk in doing so. "They were such a masculine society, they paid no attention to what any woman said or did." Just the same, each time the Germans came it was a drain on her failing strength. And it was equally wearing when there was nothing to do but wait, tense with listening and watching. At night she climbed the stairs to her room too tired to undress and go to bed. She would stand for a while at the window, staring out toward the Sound. Somewhere out there on the black, frightening water, boats were making their way toward Sweden. "Dear God, let it be dark, dark," she would pray. "Let it be dark to protect them!"

One night she sat at her mirror for nearly an hour. Could this be she, this tragicomical spectre of what she had once been—the web-work of wrinkles around the eyes, the thinning, greying hair in the dowdy net, the shabby sweater and flannel pants? She was fifty-eight, and while she was saving the lives of others her own life was petering out in ugliness. She would be an old woman before the Germans were driven out of Denmark.

The trees had relinquished their last leaves and the frosts of early November lay shimmering on the lawn before the rescue operation was completed. Two hundred refugees, alas, had been betrayed by a pro-Nazi Danish woman. Another two hundred and seventy had been caught and deported. But more than seven thousand of them had escaped, passed from house to house and set safely ashore in Sweden. Everyone breathed a sigh of relief, though another cold, dreary, difficult winter was setting in, the fourth under the occupation.

Tania lived through it less miserably than she had expected. Some new friends began to enliven the afternoons at Rungstedlund. Mostly they were a group of young writers, whose visits were intellectually stimulating. But far more important for Tania was the fact that they revived her vanity in her personnal appearance and the desire to charm and conquer, which was even more essential to her than to most women. She continued wearing pants at home as she had done since African days, despite the manifest disapproval of Alfred Pedersen, but she began to dress for effect. Illness had made her eyes seem larger than ever and she now exaggerated their size by shadowing them heavily with kohl.

However, she was busy mainly with regular hours of work. To "forget the unendurable" she had arranged with her Copenhagen publisher for an advance and had begun to compose a novel, a sort of melodramatic, romantic thriller.

"There were some moments of real comedy as this novel progressed," Tania reported later. On signing her author's contract, she had persuaded Gyldendal to send a stenographer out to the house, and she had dictated the book, improvising a chapter or two each day." The secretary would arrive in the morning, settle herself rather nervously, and I'd resume dictating: 'Then Mr. So-and-so entered the room.' The poor girl would drop her notes and wring her hands and exclaim: 'But you can't do that! You killed him yesterday in Chapter Twelve!' "

When *Gengældelsens Veje* (The Ways of Retribution) came out, in 1944, readers saw it as a political parable: the innocent young girls held captive by the villains surely stood for the Danes under the heel of the hated Germans. But such had never been her purpose, protested Tania, the story had simply invented itself day by day. The notion persisted just the same and was largely responsible for the success of the novel in Denmark, since it was daring to poke undercover fun at the Nazis, and the weary Danes enjoyed it. When Random House published it three years later as *The Angelic Avengers*, it also had some excellent reviews and joined Tania's growing list of Book-of-the-Month Club selections.

Today not even the most ardent admirer of Isak Dinesen can find much to praise in this book, which is curiously lacking in her usual atmosphere, style and wit, though it is obviously not fair to subject it to the same level of criticism by which one gauges her other books. Tania herself was quite aware of its falling below the lofty standards she set for herself. "Since I looked upon it as a highly illegitimate child, it was published under the pseudonym of Pierre Andrézel."

Unfortunately, no one respected the pseudonym. Outsiders who guessed at the author's identity pestered the publisher and newspapers to have their suspicions confirmed. Well-meaning friends rebuked Tania for writing trash. "No, you will not receive my Berlin chronicles or anything else" was her retort to Birthe Andrup, "until you have changed your Germanic (pompous, respectable) attitude toward Pierre Andrézel or at least desist from serving it up to me." Tania resented the humorlessness of it all, for, quite simply, the key to the novel was in a quotation from the book itself (printed as a preface to the Random House edition): "You serious people must not be too hard on human beings for what they choose to amuse themselves with when they are shut up as in a prison, and are not even allowed to say that they are prisoners. If I do not soon get a little bit of fun, I shall die."

In the end the critic Christian Elling came to her defense in a long and delightful article in *Politiken*, November 25, 1944. In eighteenth-century Venice, he said, persons who wished to remain incognito did not even trouble to put on a mask or disguise, but simply wore a symbolic miniature mask attached to a coat button. The tiny symbol was always respected; it gave the wearer freedom of action and rendered him immune to prying eyes. Living authors who assume a pen name have every right to the same privilege, Elling insisted, and tongue in cheek, he concluded: "*Gengældelsens Veje* must be written by Pierre Andrézel. His name stands on the title page. No doubt he is a relative of an officer mentioned in Chateaubriand's *Mémoires*."

VII

Clara

—〰〰〰—

As the winter came to an end, many of the Nazis became less despotic. Perhaps they could not remain impervious to the radiant Danish spring. Perhaps, simply, they were tired of their own aggressiveness, or lonely for other human contacts. A few even hanged themselves in the parks of Copenhagen rather than carry out the bloody reprisals against the Resistance ordered by the Gestapo in 1944.

Any personal overtures they made at Rungstedlund were repulsed with withering scorn. Tania turned her back on them when she went out-of-doors, which was more often now. Practical gardening was a wartime necessity—after all, one had to eat—but it had also become one of her greatest pleasures. She enjoyed walking along the neat green ribbon rows of lettuce and beans, onion spikes and feathery carrot tops, as she had once enjoyed walking among her coffee trees. The vegetables had been planted in a level half-acre of ground between the brook and the woods where centuries of fallen beech leaves had enriched the soil. Future gardeners would always choose this place, she decided, and the thought of them cultivating this same small patch of earth fifty or a hundred years from now gave perspective to her troubles. "The earth gave me peace" was a reflection which often came to mind. But the actual peace was still a long way off.

When reports of the the D-Day landing in Normandy filtered into Denmark, they spread across the country with such mysterious speed that Tania was reminded of the way news traveled among the natives of Africa. In the general surge of optimism that followed during the summer months, her own joy was short-lived. Within the space of a few days the entire garden was destroyed by a blight. It was a plant fungus, she wrote to Birthe Andrup, as destructive as the scourge of grasshoppers had been at the farm. Tomatoes, beans, peas, the few flowering annuals she had tended with such care, everything had shriveled down to the roots. All the similar failures in Kenya rose up again to mock her over this new calamity; but an even worse blow was a little book, *Gaasen og Ræven*, written by her sister, Ellen.

Tania was not the only member of the family to have inherited literary ambitions from Wilhelm Dinesen. Thomas had *No Man's Land* in print in England as well as in Denmark. Ellen had published *Introductioner* and *Dansk Billedbog*—acceptable pieces of writing, though somewhat naïve. Now, as Tania read her sister's parable of the Goose and the Fox, she felt that Ellen had intended it for her: the story of the foolish goose chasing after the fox and a silly, unsuitable life was meant for Tania, who had once preferred the glamor of Katholm and Frijsenborg to the more solid values of "Mama" and Folehave, and who still indulged in frivolous notions. Ellen would have denied any such intention, but Tania was in no position to discuss it with her. Her dislike for Ellen's husband, Knud Dahl, had become more unreasoning and violent as time passed, and it had finally caused a rift between the two sisters. How could Thomas find it in himself to defend Knud Dahl? railed Tania. How could Ellen tolerate such a dull, ultraconservative husband? Their prosaic outlook on life appalled her and she felt betrayed by all of them.

As autumn approached, the prospect of another year, even another day, of the occupation was unbearable. It seemed there would never be an end to the humiliation, ugliness and loneliness of it all. Paris had been liberated in August. The French had poured into the streets, laughing and crying, embracing the victorious GI's, exchanging flowers and kisses for chocolate bars and Lucky Strikes, while at home the Danes were pulling in their belts for yet another lean, miserable winter under the Germans.

On October 30, with the first frosts already dappling the lawn and the house invaded by numbing drafts and early darkness, a young girl arrived at Rungstedlund. It was Clara Svendsen, who had met Tania at a church bazaar in 1942. Since then she had been far away, teaching French and Latin in a school in Jutland. But Tania had made a deep impression on Clara, who beneath a seemingly meek exterior was an intense, determined person. She had made the journey to Rungstedlund, hoping to work there as a secretary.

"I don't suppose you can cook?" demanded Tania without further preamble. "That is the greatest need here at the moment."

Clara didn't blanch at the preposterous suggestion, and replied that perhaps she could. One way or another, she was resolved to stay, and it was in her nature to be helpful whenever a need arose.

"If you can't," pursued Tania, "then you must find me a cook as soon as possible. In the meantime, please do the best you can."

Relegated to the kitchen, Clara turned out a disastrous meal. Nor did it seem an easy matter to hire a cook who could meet the high standard which Denys and Berkeley Cole had set for Tania at the farm. As a last resort, Clara took a few cooking lessons.

"Appalling!" Tania shuddered when she recalled Clara's final culinary effort. "It was simply appalling!"

Eventually Mrs. Landgren, the former gardener's widow, took over the duties of cook for a while, and Clara stayed on as part-time secretary, though not without protests from Tania. Clara would never be happy and satisfied at Rungstedlund, Tania insisted. She might become a convenience; she was much more likely to become a nuisance.

When she assumed her new duties, Clara was a shy, even a somewhat awkward girl who blushed easily and often. If she was also rather plain, it was not from lack of natural assets but because she had chosen to be that way—teachers were supposed to be plain. The whole academic milieu was full of such constraining reservations, but although Clara conformed to them outwardly, her spirit remained fervently independent. She was an ardent Roman Catholic, one of a tiny minority in a country which was officially Lutheran. At seventeen she had fallen in love with Byron, and it was not the usual schoolgirl infatuation with a romantic poet-hero but an *affaire de cœur* for life. When Clara discovered *The Dream*, *Childe Harold* and *Don Juan*, she decided that Byron's poetry was different from any other she had ever read, "the way the sea is different from inland lakes."

And Isak Dinesen was different too. Clara had read her books and "felt, as with no other living writer, that she had inexhaustible sources outside herself to draw upon, that she had a real poetical inspiration." Meeting her had been a further revelation, for Baroness Blixen had an air about her that made all other women seem drab. She wore even her wartime slacks and sweaters with elegance. Clara observed that her face was deeply graven with lines of pain and fatigue but that her eyes spoke of equally inexhaustible sources within. "Whatever I could do to assist her in her work would be worth more than anything I could do on my own," Clara concluded.

Tania was more in need of assistance than she herself realized. The drawn-out strain of the occupation, the evacuation of the Jews, as well as constant bouts of illness, had left her very depleted. When spring came around again she would be sixty, and she approached that landmark, that Tycho Brahe day, with dread.

"I once thought or said," she now remarked in another letter to Birthe Andrup, "that there were three kinds of complete joy in the world: 1) to feel an excess of strength within oneself; 2) to be convinced that one is fulfilling one's destiny; 3) the cessation of pain." The first of these was a joy that Tania would never know again, and though she would not have cared to admit it, she was profoundly relieved to have someone to lean on, someone young and enthusiastic to dispel the chilly solitude at Rungstedlund. As a sort of defense she immediately made a habit of teasing Clara, but only the undiscerning were misled by these tactics. Clara blushed and lowered her eyes but understood quite well that the taunts only concealed Tania's growing affection and dependence.

As for Clara, at five years of age she lost her own mother, whom a stepmother had never really replaced, and at Rungstedlund she might easily have slipped into the sentimental role of semi-adopted daughter of the house. But she was far too modest and self-effacing, far too reserved. She demanded only to be of service, and in this direction her capacities seemed endless. She spoke English and French and had a scholarly knowledge of Latin; she had a drawing-room talent for playing the piano; she could edit Tania's manuscripts intelligently and type the finished work; she had a rare gift as a translator; and she could cope with the avalanche of correspondence and calls—only the art of cooking remained an obstinate mystery. And only the subject of Roman Catholicism remained a private and unassailable domain. It was a proof of Clara's strength and *grandeur d'esprit* that she could hold to her own convictions and yet understand and accept notions of Tania's which had shocked many of the more conventional Danes.

Clara had fought a long, hard battle for the privilege of believing as she wished. Her father, who lived in the Østerbro section of Copenhagen, was the descendant of a line of dour fishermen and shipbuilders. He sternly opposed Clara's ideas, as did her intractable stepmother. Her happiest days had been spent visiting her grandmother, uncles and aunts in the quaint fishing village of Dragør, but there too she found a lack of sympathy for nonconformist religious leanings. It had been decided when she was scarcely more than a child that she should be trained for an academic career, and her father, though he never allowed her even a few kroner for what he considered foolish luxuries, was at least making her studies financially possible. When she was fifteen and announced her intention of adopting the Roman Catholic faith, her parents threatened to stop her education. Given this choice, Clara simply waited until she came of age, at twenty-one, and then she quietly joined the Church. Some months later, thanks to a scholarship, she was able to rent a small apartment of her own near the university and thus establish a certain independence, and teaching supplemented her income. Just the same, her decision to give up her career and live with Tania caused another painful crisis at home.

At Rungstedlund, in spite of a strenuous routine and Tania's

Tanne, 1913

Tanne on safari, 1914/Bror

Thomas/Tanne with Eric von Otter on safari

Kamante

Abdullahi—a portrait painted in Africa by Tania

Tanne, 1915

Denys Finch-Hatton

*Tania with Dusk's son Pania/Tania at the desk where she wrote
sketches later included in* Seven Gothic Tales *and* Out of Africa

persistent teasing, Clara flowered. It was delightful to be free of the tiresome aspects of being a teacher. It was fine to be in a house which invited her spirit to breathe and grow, and to share her life with a person like Tania who lived intensely and generously, never on the surface of things. It was an enriching experience, too, to meet the rather odd parade of afternoon visitors. When they were all gathered around the tea table, Clara's silvery voice and fluttering manner were a charming foil for Tania's throaty remarks, smoldering glance and sibylline poise. Before many months had passed, it would have been difficult to imagine Rungstedlund without her.

Some of the visitors were curiosity seekers who had heard wild tales about the lady of Rungstedlund; some were fervent admirers of her writing who came simply to pay their respects; and a rare few found a permanent welcome and were assimilated into her life.

Erling Schroeder, one of Denmark's leading actors, had played every sort of role from the finest Hamlet that anyone could remember to operetta, and was finally devoting himself to producing and directing. The Nazis exercised strict censorship over the theatre, and it was Schroeder's ambition to put on plays that would not only get by the authorities but would also contain hidden messages of patriotism, rebellion and freedom. In a theatre which seated only two hundred people he had staged *The Time of Your Life* with great success. It had been running for over three years, and he was searching for new material when he decided to call on Tania and persuade her to write a play for him.

Other people, Tania told him, had preceded him with the same purpose in mind. Negotiations with one producer broke off because he insisted on getting a play in a few months' time and she refused to be hurried. A popular actress had also requested a play. "Which of my published stories do you think would lend itself to the theatre?" Tania had asked her.

The actress didn't know what to suggest. She had read the stories but unfortunately they were all period pieces.

"But couldn't the play be a period piece, set in the eighteenth or nineteenth century?" Tania pursued patiently.

"No, no! Not at all!" the actress protested. "That would be too dreadfully expensive!"

"Then what do you suggest?"

"Oh, well," burbled the actress, "The setting might be in Hell, or perhaps in Heaven."

"I see," said Tania. "Would that be cheaper?" The tone of her voice was unmistakable and the actress had made a hasty exit.

But with Schroeder, a long afternoon was spent discussing possibilities. Tania offered several suggestions and seemed eager to co-operate, but she was more absorbed in her guest than in his problems. Schroeder was said to be the handsomest man in Copenhagen. He was tall and well built, with a finely proportioned head, and his natural assets were enhanced by the suave speech and manner acquired during many years on the stage. He was all too used to having people find him irresistible and Tania was as vulnerable as anyone, but it was Schroeder, in the end, who succumbed. He became the special friend on whom she could rely for sympathy and understanding. Eventually, in 1961, he accompanied her on her last trip to Paris. He sat beside her as she lay dying. And when she was no longer alive he would talk and talk about her to any worthy listener. He had hundreds of anecdotes to illustrate her wisdom, her humor, her complex feminine wiles, and the extraordinary will power which had dominated her illness and even the debilitation of old age. She was really a witch, he would say.

During the occupation Tania had spent several Christmases with Thomas and his family at Hillerød, though she had always made a point of decorating a tree of her own. This year, with a young girl in the house, Christmas Eve was to be celebrated at home, and she had her heart set on a truce with her sister, Ellen. Clara and Knud Dahl, as the tallest ones, won the contest of blowing out the topmost candles without using a ladder; the few wartime extravagances were brought out and shared; and what with gifts and carols and family differences forgotten, the evening passed happily. Tania would have reason to remember it with gratitude, for it was Knud Dahl's last Christmas. He lived only long enough to see the end of the war.

It was Clara's presence which made the sixtieth birthday seem a less distressing turning point. Tania, who loathed the idea of growing old, would have preferred to ignore the day altogether. But any morbid thoughts that might have continued to plague her vanished when the gardener brought her his gift—a police-dog puppy, recently born in his cottage, which was given the name of Pasop, after the dog mentioned in the first of the *Gothic Tales*. Tania had always been passionately attached to the dogs she owned. Dusk, Pania, David, Dinah—they all had an almost mystic importance for her, but Pasop, she said, had the sweetest nature and he became her favorite. Wherever she went Pasop went, in the way that Osceola had gone everywhere with Wilhelm. And when Pasop died after thirteen years of rather startling adventures, he was buried with sorrow and ceremony at the edge of the plot on Ewald's Hill which was later consecrated as a final resting place for Tania.

A fortnight after her birthday, Berlin fell. And on May 4 the Liberation of Denmark was proclaimed. The Germans, those old foes of human happiness who had harried their neighbors since the days of Julius Cæsar, would now go back where they belonged. Stripped of their weapons, they sombrely began preparations for leaving while the entire Danish nation erupted into a delirium of bell ringing, singing and shouting, and general joy. All Danes had hoarded candles to use on the great day; and when evening of May 4 fell, the black-out windows were at long last unshuttered, uncurtained, and millions of lighted candles sent out their message of freedom and hope. The next morning Tania, frail as she was, bicycled the more than twenty kilometers to Hillerød to celebrate with Thomas.

On December 19 she went alone to the top of Ewald's Hill and sat on the familiar wooden bench for an hour in spite of a blustering winter wind. It was the hundredth anniversary of Wilhelm's birth. A century. It was a sobering thought. How many wars, how many public and private tragedies, how many inventions and changes did that century not embrace in its round numbers. These woods, where she had walked and talked with her father, were finally rid of Germans and she felt free again to come here as she wished; but since the enemy left there had been the atom bomb at Hiroshima. It was a grave portent of another, new era, far more dreadful, no doubt, than anything she or her father ever knew. They had both been born into a world of carriages and horses, of music performed by human beings, of fires on the hearth, of women who sewed—a world where tradition outweighed novelty and the individual meant more than the masses. Of course, she had always driven an automobile and she would have central heating installed at Rungstedlund as soon as conditions permitted, but her whole nature recoiled at the idea of machines and noise and hurry and newness. One must learn not to resist change, she reflected; one must try to make sense of it all, and laugh at it, and go along with it in a fitting manner. "The old order changeth, yielding place to new; And God fulfills himself in many ways, Lest one good custom should corrupt the world." Tennyson had said it; and flippantly or solemnly, she herself had written the same thing over and over again. She had made Mira say: "I have been trying for a long time to understand God. Now I have made friends with him. To love him truly you must love change, and you must love a joke, these being the true inclinations of his own heart." Boris spoke for her too: "The real difference between God and human beings, he thought, was that God cannot stand continuance. No sooner has he created a season of the year, or a time of day, than he wishes for something quite different, and sweeps it all away. No sooner was one a young man, and happy at that, than the nature of things would rush one into marriage, martyrdom or old age. And human beings cleave to the existing state of things. All their lives they are striving to hold the moment fast, and are up against a *force majeure*. Their art itself is nothing but the attempt to catch by all means the one particular moment, one mood, one light, the momentary beauty of one woman or one flower, and make it everlasting. It is all wrong, he thought, to imagine paradise as a never-changing state of bliss. It will probably, on the contrary, turn out to be, in the true spirit of God, an incessant up and down, a whirlpool of change. Only you may yourself, by that time, have become one with God, and have taken to liking it." What was important was to live these ideas, not just to say them or write them.

In the next few years, two deaths marked the closing of chapters in Tania's life. On Tuesday, March 5, 1946, the newspapers carried a brief notice of an automobile accident at Borringe, Sweden, in which Baron Bror Blixen-Finecke was fatally injured. Count Corfitz

Beck-Friis had been driving when the right front tire was punctured and the car went out of control and crashed into a tree. Baron Blixen died two days later in a hospital at nearby Lund. The driver was not held responsible. The account went on to say that Baron Blixen had been a planter and big-game hunter in Kenya and had taken the Prince of Wales on safari; that he had been married to the Danish writer Karen Blixen, and was himself the author of a book describing his hunting adventures. After their divorce in 1925 he had married Jacqueline Harriet Birbeck, from whom he was divorced in 1935.

For some years Bror had been living quite dismally in a dependency at Borringe Kloster, the estate of Count Beck-Friis. In a sense he was right back where he started from, thought Tania; and his death was a miserable end for someone who had faced charging lion and rhinoceros. She stored the news away in the back of her mind and never spoke of it.

When Aunt Bess Westenholz, died on May 8, 1947, it denoted the passing of an era. She was the last of the older generation of women who had fought uncompromisingly for women's rights, for the old-fashioned morality they believed in, and for what they hoped would be a better world. She was also the last of the petticoat council that had harassed Tania's girlhood, perhaps mistakenly but surely always with loving intentions. Tania had long since forgiven her. Now the irrepressible spirit of Aunt Bess had flown away to some private Unitarian paradise of her own; Thomas would mourn her, and even Tania would miss her.

With these events, with the conclusion of the war and with the arrival of Clara, there came an end to what might be termed the "dark period" of Tania's life. From now on she belonged to the world and became a legend.

VIII

The Heretica Movement

—◠◠◠◠—

Toward the end of World War II a group of young authors began to come out to Rungstedlund frequently. Compared with the eccentric worldly personalities usually attracted to Tania, most of these writers appeared at first glance to be a handful of schoolboys, but if some of them were naïve, it was only in matters of the heart. Entirely different from one another in character and temperament, they were all gifted, ambitious, energetic and idealistic, and were soon to make literary history in Denmark with *Heretica*, the magazine they founded in 1948, and through the development of their respective talents. Novelists, poets, critics and teachers had joined forces. Several were graduates of the new university at Aarhus, where they had formed a students' literary society; a few were already established authors.

Martin A. Hansen and Jens Kruuse were the two older and more aloof members of the group. Hansen, educated as a teacher, came from a family of farmers in southern Sjælland, and the novels he had written in his twenties were colored by that locale and by his socialist leanings. Later his viewpoint changed completely and he devoted himself to purely creative writing—vivid short stories and novels; and history and archaeology replaced his political interests. He was still only forty-one when in 1950 he became co-editor with Ole Wivel (who was also the publisher) of *Heretica* magazine, but he had already produced a significant effect on younger authors, a source of some jealousy on the part of Tania.

Jens Kruuse had written his doctor's thesis on "the Sentimental Drama of France" and had lectured at the Sorbonne as well as at Askov and Aarhus University. In 1942 he became the main literary critic of *Jyllands-Posten* (a position he still holds) with tremendous influence on readers all over Denmark and especially on many young writers. He expressly disliked narrow, socialist-realist books and shared Tania's special admiration for the Book of Job, Racine, Molière, and the heroic in general. In particular, Kruuse had been a staunch defender of Tania's writings at a time when other Danish critics attacked her; and he was, in all respects, the obvious person to champion *Heretica,* to which he also contributed many articles. Oddly enough, though he caused a number of youthful littérateurs to make the pilgrimage to Rungstedlund, he never met Tania until 1961, when *Shadows on the Grass* was published. When she died the next year, he had his newspaper print the headline:

SCHEHERAZADE DEAD

Youngest of the group, but one of the most dynamic, was the poet Jørgen Gustava Brandt, who was only seventeen when the war ended. By the time he was twenty-five many of his poems had been published in *Heretica* magazine. Tania believed in him and thought he had an important future, but as he began to develop a very modernistic vein in his writing, there were violent arguments like those which rent the idyllic atmosphere at the farm when Tania and Denys quarreled about avant-garde painters and writers and Stravinsky. After one especially furious discussion, Brandt sent Tania a peace offering—a bull calf hung with garlands of flowers—and she was so much amused that she forgave him for good and all. It was Brandt's ivory-tower attitude which was partly responsible for the eventual split in the Heretica group. He felt that poets should not be involved in politics. However, he remained with the magazine until its demise, publishing an article on Tania in one of the last numbers, in 1953. He founded his own magazine, *Bazar*, in 1958, and to help him promote it Tania contributed a long essay which appeared in the first two issues, but the venture failed after a year. Though he continued to be a distinguished poet, Brandt later became associated with Danish Radio. He had a rather wild bohemian nature, and his beard and humorous grin combined to give him the appearance of a young, merry Hebrew prophet. Tania always called him Elishama after the character in her tale "The Immortal Story," although the original Elishama was far too silent and circumspect for any resemblance; and Brandt fell in with the whim and adopted the name. Indeed he fell in with most of Tania's caprices and was one of the few members of Heretica who remained faithful to her till the very end.

What banded all of these writers together was their need to protest against the prevailing socialist-realist literary trend in Denmark; the enthusiasm they shared for certain foreign authors who expressed their ideals; and a longing to break the bonds imposed by the occupation, the narrow academic world, the recognized critics and the Danish middle class. They craved the heroic, the Romantic, the utopian, and most of them believed that in Tania they had found a leader. She had dared to be different and independent, they felt. She had had the courage to develop a Romantic style, to deal candidly with illicit love and homosexuality, to write with wit and humor about God and the Church and time-honored customs. She believed in the dignity of man's individual destiny and in the eternal femininity of woman. In an ugly world, she defended the beautiful.

One by one they made their way to Rungstedlund like sailors lured to the siren's rock. A few of them fell madly in love, as only young boys can fall in love with wise and experienced older women. Others were permanently influenced in their thinking or style of writing. All of them brought their manuscripts for discussion. They wrote poems to Tania and essays about her, and sat at her feet while she held forth. As she had once been a white queen reigning over her natives and adoring circle of friends in Africa, she now became a sort of high priestess to the Heretica movement. Unfortunately, it was all far too *exalté*, and much of it could only end in bitterness.

In the spring of 1948 Tania abandoned her protégés to spend a few weeks in Paris. She had gone there several times over the years, but this time she was struck by the changes that had taken place in the city since her student days. The quiet streets she had first known were crowded and noisy with traffic, and double rows of parked automobiles encumbered the Champs-Elysées. The funny, cozy old Trocadéro had been replaced by the vacuously modern Palais de Chaillot, and rattletrap apartment houses were springing up here, there and everywhere. But the same avenues of pink and white chestnuts were in bloom, and the rare jacaranda trees were spilling their violet blossoms onto the pavement. And one could still stand at the prow of the Ile Saint Louis and contemplate the loveliest view of Notre Dame with its fretwork of struts and braces soaring above this most ancient part of the city, where Celtic altars had made way for Roman temples, which in turn lay buried beneath the great cathedral. One could still meander along the *quais*, loitering at bookstalls, buying a prim, tight bunch of anemones or *muguet* at a flower stand, avoiding only the rows of bird shops, which always made Tania want to open the doors of those wire prisons and let all the poor caged creatures fly away. She had rooms at the Hotel du Palais d'Orsay; its long, dreary, impersonal corridors appalled her and a terrible clamor rose from the station next door, but from there it was only a few steps to the Louvre or the Tuileries, where she could idle away an hour or a day, watching the children—shrill little girls in absurdly short dresses and serious small boys busy with sailboats.

One morning when her visit was drawing to an end she made a telephone call to the wife of an American diplomat in Paris. "Are you Parmenia Migel Ekstrom?" asked the low, husky voice, sounding curiously like Greta Garbo. "This is Karen Blixen. I have heard from my agent of your enthusiasm for my books and your efforts to have them published in France. Why did you never write to me? In any case, I am in Paris now and should like to meet you. I shall be here for only three more days and have many people to see but could spend half an hour with you at my hotel."

Half an hour—and with every possibility that callers would prevent conversation! But perhaps Baroness Blixen would come for lunch, which would be prepared by one of the best cooks in Paris and would be served under a towering elm tree on the terrace. The weather was perfect for lunching out-of-doors, and she would enjoy a view of the Seine, Balzac's house, the Hotel de Lamballe and rambling gardens where the ghost of the guillotined Princess de Lamballe roamed at night, carrying her own head in her hands.

"Today, then," Tania decided at once. "You can pick me up at one o'clock in front of my hotel."

"How shall I know you?"

"You will know me."

The proposed "half an hour" stretched out until the whole afternoon had vanished away. In the garden, tiny blue Lysandra butterflies sped back and forth in the shimmering May sunlight, and the scent of wood hyacinths floated up to the terrace. Tania admired the wild orchids transplanted from Marly forest and spoke of the wildflowers she had discovered in Africa. After lunch, ensconced in the library, she told an early version of "Letter from a King." She reminisced about her student days, hummed snatches of French songs that had been popular in 1910, recited a poem by Béranger, and seemed very emotional about being in Paris again.

When the butler brought afternoon tea she waved it aside, and she was still talking when he came into the room again to turn on the lights and close the iron shutters against the mist and sharp chill of the Paris twilight. By then it was seven o'clock.

"I think that I have been talking for a very long time. Now I should leave," she said, and then added firmly, "but we shall continue this conversation tomorrow. I have never seen Chartres. Let us start early in the morning and spend the day there."

It was typical of her to promise fifteen minutes but then to become carried away by the stories she was telling. When she thought she had found a good listener, she often lost all sense of time and talked on and on. A sudden intimacy was established which frequently grew into an enduring relationship. This time she had also been delighted to discover the quiet, the almost dreamlike atmosphere of the house and gardens only a few minutes' drive from her noisy hotel, and it became a haven for her whenever she returned to Paris.

When she arrived in Denmark the Heretica group was waiting for her impatiently, because the movement had now gathered sufficient momentum to launch its magazine, and she was needed for consultation. *Heretica* was to be published by Ole Wivel, a brilliant young man of twenty-seven who had directed his own publishing house for three years. Under the imprint of Wivels Forlag he was bringing out not only the most promising Danish authors but also art books (among them Klee, Kandinsky, Seurat) and many foreign writers in translation. Drawn to Rungstedlund toward the end of the war along with the other "heretics," Wivel composed a remarkable poem for Tania but finally refused to become a part of what he referred to as her "ordered cosmos," a resolution no doubt strengthened by his having an enormously active life of his own and a charming wife and two children at home. As a publisher, however, he was involved with Tania from the beginning. His first project was *Farah* (subsequently incorporated into *Shadows on the Grass*). When Wivel joined Gyldendal in 1954, he continued as Tania's editor and after her death was co-editor with Clara Svendsen of *Karen Blixen,* an anthology of tributes by authors and Tania's personal friends. With all this, he had found time to teach at Askov and later at Krogerup, to contribute articles to *Heretica* magazine and serve as its editor for two years, and to write a number of books, some of which were volumes of poems.

Thorkild Bjørnvig and Bjørn Poulsen were to serve for two years as editors of *Heretica*. For the first issue they had obtained from Tania her four Berlin reports, "Breve fra et Land i Krig" (Letters from a Country at War) and were trying to persuade her to contribute some new stories. Poulsen himself set the keynote for the whole Heretica group with his article "The Ivory Tower." Considerably influenced by Jens Kruuse, Poulsen was also making a name for himself as a critic and essayist even beyond the sphere of the Heretica group.

As for Thorkild Bjørnvig, a long chapter might well be written by some future literary analyst about the sway Tania had over him, and its consequences for both of them. For more than four years he was a very rewarding as well as acutely disturbing element in her life. Like Poulsen, Bjørnvig had his M.A. degree from Aarhus University and was a driving force of the Heretica movement. His special interests were Goethe, Hölderlin and Rilke, much of whose work he translated for the magazine, besides poems of Auden and other literature from abroad. Wivels Forlag brought out the Rilke translations in book form, and further volumes were published by Gyldendal when Wivel became an editor there. Noting how gifted and prolific a writer he was, Tania somehow leaped to the conclusion that in Bjørnvig she had discovered that *rara avis*—a true genius; and without being really aware of her own motivation, all her creative instincts were aroused to mold and direct his talent according to her personal precepts.

Circumstances played into her hands when Bjørnvig's doctor prescribed a long rest for him after an accident which had caused a concussion. She invited him to Rungstedlund for his convalescence. He remained in the house for several months and came back to stay there again and again, and soon became exaggeratedly influenced by Tania's personality. For Tania he grew to be many things —not merely the patient who required her care or the fledgling author who needed her guidance; Bjørnvig was also the captive audience for the theories she wished to expound (Bror had never listened at all and Denys had countered with his own opinions); he was the personification of the son Tania had never had and the embodiment of what so often figures in her writing—the youth ideal eternally threatened by marriage, mediocrity, corruption and age. She obviously never sensed that she herself was as great a threat as any. As she became more and more engrossed in him, her imaginings even cast Bjørnvig in the role of her spiritual and literary successor.

What Clara thought of the guest who became such an obsessive presence at Rungstedlund she did not say. She was too discreet, and she was more than occupied with the morning correspondence and editing, in addition to her work in a Copenhagen library, and the influx of afternoon callers—sometimes Robert Haas from Random House in New York; or a newcomer, nineteen-year-old Bent Mohn; and "heretics," neighbors and relatives. Old Pedersen, however, made no attempt to hide his dislike and jealousy of Bjørnvig. After fifty-four years on the place it was his prerogative to be Tania's chauffeur, and he raged when she allowed Bjørnvig to drive the car. In a household of women a ridiculous fuss was being made over that riffraff, whom he flatly declined to mention by name. *"Ham derinde"*—the one in there, Pedersen would say with a scornful nod toward the house.

By degrees Bjørnvig himself began to feel suffocated. Suddenly he turned against Tania with angry accusations, and at last he broke away altogether. When she followed him to Jutland, where he had taken refuge, he refused to receive her. "If I have to see you again I shall die," he said with desperate finality.

Tania was stunned and heartbroken by Bjørnvig's defection. After a while all the enchantment and subsequent disillusion came out, transmuted into a tale called "Echoes." In "The Dreamers" (*Seven Gothic Tales*) Tania had introduced her readers to Pellegrina, the famous diva who had lost her voice as a result of the great fire at the opera house in Milan and thereafter had cut herself off from life, wandering from place to place, unrecognized and alone. Now, in "Echoes," Tania took up the thread of the story once more: Pellegrina has discovered the extraordinary gift of the village boy, Emanuele, and is teaching him to sing, and everything that she herself once was in the world of music is to be reborn in the divine voice of her pupil.

"The story suggests," says the critic Robert Langbaum, "that in her soul-searching Isak Dinesen pointed the finger of accusation against herself. For 'Echoes' is about cannibalism—literal, psychological and ritual cannibalism. Pellegrina comes to realize that her love of the twelve-year-old boy, Emanuele, to whom she has been giving singing lessons, has been cannibalistic—that she has been feeding on him in order to restore her own youth and to resurrect the Pellegrina Leoni whom she buried in Milan twelve years ago." The boy has sensed all this; he calls her a witch, a vampire, and accuses her of wanting to drink his blood when she runs after him on the street. "If you do not stay where you are, I shall throw the stone at you," Emanuele cries out, and hurls two of them at her.

When "Echoes" was published, people in Danish literary circles understood who was intended by the character of Emanuele and it became for a time a sort of cause célèbre. And echoes of "Echoes" hung in the air for many long years; in 1964 Bjørnvig published a book called *Cain's Altar* about Martin A. Hansen and it was bruited about that he had chosen this subject rather than Karen Blixen as an act of revenge and to rid himself of Tania's influence. But it was an unfair assumption, since he had long been an admirer of Hansen and had, in fact, already written a book about him as far back as 1949.

Though absorbed in Bjørnvig, Tania had always had time and affection to spare for the rest of the group. At times they exasperated her, and she was especially annoyed with them over the matter of the Pierrot costume.

Tania had felt so sentimental about this relic of one of her girlhood masquerade balls that she had packed it with her household effects when she went out to Africa. She was trying it on one afternoon at the farm when some of the natives came to tell her that the first examinations were about to take place in the little school, and she had hurried to join them without stopping to change into other clothes. The costume had made a tremendous and unforeseen impression. The natives, she learned afterwards, had thought that what she was wearing was the prescribed costume for examinations.

Rummaging through old trunks in the attic at Rungstedlund she rediscovered the costume on a day when she was expecting the Heretica writers at a party to celebrate the publication of one of their books.

"They were all assembled in the drawing room," she poured out her disappointment to Erling Schroeder on the telephone, "when I flung open the door and appeared before them . . . as PIERROT! A stupid silence was the only reaction. The whole thing fell flat."

How depressing it was when people failed to respond! At any rate, she refused to be completely cheated of her fun this time. She had promised her photograph to John Gielgud, whom she had introduced as the first actor to play Hamlet at Elsinore, in the late thirties, and who later invited her for a whole week of his Shakespeare performances at Stratford-on-Avon. She would send a picture of herself in the Pierrot costume.

Clara, after twenty years at Rungstedlund, insisted that Tania was always very reluctant to pose for photographers, and Tania herself would never admit that she enjoyed it. But seldom if ever has there been an author more photographed by everyone from the most celebrated professionals to the humblest of amateurs, and Tania posed for them like an accomplished actress with a careful eye for every detail. She had decided to have the Pierrot picture made by Rie Nissen, who had already photographed her a number of times: at the typewriter, in a dashing black silk cape, peering out flirtatiously from behind a mesh veil, and in evening dress on her way to a reception given by the King and Queen. Tania had also sat for her at the time of the publication of *Seven Gothic Tales*, the only one of her books which came out in Denmark under the pen name Isak Dinesen. "Karen Blixen asked me to make a photo for that occasion, which would express the pseudonym so that one wouldn't see if it was a man or a woman," Rie Nissen later recalled. The result had delighted Tania—a mask, an enigmatic pale shape suspended in a dark void.

Tania put on the Pierrot costume and made up her eyes extravagantly with kohl, and as it was obvious that old Pedersen would never consent to drive her to Copenhagen in such outlandish garb, she called Knud W. Jensen, a great friend who had endeared himself to her as a patron of the arts and who also had helped Ole Wivel start his publishing house. He accompanied her to Miss Nissen's studio, and after the sitting, suggested lunch at Tivoli.

"They have too many Pierrots there already," objected Tania.

Driving back to Rungstedlund, they passed the Bellevue Strandhotel and Jensen, equally affected by pangs of hunger and by a desire to show off his companion, again suggested lunch.

"It would never do in there!" said Tania scornfully.

At the Beaulieu Hotel she finally gave in. "But dressed as I am, we must pretend we are engaged in making a film," she insisted. "And we must act our parts."

Another unhappy telephone call to Erling Schroeder: "He

couldn't keep up his end of the dialogue," she lamented.

In due course, the photograph appeared in a Danish newspaper, evoking the usual censure in conservative circles.

In 1952, anyone could see that the Heretica movement was breaking up. If most of the group preferred to maintain their original stand, several were rebels who were reaching out toward more modern philosophies and techniques. A couple of them avoided Rungstedlund, or avoided each other. Erik Knudsen, with his more leftist tendencies, had caused one of the rifts, and like Jørgen Gustava Brandt, eventually started a magazine of his own, *Dialog.* "I long for people who don't have polished sentences hanging around their necks like pearls, People who stutter and use the simplest words . . ." said one of his poems. Could anything have been more at variance with Tania's manner of talking and telling, or what the Heretica writers had first admired? Brandt was against political involvement of any kind. And soon it became increasingly clear to each of the group that writers, like other creative artists, are individualists first of all, self-centered, essentially ambitious for their own ends, and seldom capable in community of producing their best work.

Bjørnvig and Poulsen, Wivel and Hansen, had completed their two-year stints as editors of *Heretica,* and the magazine was now in the hands of Tage Skou-Hansen, who would perpetuate the Aarhus-Heretica group in his novel, and Frank Jæger, who, having met Tania only twice, had escaped being bewitched by her, but whose writing revealed traces of her particular qualities. They could all feel reasonably proud of the magazine's achievements. Besides their own original contributions *Heretica* had presented many Danish authors, as well as Auden, Yeats, Sandburg, Faulkner, William Carlos Williams, Goethe, Hölderlin, Rilke, Werfel,

Saint-Exupéry, de Rougement, Neruda, García Lorca, Ilya Ehren-
burg, and others. Tania, in addition to Brandt's essay about her,
poems about her, and much material for which she was the inspiration, had been represented by her "Letters from a Country at War"
and "Converse at Night in Copenhagen," a story later included in
Last Tales. The final issue came out in 1953, but the general trend
of the magazine was taken up and carried on by *Vindrosen*, a
periodical published by Gyldendal.

As they had come, one by one, most of the Heretica writers
drifted away from Rungstedlund, a few of them with resentment
in their hearts, but all of them, they were bound to admit, much
enriched by the experience. They were not the last young writers
who would appear there, undergo a similar influence and react
in much the same way.

IX

Of Birds and Boys

—〰〰—

"Shall I go to the right or to the left?" Pellegrina asks herself when she is about to leave Emanuele's village forever to seek a new existence . . . somewhere . . . somehow. In the first shock of Bjørnvig's departure Tania, too, felt that she did not know which way to turn, but the question need not have troubled her. A small, indelible cicatrix had left its mark on the core of her affections, perhaps also on her feminine vanity, but there would hardly be time even for unremembering. "The divinity which shapes our ends," and on which Tania usually placed such reliance, was already crowding her life with new shapes and faces, new loves. One should never bother at all about left or right, Tania decided, but simply keep on going.

Now it was a very, very small boy who was insinuating himself into her heart, filling the vacuum left by the deserter. In 1949 when Fru Carlsen applied for the post of housekeeper, she brought up the problem of the three-year-old son whom she wanted to keep with her.

"No," Tania objected before Fru Carlsen could go any further. "Definitely no! It would never do." Rungstedlund was no place for a child. It was much too close to the Strandvej and cars went speeding by all day. Sooner or later any boy would be tempted to cross the road to get to the beach, and the danger was far too great. She could not accept the responsibility. No, it would never do.

Having seen the house and its lady, Fru Carlsen was determined to stay. She was positive that in spite of cooking and housework she would always manage to watch out for the boy. He was quiet and obedient; Baroness Blixen need have no fears about him.

Fru Carlsen moved in. And cavorting around the lawn, romping with Pasop, laughing and shouting like the African *totos* at the farm, was Nils. Nils, tow-headed as a sunlit haycock in June, blue-eyed as Danish summer skies, with a sudden, dazzling smile that was irresistible. Tania could never have guessed that the time would come when her lawn would be used as a football field, or that Nils would cast covetous eyes at the duck house next to the pond and that she would hand it over to him to use as a playhouse, or that her backyard and cellar would one day become a workshop for building sailboats. But she was right about the Strandvej. When Nils was six he and the gardener's boy went skipping across it with their minds on anything but where they were going, and a car struck both of them down. Nils had both legs broken and the other child was carried home suffering from a concussion. And no sooner was Nils out of the hospital than he wheedled permission to sit in Knud W. Jensen's big car, and somehow managed to release the brakes. The car rolled down the driveway, escaped a collision as it shot across the Strandvej and barely missed plunging into the sea.

The year that Nils came to Rungstedlund was also the year that Pasop ran away—not in itself a dramatic occurrence since he was doubtless off in pursuit of some amorous canine adventure, but the consequences were far-reaching. After two days, during which every frantic effort to find him failed, Clara offered to make a pilgrimage to Rome if Pasop would only come back.

"And I," said Tania, "shall offer something too. If Pasop is found I promise to donate the park of Rungstedlund as a bird sanctuary."

One hour later the unabashed miscreant came home, and Clara did indeed set out for Rome. She had left eight hundred dollars on deposit with Random House—advance royalties for *The Angelic Avengers*—which Tania had given her in return for typing the manuscript; and the money had risen to the equivalent of fifteen hundred dollars as the Danish krone declined. She devoted the windfall to redeeming her pledge.

Tania also made good her word. The plight of birds had always filled her with pity. Those that Wilhelm had taught her to love and recognize were being driven away from Rungstedlund, inland and north, as the suburbs of Copenhagen encroached on the forests along the shore. Already it was rare to hear a hawk or an owl in the woods at night, and years ago the nightingales had flown to safer, wilder places. They needed a haven here, like the pond she and Old Knudsen had made in Kenya. ". . . in the hot season, when the water-holes dried up in the plains and the hills, the birds came to the farm; herons, ibis, kingfishers, quail, and a dozen varieties of geese and duck. In the evening, when the first stars sprang out in the sky, I used to go and sit by the pond, and then the birds came home." Birds needed a refuge too from enemies who snared and caged them. Tania had never been able to forget the consignment of flamingoes on a ship which took her from Port Said to Marseille.

Packed in crowded, filthy cases, suffering and terrified, many of them died a pathetic death during the voyage, and she doubted that those surviving had fared any better in the Marseille zoo. "I want to tell you," says old Miss Malin to Kasparson as she confronts death, at the end of "The Deluge at Norderney," " . . . I, too, was once a young girl. I walked in the woods and looked at the birds, and I thought: How dreadful that people shut up birds in cages. I thought: If I could so live and so serve the world that after me there should never again be any birds in cages, they should all be free—"

The idea of a sanctuary for birds had undoubtedly been in Tania's thoughts for a long time, and the vow made when Pasop disappeared merely caused it to take definite shape. In 1958 the project became a reality; not only a place of safety for birds but a peaceful retreat for humans as well, a public park. One of the first visitors was Fru Christensen, an old lady who came out from Copenhagen and the next morning sent a complaining letter. The park was lovely and she had enjoyed it very much, she wrote, but since the paths were steep and tiring, it had been very annoying to find no bench at the bottom of the hill where an elderly person could sit and rest before going home. Tania made reparation at once. Under a shady tree near the entrance a comfortable seat was placed, marked in large white painted lettering "FRU CHRISTEN-SEN'S BENCH." The old lady came back and sat on it, satisfied and proud, and even had herself photographed there.

In the early days of *Heretica*, Bent Mohn had written requesting information for a newspaper article, and had been invited for tea. Tania's expert glance took stock of him appreciatively when he came into the drawing room. Fair-haired, tall and slender, with the keen look of an intellectual and the sensitive, tapered fingers of an artist—so might Shelley have appeared at twenty. He was also exceedingly shy and reserved, but his hostess was very skilled. She had the special gift of making each person feel that he, and only he, was worth her undivided attention. Fixing dark, almost hypnotic eyes on the guest, she talked and told stories until he felt quite at ease, and then plied him with shrewd questions, listening as raptly as she had talked.

After four years of friendship Bent brought the young Negro pianist, Eugene Haynes, whom he had met in Paris. To Tania, the blond Dane and the dark American presented a ravishing contrast as they sat facing her across the tea table. Bent had changed a great deal in the time she had known him, thought Tania. He was keener and wiser, but his comments were spiked with irony; and cynicism, premature for his years, was warping his sense of adventure. Not Shelley at all any more, she decided, but perhaps a sort of Nordic François Villon—with a touch of the demonic which, after all, was the real salt in any personality.

Deftly she maneuvered the conversation to focus upon the new arrival. He had come originally from Illinois. There, as a child prodigy, he had won some renown for composition and improvisation, and later had graduated with a first prize in piano from the Juilliard School of Music in New York. At present he was preparing for his New York debut and a concert tour in Europe.

While he was speaking Tania observed him quietly, and liked what she saw. He had kind eyes and a generous smile, and he talked of his future plans with the happy, excited look of a small boy about to open a surprise package. She nodded approvingly when he said he preferred playing the Romantic composers, and could not resist airing her own ideas on the subject. Bent was a music lover, and had heard Tania's views before, but today she was spinning her web of charm for Eugene. In Africa, she told him, she had argued with her friend Denys Finch-Hatton, who had always wanted to hear the most advanced music. "I would like Beethoven all right," Denys had said, "if he were not vulgar."

"Personally I used to listen to Beethoven with pleasure," Tania went on, "but one day I said to myself, 'I don't trust you. It's really your spirit which started all this Nazi business.' " Of course, she would always enjoy the Romantic composers, but now, at the end of a long life, she had come around to liking Mozart best of all.

Not knowing Tania, Eugene did not realize at the time all that was implicit in her remark. It was, in fact, very indicative of her character and philosophy that she had so marked a preference for Mozart, composer of aristocrats, aristocrat of composers—Mozart who had given perfect expression to the form and elegance of his age, and had what Tania most admired: the ability to sense the comic in conjunction with what a lesser genius would have seen as purely tragic. She often confessed to being merely bored or irritated by what she considered the too-insistent rhythm and the grandiose humorlessness of Bach, and had laughed with relish when Colette's remark was repeated to her: *"Bach, c'est une divine machine à coudre."*

As for modern music, it simply wasn't music at all. Not even Denys had been able to convince her. Apart from Mozart, she took a childlike pleasure in simple tunes, and it was typical of her that in later years, when she had Eugene in the house for months at a time and might have enjoyed the whole range of his repertoire, she made him improvise a piano arrangement of the English folk song, "Barbara Allen," and obliged him to play it not only every day but many times each day. It was a small indulgence which he performed for her with patience, with tenderness and gratitude, for by then he loved her like a son.

On the afternoon of his first visit Tania, as was her custom with all of her guests, walked out to the courtyard to say good-bye. She placed her thin, frail hand in his, which was warm and strong, and gave him her most encouraging smile. "We must arrange a concert for you in Copenhagen," she said. And turning to Bent: "You must come out to see me again. Soon. Both of you."

Eugene required no urging. Unlike many musicians who only evolve through brooding and self-exploration, through a secret communion between themselves and their art, Eugene had need of the world around him. He was eager and impressionable and in his desire to absorb the essence of places and people, he was gaining perspective on his own problems and acquiring the solid maturity which would add scope and depth to his playing. For a young pianist exploring the nuances of nineteenth-century music, Rungstedlund was the Romantic ideal, with its ancient beech woods and mellow gardens, its soft green lawns curving down to the edge of the sea. Tania took him to the top of Ewald's Hill to show him the place where she wished to be buried. This preoccupation with one's final resting place was part of the Romantic ideology. A whole cult of sentimental relics had grown out of it: the mementos and embroidered pictures, brooches and rings, depicting the grave, testimony of the role that death had played in nineteenth-century life. Nostalgic rather than tragic or macabre, it had infused all of Wilhelm's generation and the literature and music of his time with a gentle melancholy which Tania had always cherished. Long years ago, up in the Ngong Hills, she had taken Denys to see the burial place she had chosen for herself and he expressed a wish to be buried there too—a place high on the first ridge of the mountains with a sweeping view of Kilimanjaro in the far distance and the plains and Tania's house below in the forest. After that, when they were out in the hills, Denys had sometimes said, "Let us drive as far as our graves." Our graves. She had liked that: the sepulchral note in a landscape teeming with life, a flutter of wings of the Angel of Death in the high blue sky where African eagles soared and screamed.

Eugene walked slowly up the hillside with Tania leaning on his arm. She was nearing seventy and already seemed as pale and un-substantial as any Romantic spectre that might be wandering there among the trees. She talked about her past and Eugene's future, about Africa, and death. She was, as Clara said, "drawing out her life to the hungry," dispensing friendship and wisdom and her particular gift of storytelling. Eugene would never forget it. His perceptive ear also recorded every inflection of her voice, its low pitch and leisurely pace, and the trace of a Danish accent which she had never been able to shed. Afterwards he could always make her friends laugh with his imitations of her way of speaking.

"I suppose, Eugene," said Tania one day, interrupting the tea-table banter with abrupt seriousness, "I suppose that you will be coming back here next summer." It had the tone of a command rather than a casual suggestion. She didn't want him to refuse. She enjoyed having him at Rungstedlund. There were, of course, a dozen reasons why a young pianist at the beginning of his career should not spend another season in Denmark but before Eugene could mention them, Clara proposed Dragør.

The fisherman's cottage now belonged to Clara. Her grandmother's will had bequeathed it to several relatives, but Clara had recently managed to buy the last remaining share. Her happiest childhood memories were of the holidays she had spent there and she was very excited at having a place of her own. "Tiny and modest though my cottage is, *c'est moi la patronne,*" she said possessively, almost defiantly. It was hers as a refuge against an intrusive world, hers to do with as she wished, hers to offer. She offered it now to Eugene, and as soon as she could escape from her work at Rungstedlund, she took him to see it.

Det Gamle Dragør—Old Dragør on Amager Island—had long been one of the most picturesque of Danish villages. Many of its houses dated from the eighteenth century, when prosperous Dutch shipowners and farmers had been the overlords, but there were also survivals from medieval days when the harbor had sheltered thousands of ships that came from the farthest ports of Europe and even the Far East for the great annual herring fisheries and trade fairs; and Stone Age settlements slumbered under the swaying grey-green grass of the meadows along the beach. Since Copenhagen was only half an hour away, each year was bringing more of the sophisticated summer residents, more and more tourists were swarming into the little shops and inns, larger and noisier crowds were taking the Dragør ferry back and forth to Sweden. The village folk, however, were making great efforts to stave off the onslaughts of the twentieth century. Did their narrow, flagged streets discourage modern traffic? They made them even narrower by planting beds of hollyhocks in front of nearly every house. And when an enterprising city man attempted to put up an eight-story building (a veritable skyscraper in Dragør) he was politely but firmly told that he could move to another town.

Clara's cottage stood in a quiet angle of the street which ran beside the harbor and beach. Like most of the houses it had a steep roof, densely thatched with marsh reeds, and a diminutive, walled-in garden. The ceilings inside were so low that a tall man would knock his head on the rafters, and the smallest possible stairway led to the upper floor. For all that, it gave off a sense of space and comfort. Eugene was shown the sitting room and study and a tiny old-fashioned kitchen. Upstairs were a bedroom and bathroom, and enough extra space for eventual guests. A piano could be sent out so that Eugene would be able to work in peace at the cottage, Clara explained. And if he didn't want to bother with meals, he could always go to the nearby Dragør Strandhotel or one of the several inns.

When the little house had been thoroughly displayed and admired, they went down the street to have coffee at the Strandhotel, which was one of the places that had survived since early times. New arrivals were handed a leaflet printed in Danish, German and rather eccentric English, tracing the history of the hotel for seven hundred years (it was the oldest inn in Denmark) and listing kings and Kierkegaard among the noted guests. All the goings-on of the busy, glittering harbor could be seen from the terrace tables. Fishermen were unloading their catch while a crowd of idlers looked on and commented; others were sorting, cleaning and packing fish in baskets. Launches darted in and out of the basin and hundreds of boats with furled sails swayed in a slow, continuous dance, straining against their moorings. At regular intervals the sleek white ferry came gliding in like a huge, majestic swan, and spewed out its cargo of tourists and automobiles. Children in midget boats of their own skittered back and forth like water bugs, dodging the larger craft. And all the air seemed to vibrate with fluttering pennants and sea birds.

Clara pointed out the pier which her great-grandfather had built. To the right of it, beyond the last racks of drying nets, the beach meadows reached in a wide arc away from the port and the cottages, away from the people and bustle, out toward the distant headland and wide, enigmatic sea.

Eugene looked slowly and carefully at everything, and everything smiled back at him. There was no need for Clara to ask him if he would return to Dragør.

X

Essayist and Plagiarist

—ᴧᴧᴧ—

In 1952, Aage Henriksen's *Karen Blixen og Marionetterne* (Karen Blixen and the Marionettes) was published by Wivels Forlag, and it has generally been considered one of the most perceptive of the many essays about the author of the *Tales* and *Out of Africa*. In a way, it was not surprising that Henriksen chose the marionette theme as the basis of his analysis. Tania's writings and conversation contained many references to marionettes. In particular, there was *Sandhedens Hævn* (The Revenge of Truth) published in *Tilskueren* magazine, May 1926, while she was still living in Kenya. The little comedy expressed some of Tania's most cherished ideas and she was, no doubt, loath to have it reach only the limited public of *Tilskueren*, for she alludes to it in "The Supper at Elsinore" and she introduces it with considerable detail in "The Roads Round Pisa": "The play which was being acted was the immortal *Revenge of Truth*, that most charming of marionette comedies." It is the sort of sly humor readers have always enjoyed; Ionesco indulged in the same little trick in his play *Rhinoceros:*

JEAN: Instead of squandering all your spare money on drink, isn't it better to buy a ticket for an interesting play? Do you know anything about the avant-garde theatre there's so much talk about? Have you seen Ionesco's plays?

BERENGER: Unfortunately, no. I've only heard people talk about them.

JEAN: There's one playing now. Take advantage of it.

In "The Roads Round Pisa," however, the joke has its serious purpose too, as is often the case in Tania's writing. The marionette play is inserted in order to point out a moral and to cast light on the actions of the main characters of the tale.

A manuscript copy still exists of the first version of *The Revenge of Truth*, written when Tania was sixteen. It was staged by the Dinesen children and their friends, with Thomas and Anders playing the girls' roles, since they were very much younger, and its success with the family and neighbors was one of the reasons why "Mama" felt at the time that Tania should go on writing rather than take up painting at the Academy. The playlet was first revised in 1915, when Tania was thirty. She was forty-one before it came out in print, and another ten years went by before it was first put on, at a midnight performance, at the Royal Danish Theatre. Since then it has gained steadily in popularity. For example, in 1959, it was presented at Aarhus University; in 1960 it was shown on Danish television and at the Marsyas Theatre, Stockholm, in a translation by the poet Bo Setterlind; Oslo saw it the following year. It also appeared in book form, in 1960, under the Gyldendal imprint.

"Everybody will remember," we are told in "The Roads Round Pisa," "how the plot is created by a witch pronouncing, upon the

Tania's passport photograph, 1934/Tania and her mother at Rungstedlund

The study at Rungstedlund

Clara/Rungstedlund—view from the woods

Erling Schroeder/Jørgen Gustava Brandt (left); Thorkild Bjørnvig (right)

Tania in the Pierrot costume

Tania and Pasop (above, left); Tania with Alfred Pedersen (right)/Tania during the occupatio

Nils/Fru Carlsen with Ping Pong

Eugene Haynes/Bent Mohn

house wherein all the characters are collected, a curse to the effect that any lie told within it will become true. Thus the mercenary young woman who tries to catch a rich husband by making him believe that she loves him, does fall in love with him; the braggart becomes a hero; the hypocrites finish by becoming really virtuous; the old miser who tells people that he is poor loses all his money . . . At the end the witch appears again, and on being asked what is really the truth, answers: 'The truth, my children, is that we are, all of us, acting in a marionette comedy. What is important more than anything else in a marionette comedy is keeping the ideas of the author clear. This is the real happiness of life, and now that I have at last come into a marionette play, I will never go out of it again. But you, my fellow actors, keep the ideas of the author clear. Aye, drive them to their utmost consequences.' "

Using the marionettes and the author as symbols for man and God, the witch is expressing ideas which appear again and again in the *Tales,* and specifically in *Out of Africa:* "Pride is the faith in the idea that God had when He made us. A proud man is conscious of the idea, and aspires to realize it. He does not strive towards a happiness, or comfort, which may be irrelevant to God's idea of him. His success is the idea of God successfully carried through, and he is in love with his destiny. As the good citizen finds his happiness in the fulfillment of his duty to the community, so does the proud man find his happiness in the fulfillment of his fate. People who have no pride are not aware of any idea of God in the making of them, and sometimes they make you doubt that there ever has been much of an idea, or else it has been lost, and who shall find it again? They have got to accept as success what others warrant to be so, and to take their happiness, and even their own selves, at the quotation of the day. They tremble, with reason, before their fate."

Henriksen cites the passage from *Out of Africa;* he also discovers that *The Revenge of Truth* and Heinrich von Kleist's *The Marionette Theatre* have many points in common; and he refers at length to Thomas Mann's *Freud and the Future*. In his life as well as in his writings, von Kleist was just the person to sound a responsive chord in Tania. An Army officer and adventurer in his youth, a disheartened, embittered idealist who killed himself at the age of thirty-four, von Kleist's history parallels many of the events in the life of Wilhelm Dinesen. His work as leading dramatist of the Romantic movement and writer of picturesque tales also includes the charming and profound dialogue between its author and the first dancer of the Opera, which was one of the main themes of Henriksen's essay on Tania. The dancer asserts that marionettes have qualities which make them superior to human performers. They are not, he explains, manipulated by a puppeteer struggling with a confusion of strings, but "each puppet has a focal point in movement, a center of gravity, and when this center is moved the limbs follow without any additional handling." The advantage of a perfectly constructed puppet would be not only that it would respond precisely to the ideas of the puppeteer [as man, says Tania, should respond to the ideas of God] but that it "would never slip into affectation (if we think of affectation as appearing when the center of intention of a movement is separated from the center of gravity of the movement)."

In his critical study *The World of Isak Dinesen,* Eric O. Johannesson enlarges upon these notions: "All of life becomes a great story in which we human beings have our own little story to enact to the best of our ability and knowledge. The characters who have faith in the story are rewarded with a sign or an image, discover their identity, and accept their destiny. Some of them are tragic figures, other are comic; but whether they are villains, victims, or fools does not seem to matter in the long run, for ultimately they are all marionettes and thus in the hands of God and the story-teller. In the final analysis, the marionettes in Dinesen's world are performing in stories which illustrate two central themes in Dine-sen's view of life: the theme of aristocratic pride and the theme of acceptance."

Aage Henriksen, who was so preceptive in writing about Tania and the marionettes, was far less perceptive about his own role in the story. For a while he saw a great deal of Tania, and amongst other things, they both enjoyed discussing Kierkegaard, a favorite subject with Tania and of special interest to Henriksen, who, while lecturing at Lund, was also preparing his doctor's thesis on Kier-kegaard. But Henriksen fell deeply under Tania's influence, more so than anyone ever had. Eugene Haynes had responded in a direct, natural way to everything Tania had to offer, with re-sultant happiness for both of them. Henriksen took everything she said or wrote in deadly earnest. He confused art with life, and tried to live her ideas. Soon it was said that he was attempting to assume the role for which Tania had formerly destined Thorkild Bjørnvig. Like Bjørnvig he also turned against Tania, feeling that his whole experience with her had been fraudulent from the begin-ning. His idol fell from her pedestal and became, he concluded resentfully, a destructive siren who lured people to her, absorbed what she wanted or needed from them, and then cast them aside. She exemplified for him, in another sense, the phrase she had used in describing Miss Malin Nat-og-Dag in "The Deluge at Norderney": ". . . it was far better than it should be said of her that for her sake many men had been made unhappy, than that she should have made many men happy." One gets an inkling of the unnatural tension of Henriksen's relationship to Tania when he recounts how she once asked him to tell her something about his own life. He began . . . but lost the thread of his story because he looked up and became conscious of her face. Her customary pallor suddenly seemed to him "white as a china plate," and he was unable to go on.

Authors, like caricaturists, have a deadly weapon at their disposal when they are feeling hurt or revengeful. Henriksen's collected essays relating to Karen Blixen were not published until three years after Tania's death. When her friends and admirers read them they were indignant. They felt that he had too cleverly drawn a very one-sided picture to the detriment of the other aspects of her character which made her admirable and understandable as a whole. Because his own relationship with her had been unsatisfactory, Henriksen claimed that she repudiated normal adult relationships, that she did not even want them. She had few friends, he said, casually dismissing the whole rich pattern of her life of affection received and bestowed. In the end, one person wanted to be her friend, he conceded, and he recorded her as saying: "There is no longer room for you in my life. You should have come sooner. Now there is nothing left for me but to live out my destiny."

Eugene Haynes, in the meanwhile, was in Copenhagen again. Clara's cottage was undergoing repairs and was not yet ready for visitors, so he stayed with the well-known producer Svend Fridberg. Eugene was busy preparing his concerts, but as always was having a good time and making friends wherever he went. His one disappointment came when he gave his series of three recitals at the Riddersalen Theatre in November 1953 and Tania was too ill to attend.

As she had hoped, he was often at Rungstedlund with her and Clara during the summer months, and then the old house suddenly brimmed with life and laughter. Sometimes neighbors joined them for tea or dinner, sometimes Bent Mohn, whose presence often made the conversation take a more earnest turn. By 1961 Bent would be literary and dramatic critic of *Politiken* and already he had incisive ideas on these subjects. Tania could also pour out her lingering grievances over *Heretica* to Bent. One of her letters to him had left no doubt about her continuing displeasure: "*Heretica* is, I feel, with rather unreasonable arrogance engaged in monopolizing the top intellectual life here in Denmark. I had faith from the beginning in the group and have encouraged and supported it according to my abilities, and *Heretica* might amongst other things have had 'The Cardinal's Third Tale,' but they were stupid in their relationship to me and have, it seems to me, felt it to be a duty to reprimand me morally. That is something I don't like at all." The group, they both agreed, had grown pompous and humorless beyond all bearing. Perhaps it was just as well that the magazine would shut down this year, though it was always sad, remarked Tania, to contemplate the failing of a venture begun with hope and idealism.

The talk did not usually dwell too long on these minor irritations, for Tania, as always, told stories. Sometimes she would suggest some arbitrarily chosen topic to be discussed by all of them; or she might select characters from history or literature, one for each person at the table—a predilection inherited from her parents. Parlor games had been a main source of amusement in Wilhelm Dinesen's day, before the advent of radio and cinema. Tania continued to find them entertaining and brought such finesse to them that everyone shared her pleasure.

Nils was also constantly involved in all sorts of games with Tania. He was now a bright little boy of seven with a dense thatch of flax-colored hair. Guests or no guests, he flashed in and out of the dining and drawing rooms like a yellow canary on the wing.

"Baroness," he demanded on one of these evenings, "isn't it true that a dog is worth as much as a nun?"

"Yes, indeed," replied Tania, perfectly serious.

To the baffled listeners Clara explained that it was a counting game which Tania played with Nils when they went for a drive in her car. So many points for each soldier, policeman, nun, dog, cat, etc., that either of them saw first and knew by name, the winner being, of course, the one who had the most points by the time they reached home.

The Lindemann lawsuit cast a blight over all of these gently pleasant evenings—over everything, in fact. Looking back upon it after a long lapse, one is at a loss to understand how it could have caused such acute distress to Tania, who had weathered many real tragedies with calm and courage. But so it was. She brooded over it for years and never ceased speaking of it resentfully.

Tania's name and her pseudonyms were by now household words in Denmark. The country was proud of the success of her books abroad and at home, and though she had published no major work during the eight years since the end of the war, she was continually before the public with stories, articles and interviews in foreign and local papers and magazines. Her radio talks had also made her voice as familiar as the names she used. Two writers decided to take advantage of this popularity by adopting pseudonyms of their own and managing to have their works attributed to Tania. The first one she dismissed as an insignificant prank.

"But there was another book which was rather more of a problem," wrote Eugene Walter, an expatriate American writer in Rome, who was to play a whimsical role of his own in the affair. "Tania was reluctant to discuss the matter, but I heard from Danish friends that it had saddened her, seeing herself stolen from and copied in a very inferior manner. It seems that a certain writer, a kind of adventurer who had knocked about the world, went to great trouble to be introduced to Tania, who received him with the usual generosity she showed to writers and painters and musicians. After she had known him for a year or so, her bookseller called one day and asked her, 'Is it true that you have a new book of tales coming out under a completely new pseudonym?' She insisted that she hadn't, but the bookseller said he had been very reliably informed. A radio interviewer telephoned to ask the same question. The publishers recorded a large advance sale for the book, which was a series of tales of a plague year in Europe. Controversy raged. Indeed, the author had lifted bits and pieces from the *Seven Gothic Tales*, giving himself away in an amusing fashion. Tania kept and smiled ruefully over a note the younger writer once sent her. 'Dear Baroness,' it purred, 'every time I visit you, I take something away with me.' "

The villain was Kelvin Lindemann. His book *En Aften i Kolera-Aaret* (An Evening in the Cholera Year) was published by Carit Andersen under the pseudonym Alexis Hareng. Tania didn't know what action to take. At one point she thought it a great joke to stage an interview with Lindemann, pretending to be completely innocent about his plagiarism. Clara fled; she wouldn't have been able to stay and keep a straight face. Lindemann, immediately on leaving Rungstedlund after the interview, went to the offices of a rival newspaper, asked a brazen price, and telephoned to Tania to get her to modify something she had said in order to make it even better promotion for the book. Tania and Clara realized then that people would think it had all been staged for mutual publicity, so Tania withdrew the interview, remarking that it was only possible to have fun with one's peers. "Fine manners need the

support of fine manners in others," said Emerson, and Lindemann's ways were too underhanded for her. She would have no
further dealings with him. In the end, she felt impelled to sue the
publisher, with all the painful publicity that was bound to follow.
But to the surprise of most people, and particularly Tania, she did
not win the case.

Even Walter's shenanigans, although they amused her very much,
could not completely dispel the unsavory aftertaste of Lindemann's
treachery and the futile lawsuit. Walter, who was editorial assistant for Princess Caetani's literary review *Botteghe Oscure,* and a
person of real ingenuity, had managed to lay his hands on the
original manuscript of Lindemann's book. Tania and Clara had
just arrived in Rome in November 1957, and they were all in a taxi
on their way to a party when he suddenly produced it like a
prestidigitator. "I thought we might begin festivities by dumping
it into the Tiber," he suggested. Afterwards he wrote an account of
the incident.

"It was about 7:40 in the evening, when traffic is heaviest in
Rome, but the taxi driver obviously knew, seeing Tania's bearskin,
that no ordinary mortal was his passenger, so he obediently
stopped smack in the middle of the narrow bridge that crosses the
island, and we very ceremoniously got out. It's always a pleasure to
hold up the business of the world, and the more impatient and
irritated that world is, the greater the pleasure in making it stand
still. We stopped traffic for two blocks, and they blew horns and
shouted Roman insults, but our taxi driver just looked wide-eyed at
us as we went to the side of the bridge and performed our ritual.
Tania, Clara, and I each held a corner of the manuscript and
recited together, very slowly and solemnly:

> *Rat shit,*
>
> *Bat shit,*
>
> *Three-toed sloth shit,*
>
> *Tiber and Oblivion*
>
> *Receive this book and its author!*

"And we dropped the manuscript and watched it sink. Since the author died shortly thereafter, I am now very careful with magic of this sort."

Eugene Walter was one more who had capitulated to Tania's fascination. "Do I sound as if I fell in love? I did," he said after he first saw her, in 1956. "Here was some eternal human mystery, crystallized in a ninety-pound Danish lady of any age you might care to guess. A sibyl." A witch, Erling Schroeder had said. A siren said some. And others would come along who would find new, extravagant epithets or none that would do at all in expressing what they felt for her. And at this time she was seventy-one years old!

It was gratifying to her vanity both as a woman and as an author to receive the constant adoration of all the young men. More important was sharing their youth and vitality, but even her need to renew and cling to her own youth was only part of it. Essentially it was an unconscious quest for someone to fill the place of Denys. She had enshrined him within the printed pages of *Out of Africa* and now the world of readers possessed him. But did she? Every painter, composer and writer knows that a haunting image once externalized no longer belongs to the artist. "You can stand pain if you can write about it," said Hans Christian Andersen; he might have gone further and said you can stand it because you no longer have it, because it has lost its reality in the process of becoming literature.

Tania was constantly quoting Denys and telling stories about him to everyone she met, but none of that really conjured him up for her. Perhaps at night, when she was alone, she saw him more clearly. Clara, who was observant, had soon noticed that before going to bed Tania invariably went to the study and closed the door behind her and then opened the door to the courtyard and stood there quietly for a while. "As I am the most uncurious of persons," related Clara, "I only found out the explanation after I had lived at Rungstedlund for fourteen years" (and Denys had been dead for nearly thirty). On the side of the desk in the study hung a framed map which showed the farm and the Ngong Hills. Every night Tania looked at the map and at her photograph of Denys. The courtyard door faced south—toward Africa. The nightly rite completed, she could go to her room and sleep.

Part Four

—⁐⁐⁐—

Journeys and Work

I

"Queen of the Northern Monkeys"

—◊◊◊—

The last twelve years of Tania's life were a sort of continual safari. What she was pursuing during all that travel, which placed such a strain on the tattered remnants of her health and strength, it would be hard to say. Some of it was simply the old urge to escape, conscious or otherwise. Occasionally she was seized by a longing to see more of the world before she died, and she constantly received invitations from abroad.

In 1950, at the end of June, she went to Paris again. As her stay was to be very short, friends were anxious to make careful plans for every hour of each day and they asked her what she wanted to do, whom she wished to see. Her ideas were very positive. She wanted, she said, her eyes shining with all the excitement of a teen-age girl, to dine at the best French restaurant—caviar and champagne, muted lights and sentimental music, beautiful women in chic Paris gowns; she wanted to see the best plays—the Comédie Française and *Le Maître de Santiago,* one of the hits of the season; she wanted to buy French perfume—lots of it; she would see her friends, and walk around the streets as she had done as an art student. She must also visit some studios with a view to finding a painter to make a portrait of her which was needed for Denmark's Hall of Fame. No conventional portraitist was finally found whose work seemed more suitable than that of Danish artists, but she did have a very touching encounter with Pavel Tchelitchew.

After an absence of more than fifteen years in the United States, Tchelitchew had just returned to Paris, where he had enjoyed considerable success as a young painter and designer for the theatre. Paris has, however, more than any other city, the faculty of forgetting those who depart for other lands. Many of Tchelitchew's former companions had died or gone away; the ones who remained were absorbed in their own affairs and few were impressed by or even aware of his triumphant career in America. At forty-three he had both been honored with a huge one-man exhibition of his paintings and drawings at New York's Museum of Modern Art and received extravagant praise for his sets for ballets of Massine and Balanchine: *Errante, Ode, Balustrade, St. Francis.* "At times he simultaneously designed ambitious stage productions and executed large-scale compositions in oil or gouache, and neither effort has shown a trace of the other. He does not transfer pictures to the stage and, more important still, he never permits the theatre to infect his paintings with its specialized drama and artifice. He understands instinctively and as a matter of theory that there are things which may be said in the one place and not in the other," wrote the art historian James Thrall Soby, who described Tchelitchew as "one of the few great stage designers of his period." And here he was now, lonely, apparently unknown, and already suffering from the early symptoms of the illness which would cause his death.

"I have come back to Europe to die," he told a friend who was making efforts to rouse him from despondency, "and I hope I shall die soon. Life has no meaning for me any more. I have traveled everywhere, met everyone, and whether people grasp it or not, I have solved to my own satisfaction the final problem of putting the fourth dimension into a drawing or painting."

He kept shuffling around the room, and his habitual nervous tic made him squint and frown more than ever. "Look at that drawing on the wall," he demanded almost angrily. "Is it static? No, of course not! It moves! After a few minutes you see something utterly different from your first impression. Anyone ought to be able to see it. It isn't limited to height and width and depth plus the trumpery of perspective. It moves, moves in space!"

At last he subsided into a chair. "I do have a regret," he sighed after a moment. "I should have liked to know Baroness Blixen, but I am too ill now to go to Denmark even if she cared to see me. I understand she is ill too, so she certainly would not come to Paris."

"But she is here!" exclaimed his caller. "I can bring her to see you tomorrow!"

Tchelitchew had his wish. When they met he talked excitedly and uninterruptedly for three hours about his boyhood in Russia, his early abstract paintings, his portraits and stage designs, his years in Paris, and the life he had made in America. Most of all he spoke of his recent preoccupation with Einstein's time-space theory, and his efforts to work out a formula for expressing it in visual art. Tania, who loved to talk herself, sensed that there was a great urgency in what he was trying to tell her, and she listened to him in silence. He had, in any case, a splendid and uninhibited gift of speech. Everything he said was pointed up with vivid, original imagery, and his sense of humor, deft and malicious, only failed him when he was very sick. As she was leaving, Tania asked if he would consider making a portrait of her.

"I have finished forever with all that," he replied, without histrionics, quietly and simply.

They never saw each other again, but this meeting meant a great deal to both of them. Tania, who was used to doing all the talking, had hardly said a word all afternoon, and Tchelitchew felt that he had found the perfect listener embodied in the one woman he had longed to meet. At first Tania had been rather shocked by his categoric refusal to paint her portrait, but when she learned how anxious he had been to know her she was mollified, and she felt a sense of real loss when, in 1957, he died in Italy shortly before she arrived there.

The next summer Tania flew to Greece with Knud W. Jensen and his wife. Jensen was an ideal companion for a trip of this sort; he was not only a friend of hers but a friend of all artists, and he was soon to give Denmark Louisiana, one of the most beautiful museums in the world. On the return journey they stopped in Rome. Tania had an audience with the Pope, and renewed nostalgic memories of her first visit there with Daisy Frijs in 1912. After this excursion, work and sickness combined to prevent her traveling until she began her series of strenuous yearly treks in 1956.

The various illnesses which had plagued Tania since African days had aftereffects which now became alarming. In a first spinal operation in 1946 the surgeon had severed certain nerves in order to give her some relief, but the benefits had gradually worn off, and she was once again the prey of pain and nausea. She was exhausted and unable to eat enough to be properly sustained; only grim determination kept her at her writing desk. Always small and frail, she now declined to a weight of eighty-five pounds, and in 1955 her physican informed her that another operation was unavoidable. On August 11 the *New York Times* reported that her condition, after a second spine operation, was critical. And while her family and public waited anxiously for news, the doctors discovered that a further problem was an ulcer which also required surgery. She was far too weak, however, to withstand another ordeal, so she was allowed to return to Rungstedlund to convalesce.

Once at home, her only thought was to resume her work. Up till this time she had done her writing occasionally in longhand but mainly on a battered old typewriter which was a precious relic from the farm. Now she could not sit up at all, so she began dictating to Clara the remaining stories which would appear in the volume entitled *Last Tales*. She dictated lying in bed or even flat on the floor, ignoring pain or fatigue. In less than a year she was in the hospital once more. As a result of the final operation she was never again able to eat a normal meal, since part of the stomach had to be removed along with the ulcer.

With so much suffering, her will to live and her avid interest in life never wavered. She continued to see as many people as possible, expending herself but mysteriously absorbing strength from efforts which the doctor was sure would exhaust her utterly. She needed people, as she needed to work, to read, to see and do. Often she also felt a need of music, and Eugene was there to play for her. He had rented a flat for the summer in Copenhagen. Together they would repair to the green sitting room of Rungstedlund's guest apartment, where Clara's spinet stood surrounded by souvenirs of the Dinesen and Westenholz families, and Eugene would play Scarlatti and Schubert.

In November 1954 the *New York Times* had published a photograph taken in Copenhagen of Tania with Nobel Prize-winner Albert Schweitzer. At this time she had one of her most gratifying experiences as an author, for this was also the year when

Hemingway received the Nobel Prize in Literature. In his acceptance speech he said: "As a Nobel Prize winner I cannot but regret
that the award was never given to Mark Twain, nor to Henry
James, speaking only of my own countrymen. Greater writers than
these also did not receive the prize. I would have been happy—
happier—today if the prize had been given to that beautiful writer
Isak Dinesen . . ."

Tania's relationship to Hemingway was one of curious con-
trasts. Her admiration for him had begun when she read *The Sun
Also Rises.* But it was difficult for that admiration to survive the
bluster and swagger, the human immaturity, the insensitivity of his
book on Africa—Papa on safari, competing and bullying, needing
to kill in order to prove his manhood, in order to extirpate the
insecurity which he never did really conquer.

For Hemingway everything in Tania's personality and writing
represented the absolutely unattainable. In Kenya, though she was
a crack shot, she had almost immediately outgrown the necessity of
killing for the sake of killing and had come into an understanding
of the game, the natives and the country which was far more
meaningful than Hemingway's know-it-all hunting lore. "In my last
ten years out there," she wrote "I did not fire a shot except in order
to get meat for my natives. It became to me an unreasonable thing,
indeed in itself ugly or vulgar, for the sake of a few hours' excitement to put out a life that belonged in the great landscape and had
grown up in it for ten or twenty, or—as in the case of buffaloes or
elephants—for fifty or a hundred years." Though he praised her
"beautiful" writing, Hemingway would not, of course, have exchanged her style for his own succinct and original one, but he
could not help envying her poise and sophistication, nor being impressed by her offhand endorsement of homosexuality which for
her was simply another aspect of life but for Hemingway was at

the very roots of a morbid hatred and fear that had dogged him since boyhood.

His spiteful portrait of Ford Madox Ford in *A Moveable Feast* is almost pathetically self-revealing.

"Am I a gentleman?" he inquired of Ford, who was sitting with him at a Paris sidewalk café.

"Absolutely not," Ford said.

"Then why are you drinking with me?"

"I'm drinking with you as a promising young writer. As a fellow writer in fact."

"Good of you," Hemingway said.

Even in jest, Tania's easy aristocracy would never have descended to such clumsy questioning.

She and Hemingway did not meet, so one may wonder if they would have become friends, each respecting the other's qualities, each politely ignoring the other's shortcomings. It seems more likely that Papa, clinging to the public image he had built up for himself as a gruff sportsman and big-game hunter, would only have reminded Tania distressfully of Bror von Blixen.

In 1956 Tania decided to go back to Rome. She was still weak and emaciated, and she had reached the limit of her endurance. But the seeming impossibility of working during her convalescence had been the very challenge that made her attempt to do more than ever. It was also a harrying thought that death might catch up with her before the unwritten tales were safely set down on paper. "Oh, I am so full of untold stories," she said to Nancy Wilson Ross, the gifted young writer who had come with an introduction from Denys Finch-Hatton's family, "I am so full of untold stories! Sometimes I feel—prick me with a pin and they will just flow out." But now she must stop and take a holiday, ordered the doctor. She had tried to choose one place out of all those she still longed to see, and perhaps would never see. Then one day, looking from her window out over the Øresund, she had caught sight of a little boat with two fishermen, their outlines brushed with light by the slanting strokes of the evening sun. It somehow evoked Guardi's boatmen, limned in their perennial Venetian glow, and she knew then that she had to see Italy again before she died.

Further incentive for the journey was Eugene Walter. He wanted to interview her for the *Paris Review,* of which he was now associate editor; and he had also written to ask if there were any unpublished Dinesen stories which might appear in *Botteghe Oscure.* Thus began what was surely the most unconventional correspondence ever engaged in by editor and author.

Clara was to go along, and this was the first time she would accompany Tania on a trip, although she had been with her since the end of 1944. Clara also needed a holiday. She had gone through the sad experience of losing her father, who had died early in 1955. And no one could have imagined the strain of living with Tania when she was ill, with the responsibilities of nurse added to those of secretary and companion. At such times Tania could be cruelly sarcastic and capricious in her demands. Angered and frustrated by lack of strength, she kept goading herself on, and sometimes she dictated to Clara until her eyes began to close in what resembled a coma more than natural sleep. When she was really asleep Clara hurried to her room, a hideaway in the farthest wing of the house, up under the moss-grown, red tile roof. Casement windows looked down on the pond and woods; bookshelves lined one entire wall, and an overflow of books, magazines, manuscripts and correspondence was heaped on every available piece of furniture and piled on the floor. There, in a clutter which astounded the rare guest permitted upstairs but where Clara could lay her hand instantly—miraculously, it seemed—on any information that anyone required, there she would snatch what time she could for writing of her own—an hour or two perhaps, but often a scant few minutes before she was summoned again.

Clara was so modest and her dedication to Tania was such that she never spoke of the extraordinary amount of work that she managed to accomplish during these brief interludes. She had, nevertheless, contributed articles and book reviews to magazines regularly every year; besides editing all of Tania's books and translating them into Danish, she had translated Christopher Dawson's *The Judgment of Nations,* Graham Greene's *The Power and the Glory,* and Rosamund Lehmann's *The Gipsy's Child* and *The Echoing Grove;* and she had translated two stories by Paul Bowles for radio broadcasting.

During the twelve years she had lived at Rungstedlund, Clara seemed to have changed hardly at all. One might safely have ventured the guess that she would still be quite the same long after she had left middle age behind. The unrestrained giggle and sudden blush which animated an almost naïve earnestness, the clear boy-soprano voice and the tip-tilted nose were traits to defy age. She had addressed Baroness Blixen formally at first, but for a long time now she had been calling her Tania. Like a daughter of the house she took part in every phase of Tania's life, receiving callers, serving tea, arranging flowers. Tania, in the way a mother shares her belongings with a daughter, often gave Clara a coat or fur of her own, and then would borrow them back to wear for some special occasion. It was a sign of their close, affectionate relationship.

Now they were both excited about the trip, which had an added importance for Clara, since Rome was the center of the Catholic world. Eugene Walter met them at the bus terminal when they arrived. "By the last light of day in Piazza Navona," he wrote, "the obelisk which crowns Bernini's Fountain of the Four Rivers seems darkly solid against the pale chalk-blue of the sky. But as the sky turns to an iris color, the obelisk turns pale and weightless, and just for an instant seems made of paper against the twilight. On our first outing at a sidewalk restaurant, Tania, Clara, and I sat watching this before we dined and began to make plans.

" 'I ought not to undertake too much,' " said the Baroness. " 'I've been ill for over a year and in a nursing home. I really thought I should die. I planned to die—that is, I made preparations. I expected to. I even planned a last radio talk . . . I have made a number of radio talks on all kinds of subjects, in Denmark. I planned a talk on how easy it is to die. Not a morbid message. I don't mean that, but a message of, well, cheer . . . that it is a great and lovely experience to die. But I was too ill, you know, to get it done. Now, after being so long in the nursing home and so ill, I don't feel I really belong to this life. I'm hovering like a sea gull. I feel that the world is happy and splendid and goes on, but that I'm not part of it. I've come to Rome to try and get into the world again.' "

From that moment on Eugene Walter devoted himself to the task of getting her "into the world again." Tour manager, major domo, impresario, court jester, social secretary, press attaché, he filled every role, sweeping her along in such a rush of enthusiasm that she forgot how tired and feeble she really was. Visits to galleries and museums alternated with dinners and parties of all kinds— surely none of it was what the doctor had had in mind in recommending a change of scene for the semi-invalid. As they sped from one amusement to another, Walter was quietly questioning Tania about her life, her work and opinions. His findings came out a few months later in the *Paris Review,* illustrated with Michael Batterberry's delicate pen drawings (all kohl-rimmed eyes, with only a suggestion of the subject's slightly twisted ironic mouth). The interview was the fourteenth and one of the most successful in a series of dialogues with contemporary fiction writers, including E. M. Forster, Graham Greene, Joyce Cary, Moravia and Mauriac. Hemingway was scheduled to follow Isak Dinesen.

By the time she left Rome, Tania was hardly in better health, but she was rejuvenated in spirit. Walter, quite unabashed, remarked to her that she looked like a monkey, and he bestowed upon her the title "Queen of the Northern Monkeys." "I love monkeys above all creatures," he hastened to reassure her.

II

"A Magnificent Spectre"

—⁓⁓⁓—

The Christmas ship, the steamer which lands its joyful passengers just in time to celebrate at home, brought Eugene Haynes for his fourth sojourn in Denmark, and his return was the best of all Christmas presents for Tania. Seeing her for the first time after an absence of nearly two years, Eugene was shocked by the change that illness and virtual starvation had made in her appearance, but even in her wasted condition it was admiration rather than pity that she aroused. She had become a magnificent spectre, he said, though her voice had kept all of its former deep resonance, and her eyes kindled, as they always had, when he began to describe the great things that 1957 was holding in store for him. He would see her often, since he was planning to live near Rungstedlund for almost a year and would go from there on U.S.I.S.-sponsored tours across the country and to Holland and Norway. Two concerts were scheduled for the summer festival at Denmark's historic Hindsgavl Castle and, of course, he would also play in Copenhagen.

Clara's cottage had at long last been redecorated; it boasted a modern bathroom, and a small grand piano was being sent out from the city. When the day finally arrived for the ushering in of the first guest—one of those sentimental occasions so dear to Danish hearts—a priest was present to bless the house; Majken, a little cousin of Clara's, appeared in regional costume; and Bent Mohn, "Elishama" Brandt, Robert Hunt and others, came out to join in the festivities.

By spring Eugene had entered happily into the life of Dragør; by June, when the nights were long and pale and beautiful, he would stay up late, dancing at the inn, laughing and drinking with the sailors and local characters, speaking Danish fluently with all of his new friends. He had the same carefree verve as that dean of pianists, Artur Rubinstein, at a ball, dancing the polka at 2 A.M. on the eve of a concert at Carnegie Hall. The village adopted Eugene and only the small children continued to regard him with amazement. "Children," he later remarked to Tania, "have the capacity for being perpetually astonished. For weeks after I moved out to Dragør, no matter how often they saw me during the day, they were astonished, gleefully following me about. I might have been the Pied Piper himself."

No one could have doubted, by the beginning of summer, that Tania had indeed succeeded in getting into the world again. After an interval of fifteen years, during which she had published no serious full-length work, *Last Tales* (thus entitled when she thought she was about to die) was on the presses in Copenhagen and New York. In an access of stage fright about the impression the book would make after so long a lapse and how it would stand up in comparison with her earlier works, she had implored Robert Haas of Random House to publish three new books simultaneously —"The Cardinal's Third Tale" (which she had withheld from *Heretica* magazine) and two volumes of short stories. Haas quite naturally rejected the proposal as too impractical and unconventional. His more sensible plan of presenting *Last Tales* in 1957 and following it up with *Anecdotes of Destiny* one year later certainly had a far greater impact.

As if to alleviate Tania's anxieties, news arrived in May of her election as an honorary member of the American Academy and National Institute of Arts and Letters, a distinction bestowed upon writers who have made unusual contributions to literature, the membership being limited to fifty authors in all. "Under the pseudonym of Isak Dinesen you have written some of the finest works produced by a woman in our day," declared the citation. "Your autobiographical volume, *Out of Africa,* has quietly made its way into the ranks of modern classics, along with your *Seven Gothic Tales* and *Winter's Tales.* In your work you combine extreme subtlety with the warmest and broadest humane feeling; you write 'fables' which contain a living center of timeless truth; and you look upon man and nature with a realistic eye and a mystic's penetration into timeless value."

Previously she had been the recipient of other honors. In 1950 she won the Ingenio et Arti medal, which is granted by the King of Denmark, and she applied for an audience to express her thanks. It was an old friend of hers who was directing the line of people in the antechamber, and while she was waiting for her turn, Tania had a discussion with him about a huge Asiatic drum or gong which stood nearby. She could not resist the impulse to give it a light tap with the drumstick that hung beside it, and was horrified to hear it give forth a loud boom.

In 1951 she was honored by the Henri Nathensen's Memorial Fund; in 1952, the year that "The Cardinal's Third Tale" and "Babette's Feast" were published in Denmark as separate small volumes, she was awarded The Golden Laurels. She won the Hans

Christian Andersen Prize in 1955, and in 1957 was the first author to receive the Danish Critics' Prize. There was, however, something especially touching about being honored by the American Academy—America had been the first country to publish a book of hers and had been the first to give a warm, enthusiastic welcome to her efforts as a writer. It was a country she wanted very much to visit, although that seemed too great a journey now.

In September the "Queen of the Northern Monkeys" dispatched a missive to Eugene Walter:

"Dear Monkey Prime Minister,

"My book is coming out on the fourth of November, and I want to be away from Denmark on that day. Otherwise people ring you up too much. I have considered flying to Rome—with Clara—just for three or four days. Do you think there would be people in Rome prepared to make those three or four days really sweet to me, so that I should think of them later on with tears of joy in my eyes? Would anybody ask me for dinner on the fourth in that pleasant place where the pictures all need straightening, and tell me I look just seventeen years old? Or would anybody ask me for supper at the darkest den of Trastevere, haunt of thieves and murderers? Or could you possibly arrange a rendezvous with a Cardinal for me in moonlight in Piazza Navona? Do send me a word . . . The swallows and nightingales are now leaving us to go to Africa. I have asked a swallow, in passing Rome, to drop a light Louis XVI kiss on you . . ."

She would see Italy once more, but not the summer Italy which has an almost fatal allure for Scandinavians—the hot, sunny afternoons of Rome, clamorous with passionate Latin voices; the cascades of flowers, sloe-eyed bambini, officers and bare-legged girls, wrinkled hags and tourists, all spilling down the Spanish steps;

fountains plashing; and night skies blazing with southern stars. This time it would be a new Rome, chilled and muted by early winter. Rome in the rain, perhaps. In any case, Eugene Walter would add the life and sparkle she craved, of that she felt sure when she got his reply with a detailed program for her visit.

"One does not *travel* by plane, one is merely sent like a parcel" was an observation that Tania repeated from time to time, her voice hard with contempt, her eyes dark with visions of ships sailing on tropical seas, carriages careening along romantic highways. Just the same, flying had its advantages. Without too much fatigue, she could even stop in Paris and London on the way home from Italy. So letters were sent to British friends; a summons went off to New York also, typed on the familiar pale-blue notepaper:

"Dear Parmenia,

"I am planning to fly from Rome to Paris on November the 9th and shall be staying at the St. James & Albany—a good old hotel, where I used to stay on my way to or from Kenya because they had a Danish portier, who had once been butler to an old uncle of mine . . ." A wistful postscript was appended by hand: "I look a hundred years older than when you last saw me!—"

A wonderfully rewarding final event before the departure was Eugene Haynes's concert in Copenhagen. Eugene, as modest by nature as was Clara, attributed its entire success to Tania, although he had by now given half a dozen recitals in Denmark and had built up an enthusiastic, devoted following of his own. "Tania literally made my concert of October first," he said. "Word got around that she would be there—so naturally everyone came for a glimpse of her. Afterwards there was a small party at Bent Mohn's. We had cheeses and wine. Tania declared October first 'Eugene's

Day,' made a charming speech, recited a poem to me, and kissed me. It was a magical moment."

In Rome the tributes were all for Tania, and as *grande vedette* of the three-day festival, she looked the part from the first moment. She was wearing a great, fantastic bearskin coat when she stepped off the plane. Georges Garcin photographed her in it a few weeks later at the terrace café Les Trois Frères in Paris, and it was also the inspiration for one of Avedon's best portraits. It was a monumental coat and would have given her the look of a shaggy deity from the northern ice floes had she not had the humor to wear with it a stocking cap rakishly caught up over one eye with a jeweled pin.

Walter had given full rein to a febrile imagination in organizing three evenings that were Gothic tales in themselves—a dinner and reception for artists, writers and musicians, at the house of Countess Mitty Risi d'Ambra, which was an ancient building on the island in the Tiber that had once even served as a morgue for the suicides who had drowned themselves in the river; a marionette play about Tania, written by Walter and performed at the apartment of the writer John Becker; and a *soirée musicale* given by Princess Brianna Carafa d'Andria, also a writer. Each day bouquets and gifts of all sorts were showered upon Tania. Clara came in for much attention too, and in recognition of her scholastic achievements, was everywhere presented as Dottoressa Clara Svendsen.

Two days later, in Paris, after a short rest, Tania was eager for another round of parties and ready to begin working again. But this time she had overestimated her strength. She talked gaily through a luncheon given for her at the Vert Galant. From there she walked to her next appointment at one of the old houses on the Ile Saint Louis, and had just settled down to a long session of giving notes for her biography when she was overcome by pain, nausea and fainting spells. For the rest of the afternoon, in a semicoma, she lay on an alcove bed, her small skeleton a barely perceptible shape under the coverlet, eyes closed and hands crossed—an improvised gisant. When at last she opened her eyes she merely apologized for causing bother. Work, she said firmly, could be resumed the following morning in her room at the hotel.

It was a tiring and tiresome task, this dredging up memories from the past, trying to be accurate, attempting to situate a hundred details of facts and dates. Sad events and humiliations, put out of mind long ago, were once more dragged into view, elusive faces and places were lured into focus again . . . but then, after a while the story would take over and she would be raptly telling a tale, telling an African, Gothic, Danish tale.

In Paris too, though the state of her health should have prevented further projects of any sort, she was persuaded to read from her books for M-G-M records. "I put in a bit of extra work on that occasion," a long letter from Clara reported, "and typical of Tania, she said she would give me something in return, and it was to be a cameo with Byron on it—if I could find one myself. In London I used my first free moments to look up Sir John Murray and saw his Byron manuscripts and other relics. On my way back to the Connaught Hotel, actually as soon as I left Murray's and found myself in Albemarle Street, I thought I would start looking for the cameo. The next moment it was there, in the window of a shop called Collector's Corner. The woman in the shop said: 'We think it is Lord Byron' before I had asked about that myself. It was lovely, probably almost contemporary, an agate cameo, fine gold and cabochon rubies." This was the sort of coincidence that Tania delighted in. Like the heart-shaped smelling bottle presented to Augustus by the old Contessa of "The Roads Round Pisa," it savored of minor magic. Her gift took on a special significance. The brooch became—for a brief time, alas—Clara's most treasured possession.

Each time Tania returned from her travels to Rungstedlund she felt a deeper attachment and love for her home. Coming out from Copenhagen along the Strandvej, her heart would begin to lift when she saw the familiar landmarks—the last sharp curve in the road, the three ancient willows trailing garlands over the pier across from the house, and then her own high hedge of Nevada roses. There, awaiting her at the courtyard door, was Fru Carlsen with Nils, taller each time; there was Alfred Pedersen, gnarled and older but still erect, smiling a greeting after his own dour fashion; and finally Pasop, almost knocking her down in a frenzy of recognition.

The welcoming over, there would be tea in the drawing room and the wonderful rediscovery of loved and familiar things: the froth of white lace around the tall windows, drifting down over the floor, the little table where she and Clara would be playing bezique after dinner, the eighteenth-century chairs salvaged from Mrs. Dinesen's kitchen basement, and all the small objects which had become part of her life over the years, symbols of family, friends or events.

"Wouldn't it be wiser to lie down and rest?" Clara knew that her plea was useless because Tania could not resist a few minutes' walk in the garden. She must look at the old, old lilac tree and take some bread to the ducks in the pond, she must see what flowers were in bloom to cut for the house, and at least cast a longing glance up toward Ewald's Hill.

"Here is a four-leaf clover," she would appease Clara when she came in again. The one she had found on Clara's first day at

Rungstedlund was carefully pressed in the pages of Ewald's *Poems*, and it was a constant wonder that she kept on finding them where no one else could see them at all. Tania herself was very proud of her sharp vision. Her father had taught her to be observant and she was far-sighted too, she often explained, and even in Africa the natives had asked her, when they detected a barely visible something in the distance, "What do you see, msabu?"

Greatest of all the pleasures in being at home again was making flower arrangements. The creative energy that had once expressed itself in portrait and still-life painting now went into composing bouquets of such artistry that many of Tania's friends collected photographs of them. For the salon, huge brass basins and faïence tureens were filled with branches, armfuls of flowers, and the tall decorative grasses that are a specialty in Denmark; goblets and bowls spilled over with roses and smaller blooms; and equal attention and artistry went into the making of miniature bouquets. All the while her hands were busy with flowers, her thoughts were running along the track of some new piece of writing, and as soon as every room in the house had its appropriate vase, she was impatient to get back to her desk again.

III

Work and Repose

—〰〰—

Work, work, work. There was no end to it. Stories and articles, book reviews, prefaces, essays, interviews, radio talks, lectures, and more. As far back as 1943 Tania had begun contributing to American periodicals, with "Sorrow-acre" in the *Ladies' Home Journal,* followed in 1949 by "The Uncertain Heiress" in the *Saturday Evening Post.* In 1950 the *Ladies' Home Journal* also published "Babette's Feast," a tale which was the result of a wager that Tania would never be able to write popular fiction and which acquired a particular fame in Denmark because of the brilliant radio readings by the great actress Bodil Ipsen. In all, the *Journal* published ten stories, including a part of *Ehrengard,* which was only published in full after Tania's death. "Echoes" in the *Atlantic Monthly* and "The Nobleman's Wife" in *Harper's Bazaar* both appeared in November 1957. And, of course, there were other tales for Danish and foreign readers, such as "Dykkeren" (The Diver) in *Vindrosen* magazine, as well as "A Country Tale," the one previously mentioned for *Botteghe Oscure.*

Many of these stories were among the twelve which Random House brought out as *Last Tales*, and Gyldendal as *Sidste Fortæl-linger,* in 1957. Tania continued, incidentally, to use the pen name Isak Dinesen for all her American publications, but after her first book, had reverted to using her own name, Karen Blixen, in Denmark. *Last Tales*, in spite of all her misgivings about it, received excellent notices, one exception being the derisive comments in the British magazine *Encounter*. *"Au vrai les excès, de luxe et de style, choquent un peu"* was Maurois' judgment of Balzac's *La Fille aux Yeux d'Or*. This was also the accusation sometimes directed at Isak Dinesen, especially by English critics. However, as with the fioriture of Renaissance façades, it is not necessary to probe far before discovering the solid substance and formal structure beneath the decorative surface. Why, anyway, one may well ask, should a number of today's literary critics feel an almost silly embarrassment when faced with a style which is flavored with earlier traditions and classicism? The art critic experiences no such inhibition, nor does the music critic, since composers from Bach to Stravinsky have never hesitated to lean heavily on their predecessors and make use of the classic forms. Eudora Welty's review in the *New York Times* did not dwell on this but made a point of Isak Dinesen's "marvelous gaiety, and what makes it more marvelous still are its transpositions, true gaiety's other key. Her tales are glimpses out of, rather than into, an extraordinary mind. Sometimes one feels that Isak Dinesen's stories come toward one like the flashes and signal-beams from a lighthouse on a strange and infrequently sighted coast—a coast beautiful and precarious, for it may be the last outreach of magic, but resting on bedrock." Dolbier in the New York *Herald Tribune* said: ". . . There is a strength behind the strangeness, a reality behind the phantasmagorical scenes. Running like steely, unbreakable threads through these imaginative creations of Isak Dinesen are the themes of honor—family pride, marital fidelity, the loyalty of disciple to master—and of the compelling power of art."

Other themes were explored by Tania on the radio or in the newspapers. Gyldendal published a little book, *Daguerreotypier* (Daguerreotypes), to preserve two radio talks of January 1951, which compared the values of aristocratic times past with the new democracy. This subject preoccupied Tania as she observed the leveling and numbing effects of nationwide ease and comfort. "You will see here in Denmark," she had said to Hudson Strode at their first meeting, "the plus and minus of true democracy. When I returned from Kenya it struck me how things come out so right on paper, but seldom in life. With democracy, we seem to give up all ideals that are higher than those that can be reached. It's a mediocre happiness, I think, that is purchased at the price of no great art, no great music. With complete democracy the quality is bound to come down. I don't think it's well for a nation to give up completely its elite. There should be a few versed in the classics."

In 1952 she was involved in a newspaper controversy about the use of animals for experiments. Her views on this subject in regard to an article by Professor E. Lundsgaard appeared in *Politiken*, and a few weeks later the same paper printed her reply to Professor Holger Møltgaard in the debate on vivisection.

In the late 1930's she was to have addressed a women's rights congress but could not think of what to say; she was much more concerned with the English players who were performing at Elsinore with John Gielgud as Hamlet. She discussed women's rights with an older relative, of the Hansen branch of the family, who had been an active pioneer in the field. Tania told her that she had never really thought out the problems and made up her mind about them, and Estrid Hein replied, "Then you ought to do it now." But it was only years later that she did so, and for this reason her little volume on the subject is called *Baaltale med 14 Aars Forsinkelse* (Bonfire Speech 14 Years Delayed). "Mama" and Aunt Bess might well have smiled over what she wrote then, for they had championed extremely advanced ideas for their day, whereas Tania's opinions could have been considered very old-fashioned in the mid-twentieth century. After alluding to the *Kirche-Kinder-Küche* suppressive attitude toward women of Kaiser Wilhelm's Germany, she said that nevertheless, even in the freer, modern world, women should fulfill their roles as women. Her remarks, first delivered at the N. Zahles Seminarium, appeared in *Det Danske Magasin* and were radio-broadcast in 1953, and were afterwards printed in book form by Berlingske Forlag.

She wrote a review of Sacheverell Sitwell's *Denmark* for London's *Sunday Times*, May 6, 1956; and of the countless interviews she gave, one of the best was a dialogue with Bent Mohn which appeared in the *New York Times* in November 1957—it not only expressed thoughts about herself, her writing and philosophy of life but also spoke in detail of her hope of going to the United States. One of her great desires in connection with the projected trip was to see the place "I have often thought of and also visited in my dreams." This was the little township which had grown up around the hermit's hut in Wisconsin where her father had spent his two years of self-imposed exile among the Indians. The village was called Frydenlund, the name Wilhelm had given to his cabin.

When the tempo of the work and the number of visitors became too much, even for Tania, there were two places in Denmark where she could go to rest and find a change of mood. One was Leerbæk in Jutland, where her brother Anders lived; the other was

Wedellsborg on Fyn Island, the castle of Count Julius Wedell, who had married Daisy Frijs's sister Inger.

The ferry crossing from the west coast of Sjælland to Jutland took three hours. But even this banal contact with the sea gave Tania a sense of adventure—of sailing away to another world which, in fact, it was, for the mainland was rugged and wild compared with the serene landscape that surrounded Rungstedlund. Tania liked to stay on the passenger deck to watch the birds and gaze at the sea, where a siren or a mermaid might appear (why not?). Hundreds of sea gulls followed the ferries back and forth across the channel, wheeling and drifting in the air currents or perched in the rigging. At times the sea was so glassy smooth that the low-flying gulls were reflected as in a mirror. Small brown ducks floated gently up and down on the waves, and now and again they dived in pursuit of fish, remaining submerged so long that the boat had left them far behind before they surfaced again. How wonderful, Tania thought, to be so equally at home in the two elements of water and air.

Anders' property was on a high plateau above the port town of Vejle and only a few miles from Jelling, where the great rune-stone stood, carved a thousand years before by Harald, who "won all Denmark and Norway and made the Danes Christians." Leerbæk had been laid out in the style typical of old Danish farms: the stable-and-barn building framed three sides of a large yard, with the manor house facing it and constructed around three sides of its own courtyard. Early engravings showed a circular pool in the yard with a neat border of clipped grass, but long ago this had become a shapeless, untidy pond, spurned even by ducks. The moat around the house had grown stagnant and choked by water weeds, vines grew rampant over the walls, and the gardens seemed asleep in the afterglow of a lost century. Forests closed all of it in on every side, giving it the secluded, spellbound atmosphere of *La Belle au Bois Dormant*. Anders had come there as a very young man to run the estate for Georg Sass, whose wife was Aunt Lidda, Mrs. Dinesen's youngest sister; he had lived most of his life in a forester's lodge on the place and had never married. Mr. Sass had lingered on until he was more than ninety years of age, and it was only after Aunt Lidda also died that Anders fell heir to Leerbæk and moved into the manor house.

Tania had a particularly tender affection for this brother, whom she saw less often than Thomas only because he lived too far away. He was as different from Thomas as Wilhelm Dinesen had been from his brother, Laurentzius. Though Anders was only ten months old at the time of his father's death and had not been taught by him as Tania had, he had nevertheless inherited many of Wilhelm's traits and preferences. He had an inborn love and understanding of nature and was happiest out in the forest, with or without his gun. It was he who had allowed nature to have its own way with the pond and farm and gardens. He was also a rather silent man, less because of a slight impediment of speech than because people who commune with trees and animals have little need of talk. As if in deference to his wants, the house kept silence also, dreaming away the years under the summer sun and the long, sad rains, or swathed in winter snow.

In the hush of Leerbæk, Tania too became quiet. She walked with her brother in the park, where not a sound was to be heard save the crunch of the caretaker's clogs on the gravel paths, and the wind and birds in the treetops. Anders' eyes and hers would follow the flight of a bird or dragonfly, take note of a striped black-and-amber snail on a leaf or a spring of mushrooms in the grass where none had been the day before. Each knew what the other was seeing and thinking. They had no need of words. But then, unlike Anders, Tania would suddenly crave people and talk and activity, and after a few days she would be off again, usually for Wedellsborg.

The place she would rather visit than any other she knew, was Wedellsborg. The castle was one of the most beautiful in Denmark. Dating in part from the 1400's, it was completely white and of such noble proportions and pure lines that it entirely belied its vast size and suggested intimacy and simplicity. Velvet lawns sloped away from it toward a park of larch, spruce and beech, tall as sky-scrapers, and through which vistas half a mile in length gave glimpses of the sea. Le Nôtre might have been the inspiration but this park was less formal and artificial, with a wild grace of its own.

Inger, Countess Wedell, had gradually taken the place in Tania's heart where in years past her sister Daisy had reigned alone; and as once everyone had adored and envied Daisy, now everyone loved and admired Inger. "She is an extraordinary *grande dame*—one of the last," said a foreign writer who had been a weekend guest at Wedellsborg. "She rises at dawn, walks miles, rides, swims, drives a heavy car, typewrites her own correspond-ence, embroiders, and is personally repairing all the broken an-tique tiles. She has been lady in waiting to the Queen, and now she runs this huge place as efficiently as a man, is busy with church and village affairs, and is up to the minute on everything going on in the world—politics, society, books, music and ballet. At seventy-five, she is as slender, as lively and gay, as a young girl."

Inger, besides, was one of the few remaining friends who had known Tania since childhood. As young girls the Frijs sisters had considered Tania very eccentric—they thought her manner of speaking affected, and remarked on the way she had of opening wide her abnormally large, dark eyes. They also thought it strange and perverse of her to have married their cousin Bror, whom she didn't care for at all. It had been obvious to them at the time that it was Bror's twin brother whom she really loved, even though he took no notice of her. This, then, was the first love she had put so firmly out of mind as she looked at Bror during the marriage ceremony in Mombasa. Now, after all these years, Tania and Inger were devoted, admiring and uncritical of each other, and Inger respected Tania's courageous disregard of illness.

Tania's rooms were at the far end of one of the guest wings, down a long corridor later carpeted in fiery red, with the customary parade of antlers and portraits along the walls. At breakfast time Inger appeared there and inquired of her, as she did of all her guests, whether she had everything she needed and what plans she wished to make for the day. There were endless pleasures from which to choose, but first of all there would be the luxury of a leisurely hot bath (Rungstedlund had no modern bathrooms as yet and the ritual of Tania's bath at home was still a tedious business of filling a portable tub with never-sufficient kettles of steaming water). Then she might visit the stables with Count Wedell, an ardent horseman. On the way out they would meet the gardener coming in, loaded down with iris and lupines, oriental poppies, campanulas and roses from the garden, and baskets of amaryllis and callas from the greenhouses. Inger's gift for arranging flowers rivaled Tania's, and while she was busy with this, Tania would wander off to the woods. There the shy deer ran with hardly more than a whisper of sound, their spotted pelts almost invisible under the dappling of leaf shadows and filtered sun; a pheasant might pilot her chicks across the path; and the path itself would yield up the familiar but always new prodigies of ferns and mosses and pungent asphodel, the fragrance of violets and even the sudden acrid stench of wild garlic.

As the castle stood on a point of land, it rained often, a rain scented with new-mown grass and pines and the sea; and in springtime, showers of perfume fell from the sky, since all the fields and roads of the countryside were hedged with lilac for miles around. The rain was a pleasant excuse to sit indoors, talking and laughing with Count Wedell. An adored friend, he was a person of exquisite taste and knowledge, a creative artist whose aim it had been to bring Wedellsborg to its state of perfection. He had dedicated an existence to collecting boiseries, rugs, paintings and porcelains, and he fondled the objects with the delicate hands and rapt eyes of a lover.

A day, three days, a week—one lost track of time at Wedellsborg—slipped quietly by to merge with all of those other days that were gone, forever gone, into the irretrievable past. Tania, haunted by the thought that her life was ebbing away, was reluctant to prolong her visit. She felt compelled to hurry back to Rungstedlund, and work.

IV
Anecdotes of Destiny

—⁓⁓⁓—

Whenever Eugene Haynes was on tour, Clara kept him informed concerning events at Rungstedlund. In June 1958, when he was about to return for two more concerts at the Hindsgavl Castle festival, she wrote to say that she hoped it would become a tradition for him to spend a week at her cottage in Dragør each time he came to Denmark. "The reason I cannot spare the house for any longer period," said her letter, "is that I have to take refuge there now and then or I shall go mad from being secretary at Rungstedlund. Being with Goethe at Weimar could not have been more strenuous. I rarely step inside my own rooms and close the door without someone coming to fetch me the next minute; someone who wants a bill paid, someone who wants someone else to meet Karen Blixen—people even telephone from U.S.A. to ask if they may call on her, and the telephone rings at three in the morning, and the poor housekeeper jumps out of bed thinking her old father in Jutland is dying, etc., etc., etc. . . . The Baroness, who was in bad health in February, is better now and working hard to finish her new book, *Anecdotes of Destiny,* for publication in the autumn, also working hard to plan Rungstedlund's future, it is going to be preserved as a bird reserve . . . The Baroness has bought a tiny house in town which she is planning to rebuild for winter quarters."

Tania had indeed had another collapse. In a letter of April 25 she admitted it, but if she betrayed signs of discouragement in one paragraph, in the next she already spoke of ambitious plans for the not-too-distant future. "I have been terribly ill ever since Christmas, on my back in bed, feeling weaker with every day. I cannot eat anything but oysters, and I cannot get my weight above 35 kilos [77 lbs.]. I am up a little now, but I am really only longing to get back in a horizontal position, I am still unsteady on my legs and sway about from right to left. Every day I think: 'If the salt have lost its savour, wherewith shall it be salted? It is thenceforth good for nothing but to be cast out and to be trodden under foot of men.'

"All the same, I still cling to my plan of going to the States in September or October. I should like to stay in New York for about three weeks, then our Ambassador has asked me to stay with him in Washington for a fortnight, then again I should go south to a really nice place, and sit down there quietly with a few trips and excursions, and people to come and talk to me if they care to . . . If only I can get my strength back.

"I have been made a present of a small house in Copenhagen, the smallest house in town, two hundred years old, and I think I shall go and live there in the future, at least in winter . . ."

What her letter didn't mention at all was her grief over the death of Pasop, whom she had buried on April 19. For months, every time she looked at him, feebly wagging his tail and unable to run, she had thought, "Poor fellow! You are deaf, so you think I don't talk to you any more. We are both of us old, and you are as thin and weak as I am!" Now he was up there on Ewald's Hill, deep in the earth beneath the great spreading beech tree. And he hadn't even a stone to mark his grave because it was next to the place that she had laid out for her own grave, and what would the bishop say when he came to consecrate the ground if he found that Pasop would be lying beside her? She told Clara and everyone who condoled with her that she would never have another dog. It would be an infidelity to Pasop, whose memory she wished to keep green as the most lovable, faithful creature she had ever owned.

But soon something seemed oddly lacking at Rungstedlund without a dog around the place. So Nils received Ping Pong, a chow puppy with a wonderful hyacinth-blue tongue. Ping Pong quickly became enormous, and his tawny pelt stood out in a dense ruff around his neck, making him seem almost as wide as he was long. Because of this he also became the subject of a great joke at Rungstedlund. A visitor to the park was about to leave when she caught sight of Ping Pong chained in the backyard.

"May I photograph the lion?" she inquired of Fru Carlsen, obviously confusing everything she had heard on a broadcast about Baroness Blixen and Africa. "It is a lion, isn't it?" she insisted.

Fru Carlsen's expression almost gave her away but she composed herself in time.

"Of course," she reassured the woman. "Indeed it is. An authentic Chinese mountain lion!"

Raising money to safeguard the future of the park was one of Tania's main projects in 1958. She had already set up the Fund of the Rungstedlund Foundation, deeding to it all the fees and royalties from her books. She knew, however, that fifty years after an author's death the rights are no longer protected, and she wished to make sure that the park would be available to the public in perpetuity. Danish Radio came to her aid and gave her permission to make an appeal one Sunday evening.

"Will each of you," she asked her listeners, after telling the story of Rungstedlund and the bird sanctuary, "will each of you who feels that you have got one krone's worth of pleasure from my books or my radio speeches, send in *one krone* to the Rungstedlund Fund? None of you may send more than just one krone, for I want to find out how many friendly readers I have got in Denmark. The money thus obtained will be put aside untouched to multiply until fifty years after my death, in order to avoid my birds being chased off their green shades and the old tired people, the mothers with their children, and the young couples who have walked under my trees being turned away onto cemented roads." With her flair for human psychology she concluded the talk with a little challenge to the curiosity and sporting instinct of the radio audience: "Now each of you may tonight be making your own guess at the number of kroner that my appeal to you will bring in. In four weeks' time, at this same hour, I shall come back on the radio to give you the exact amount."

During the four weeks a deluge of coins arrived by mail at Rungstedlund, and every time Tania went to the city, people who recognized her handed her krone pieces until her bag and pockets were filled to bursting. "As I was one day lunching at a hotel with American friends," she related, "a sedate and distinguished old gentleman nearby on leaving his table raised his hat to me and without a word handed me a krone. My friends saw me off to the taxi, and the driver as I gave him the address stuck his hand into his pocket and handed me his coin. The doorman then with a deep ceremonial bow made the same gesture. I had got to catch a train and had no time to explain the matter, and I wonder whether my American friends are living on in the belief that people of Copenhagen, around Saint John's Day, when witches are supposed to swarm in the air on their way to the Sabbath at Bloksbjerg, will be safeguarding themselves against the evil of witchcraft by handing old ladies in the streets and restaurants a krone piece." She was able to announce at the end of the month that nearly one hundred thousand kroner had been added to the fund, and for a long time afterwards the coins kept coming in.

In June, as Clara had written to Eugene, Tania was still hard at work correcting details of *Anecdotes of Destiny*, which was to include five tales: "The Diver," "Babette's Feast," "Tempests," "The Immortal Story" and "The Ring."

"Tempests," quite exceptionally, had first been written in Danish. "I discovered," said Tania, "that I didn't have it in English at all when I was going to send it to my good friend, John Gielgud, as my thanks because he invited me last year to a performance of *The Tempest* at Stratford-on-Avon. It was, by the way, the first time that I had actually seen *The Tempest* performed."

To celebrate the appearance of *Anecdotes of Destiny* (it was published in the autumn by both Gyldendal and Random House) there was a party at Rungstedlund for Gyldendal and representatives of the press—sherry followed by tea with the pancakes that were a specialty of the house.

"It is with this book as with its author—it should be somewhat fatter to look like anything," she told her guests, "but since I've been in hospital where they tried to cut me up in little bits, I have not had much time and energy for writing. There should have been two other stories. One is 'The Bear and the Kiss,' the other a story about the difference between people of genius and a genius. Well, some other time."

She was far more anxious, however, to talk to them about the new novel she had been planning for a long time, several parts of which had already been included in *Last Tales*. "The novel will be finished before I die, but only just before. There will be lots of nonsense said about it. Not because it's a key novel or because it's pornographic, but people will say that it doesn't make sense at all; it is much too fantastic. There are an awful lot of people in it and it will be mighty long. I was inspired to write it by reading Jules Romains' *Les Hommes de Bonne Volonté*. It is good reading when you are in hospital. I think there are twenty-seven volumes. My new novel isn't going to be quite as long as that. But just as each volume of Romains' work can be read separately, my book can be read chapter by chapter independently. The story takes place in the beginning of the last century. The title is from *The Arabian Nights*, where the Caliph Haroun al Rashid takes the name Albondocani."

It hardly seemed possible that she would really finish it before she died; and yet, with each illness, when death appeared to be imminent, she had rallied in such a spectacular way that people were beginning to say that she was indestructible. Curtis Cate, author of the splendid essay *Isak Dinesen: The Scheherazade of Our Times*, was hopeful: "It is a monumental tapestry she is working on today—a tremendously long novel, made up of connected short tales, about two hundred of them, each chapter forms a whole that can be read on its own . . . this mosaic of a novel, which is set in Naples at the time when it was ruled by Bourbon kings. If the live, creative spark that has sustained her through the maladies of the last few years can give her the strength to complete this ambitious design, it will provide a fitting *grande finale* to the life of one who, though small and frail, has always been a *grande dame. Albondo-cani* is Isak Dinesen's swan song, her triumphant Ode to Joy, her own Ninth Symphony."

"Are you going away this time, too, when your book appears?" asked one of the press representatives as the party for *Anecdotes of Destiny* came to an end.

"I am. And on the thirteenth. I was planning to go to the large bird sanctuary in Jutland, but that's probably too strenuous at this time of year."

Jutland was much too bleak and wild in the aftermath of the equinoxial storms. The peninsula reached up into the northern seas like a gnarled, weather-beaten fist, and howling gales and drenching rains swept over it at this time of the year. She was persuaded to settle instead for Amsterdam, scene of the story she had written as a young girl—"The de Cats Family." The trip was a gift from Gyldendal and she left on October 11, accompanied by the head of the firm, Otto B. Lindhardt, his wife and Clara, and returned two days after the publication of *Anecdotes of Destiny*.

The journey that made 1958 memorable for her, however, was the one she had made with Thomas at the beginning of summer to visit General von Lettow-Vorbeck. A childish sense of excitement had stirred her at the thought of a reunion with the general whom she had first met in 1913, shortly before the German nation became involved in hostilities with the Allies, and whom she had seen briefly again in 1940 when the Germans were about to invade Denmark. In spite of her dislike of Germany and all the evils it stood for, she had preserved respect and a tender regard for this friend of forty-four years.

On May 24 the general and his son-in-law, Count Christian von Rantzau, met Tania and Thomas at the airport in Hamburg, and then drove them to Pronsdorf, the count's estate in Holstein, where they spent the afternoon and had dinner. The following morning Tania and Thomas left their hotel to call on von Lettow, who had rooms in a villa on a quiet street in Altona. "We had three delightful hours with the general, a most charming old man," Thomas later recalled. "It was extremely interesting to hear him explain the whole campaign in East Africa in the First World War. I have talked with many people from Kenya about this war, and they have all shown a very great respect and even admiration for von Lettow's leadership. His later years were very sad: as a pronounced enemy of Hitler and Nazism he was kept, during the last war, under strict control, very harshly treated—and his only two sons were killed fighting for Hitler! But his spirit was not broken. One incident: he had been explaining to us very animatedly and sincerely how very close the German Army came to victory in 1914 before Paris—if only General A and General B had understood . . . extremely regrettable . . . we might have won the war! —and then he looked up at my face, and we both laughed heartily."

While they were speaking, Tania observed the general. He was eighty-seven and like fine old parchment. Looking at him, she thought, "Shall I ever reach his age? Shall I ever look as old and worn?" and then bit her lip, remembering the multiplicity of wrinkles, the gaunt face, which the ruthless mirror flung back at her these days. "Perhaps already I look far older than he does."

Just the same, she could not resist making a coy reference to the kiss, a private joke between them which dated from 1940 when she had written to announce her arrival in Bremen. She had, her note said then, always regretted not having kissed him good-bye in Mombasa on the eve of World War I and this time would ask his wife's permission to do so. Now, in 1958, they laughed about it, and it would come up once again: in 1961 Tania sent him flowers for his ninetieth birthday, reminding him of the kiss which she was herewith sending by letter, and evoking a gallant reply from him that she would have to come and fetch the next one, and what did she think of an old man of ninety making such a proposition to a lady of seventy-five?

But now their talk, of course, was mostly of Kenya, the general being one of the few persons still alive who understood her nostalgia for Africa—the Africa which, like his youth and hers, belonged to the vanished yesterdays. When they said good-bye he bowed over her hand and held it lingeringly in his but their proud natures kept then both from saying more. They knew they would not meet again.

V

New York

—∿∿∿—

When the ballerina Fanny Elssler made her tour of the United States in 1840, the citizens of Baltimore strewed the pavements with flowers wherever she was expected to pass, and then un-hitched the horses of her carriage and they themselves pulled it through the streets; Congress adjourned for the day when she ar-rived in Washington; New York greeted her with frenzied enthusi-asm; and since Daguerre's invention of photography had not yet reached American shores, thousands of lithographs were published by Currier as souvenirs of her visit.

A hundred and nineteen years later such picturesque gestures were no longer in vogue, but whatever glamorous excitement New York could provide for a foreign writer was lavished on Tania. Nothing like it had been seen, said a newspaper correspondent, since Dickens and Oscar Wilde condescended to show themselves here. Isak Dinesen was more than a visiting literary lion; she was a strange, compelling personality who, without any great publicity campaign, had captured the public imagination.

"Baroness Karen Blixen arrived in New York January 4th on her first visit to this country," reported *Publishers' Weekly*. "At a press conference on January 5th at Random House, her publishers in the U.S., the Baroness said that her plans are flexible. 'I've been asked to lecture,' the 73-year-old author said, 'but I have no faith in myself as a lecturer—or as a reader, either. I'm a storyteller, and I've come to tell you some stories—some old and some new. I hope that you will like some of them. If you don't, don't worry; you'll get rid of me before long.' The Baroness' principal activity during her stay here will be to make a number of films for Encyclopaedia Britannica consisting of readings and lectures, which will be made available to schools and colleges. In addition, she has been asked by the American Academy and National Institute of Arts and Letters to be guest of honor at a dinner late in January . . . She was invited to visit the U.S. by the Ford Foundation's Fund for the Advancement of Education and the Institute of Contemporary Arts. Her schedule includes visits to Washington and Cambridge, Mass."

The distinguished audience which heard her deliver her speech, "On Mottoes of My Life," at the American Academy in New York, found her witty and wise, but above all was deeply moved by her physical being. "She was very, very frail and old but as she talked her face was lit like a candle in an old church. My heart trembled when I saw her fragility," said Carson McCullers. "When she spoke at the Academy dinner that evening, something happened which I had never seen there before. When she finished her talk, every member rose to applaud her."

Tania spoke of how important it had been for her to have a motto at various stages of her life. " 'In the beginning was the Word,' " she quoted, and was it not a fine thing to have a word or a motto to live by? At seventeen she had chosen "*Navigare necesse*

est, vivere non necesse," the command of Pompeius to his timid
Sicilian crew when they were afraid to set out in a gale—literally:
to set sail is necessary, to live is not necessary, or in other words:
one must set out and do things and not be held back by danger,
even to one's life. This motto carried her as far as Africa, she said,
where she replaced it with another when she met Denys Finch-
Hatton. She continued until 1950, however, to inscribe *"Navigare
necesse est . . ."* in books she was asked to autograph; and she lived
by this motto, as her friends well knew, until the end, risking her
life a hundred times in order to set out and do more. The Finch-
Hatton motto was in Old French, *"Je responderay,"* and when she
asked Denys if she might use it as her own, he not only agreed but
had a seal made for her with the words carved into it. *"Pourquoi
pas?"* had encouraged her to overcome her doubts about beginning
a new existence in Denmark and to write her first book. And now,
with the acceptance of age, she was settling for the less daring
advice taken from three portals of a citadel in Spenser's *Faerie
Queene* and counseled too by Longfellow in his *Morturi Salu-
tamus.* "Be bold" was inscribed over the first gate, "Be bold" over
the second, and above the third, "Be not too bold."

The audience also rose as a mark of respect and admiration when
she made her first appearance at the Poetry Center of the Young
Men's Hebrew Association on February 11. In describing the event
one could do no better than cite at least some phrases from one of
America's most distinguished writers, Glenway Wescott. He referred to the Center as "the chief platform in the world for poets
and poetical prose writers, and "As she came on stage there, walking very slowly on the arm of a young staff poet named William
Jay Smith, then pausing and turning and, by way of salute to the
maximum audience including standees, outstretching her fine-

boned arm in a gesture of some singularity—as of a hunter beckoning with a riding crop, or as of an actor in the role of Prospero motioning this or that airy creature into existence, or perhaps back out of existence—we all spontaneously stood up and acclaimed her.

"As soon as we kept quiet she established herself in an important straight chair, spot-lit, and after catching her breath in physical weariness for a moment, and gazing around the auditorium with a royal gaze, a gypsy gaze, began the evening's narration. She has an ideal voice for the purpose, strong, though with a kind of wraithlike transparency, which she is able to imbue with emotions, but only narrative emotions. She rarely indulges in mellifluousness in the way of poets; neither does she do much Thespian mimicking . . . What especially colors Isak Dinesen's voice, what gives it overtone and urgency, is remembrance or reminiscence. With soft strong tone seeming to feel its way, sometimes almost faltering, shifting its direction as power of evocation sways it, not perturbed by her listeners, perhaps helped by them, she seems to be re-experiencing what she has to tell, or if it is fable or fantasy, redreaming it. She never gives the impression of having memorized a text and recalling the sentences and paragraphs. When I heard her tell a given story a second or third time, it astonished me to realize that it had been verbatim, or nearly so." Tania had also learned a trick from the natives in Africa. "One must imagine," she says in describing a conversation with Kamante, "a long, pregnant, as if deeply responsible, pause before each phrase. All natives are masters in the art of the pause and thereby give perspective to a discussion." Consciously or unconsciously, Tania had acquired this manner of making the deliberate pause, and the slowed tempo added weight and drama to her storytelling.

At the Poetry Center the audience was far more diversified than the literary assembly had been at the dinner of the American

Academy. Of all ages, all walks of life, most of them had read and fallen in love with her books; many knew her face from published photographs. But they were not prepared for the seduction of her presence and voice. Crowds gathered afterwards on the sidewalk to catch a glimpse of the diminutive teller of tales leaving the auditorium in a wheelchair, swathed in black, her eyes luminous with a sort of trancelike excitement, her arms filled with red roses. And though by going back to one or another of her books, her listeners could quite simply have read the stories she had told aloud, they wanted to hear her again. And again. "ON MARCH 31ST, THIRD APPEARANCE BY DEMAND—ISAK DINESEN," the papers announced.

After the romantic atmosphere of Rungstedlund, any hotel would seem banal. But wherever she might stay in New York there would be the sybaritic joy of a hot bath to be had at any hour one desired, and effortlessly. First she tried a large hotel which was *très à la mode*. Then she tried a small hotel known to be very exclusive and very expensive. Finally, through the kind offices of Bruce and Beatrice Blackmar Gould of the *Ladies' Home Journal*, she was offered the two weeks' visiting privileges of the Cosmopolitan Club, and after she returned from Boston she was made an honorary member, which enabled her to stay on and have Clara as her own guest. Everything possible was done for her. She was given a large quiet room with a big four-poster bed where she could lie while dictating or receiving friends whom she did not have to see more formally. Clara spoke appreciatively of the copious American breakfasts, the patient maids, efficient telephone service, and particularly the many kind attentions paid Tania by various members of the club and the fact that Dr. Samuel Standard attended her without a fee—all in all a delightful contrast with the woeful

Boston-Cambridge experience. In addition to the general discomfort and the unjustifiable demands made upon her as a lecturer there, the hotel had neglected to send up part of her mail, including a letter written by Thomas to break the news that her sister, Ellen, was dying.

Tania was a very grateful guest at the club, but as she waited in the lounge for people to come to see her or to pick her up for appointments, her cruelly perceptive eyes could not help but take note of the women coming and going. It struck her that for the most part they looked middle-aged and of a sameness that hardly seemed possible—the same gestures and voices, the same clothes. Tania loved hats. Every hat, she said, should be a kind of outgrowth of its wearer's mood: flamboyant, seductive, droll, challenging—an added dimension to one's personality. These clubwomen wore drab, nondescript hats, or if they were a bit more daring, hats that were all alike and slavishly following the current fashion. The younger ladies bustled in and out with identical shrill little cries; the older ones reminded her dismally of the women who sat at the cafés in Danish hotels. In Denmark they consumed pastries and coffee and puffed on big cigars; here they had tea or cocktails and ate nothing but smoked a feverish succession of cigarettes—that was the only difference.

With the club as headquarters, Tania set forth to fulfill her scores of engagements, accompanied by Clara and her cousin Tove Hvass, who was part of the traveling retinue. The program arranged for her before she arrived in New York was already overly taxing for a person of her age and delicate health, but it was not enough for Tania. Nothing was enough. She had always been eager but she was insatiable now, avid to crowd what was left of her life with new scenes and sights, new experiences, more and more people.

She had expressed a desire to meet E. E. Cummings; also Ernest Hemingway, whom she wanted to thank for his kind words about her and the Nobel Prize. Hemingway was not in New York, but Glenway Wescott asked Cummings to join him in escorting Tania at the American Academy and Institute. At the same dinner she confessed that she would like to meet Marilyn Monroe, so Carson McCullers obliged with a memorable luncheon at her country house in Nyack, and Miss Monroe was there, delighted if somewhat bewildered. Ruth Ford had met Tania in 1949 when she played Ophelia in an American production of *Hamlet* at Elsinore, so she and her husband, Zachary Scott, gave a party at which Tania told an unpublished story. The Sidney Lumets entertained her in their penthouse. She was taken to Carnegie Hall to hear Maria Callas in *Il Pirata,* and later to hear Lena Horne. Tania also wanted to go to Harlem to listen to jazz, but that was never arranged. Friends invited her to spend an evening with the poet Marianne Moore, and she dined there, as elsewhere, restricting herself to her chosen regimen of a few oysters and grapes, a glass of champagne, but generous of anecdotes and humor. "Incomparable Isak Dinesen," Marianne Moore said of her later. And there was meeting after meeting with celebrities and simple folk, artists and intellectuals, café society and those who consider themselves America's aristocrats, students, expatriate Danes, radio and television men, critics and autograph hounds.

Tania was also photographed by author Carl Van Vechten, by Avedon, Brofferio and many others, and had her portrait painted by René Bouché. When she arrived to sit for Brofferio, Clara followed behind her with half a dozen hat boxes slung over her arm like a Paris midinette, and pictures were made using all of the contents in all of the boxes. But what had Clara done! In one of her rare free moments she had gone out and bought a hat for herself, a large dashing fur hat which everybody admired. Tania pouted, sensing some sort of rivalry, but Clara was photographed too.

"How can the Baroness stand the pace?" asked the younger persons who trailed after her, themselves worn out by the continual rush. Clara, gravely concerned, saw Tania getting even thinner, and noted familiar and dangerous symptoms of total exhaustion. Tania had once teasingly referred to her as "my Sancho Panza" and was perhaps not so far off the mark. For Tania was tilting, if not at windmills, then at everything that came her way in New York while Clara, helpless to prevent what she knew would be the inevitable debacle, grew pale and nervous over the responsibility.

Nancy Wilson Ross would bear out this contention. "Although I had seen her only the week before, I was greatly shocked by her changed appearance," she said of the time when she went up to Tania's room before her talk at the Cosmopolitan Club. "With difficulty, as I looked into her ravished face, I resisted an impulse to beg her to cancel the afternoon's engagement. It was quite plain that Clara, too, felt an acute, though also unspoken apprehension about the demands of the hours ahead." Tania narrated two of her *Tales*, though it was agreed that she should stop if she felt too tired after the first one, and then she was carried from the speaker's platform up to the library. "It had been decided, in order to spare her any further exhaustion, that the usual formal tea for club members would not be served. This change of plans, however, did not suit Tania in the least. Still possessed by the power I had seen in her eyes—the invisible magnetic bond between storyteller and audience not yet severed—she inquired of me in a tone bordering on severity, 'Where is everyone? Where are your literary friends?'" Some club members were called together and Tania went on talking. She was happy, and she forgave them their dreary hats in the warm knowledge that they were eager listeners while she *had* to go on telling stories. When they finally left, "she was still like someone possessed. She did not want the magic to slip away, to find herself suddenly alone, charged with all this creative force, but without attendant ears. She begged me to stay and dine with her . . . and I left with the uneasy feeling that I had somehow failed her."

The morning after the Cosmopolitan Club program she was taken to the hospital, where the doctors found her on the verge of death from prostration and malnutrition. "Unfair clubwomen in Boston having imposed on [Baroness Blixen] more engagements than she had agreed to, she had to be put to bed in a hospital for ten days, where the doctors decided that the champagne was counter-indicated and prescribed milk instead" was Glenway's explanation for her enforced temporary retreat, but it is likely that Tania herself was as much to blame. Indeed one might have thought that she was bent on self-destruction.

Even at the hospital the carnival continued: between blood transfusions and intravenous feedings visitors appeared, the Paleys sent a television set, René Bouché sent a large painting to make the room more cheerful, and the telephone rang incessantly. In less than a fortnight she was on the New York merry-go-round again, and Clara, though outwardly calm, felt deeply troubled. She lost her Byron cameo then—probably, she said, because she was so worried about Tania that she had grown careless about things of her own. Glenway Wescott, sensing that it was no ordinary loss, gave her as consolation a book that had belonged to Byron and had his autograph on the flyleaf and later sent her a Staffordshire portrait figurine which bore the legend "L. Byron."

"Tania," asked the Ekstroms, who were now living in America, "have you been disappointed by any aspect of your stay in New York? Apart from not finding Frydenlund, is there anything you longed to see or do which hasn't been accomplished?"

"Yes, indeed," Tania replied quite candidly and without hesitating a moment. "I have always wished for a meeting with Pearl Buck, whom I greatly admire. I should like so much to hear what she has to say."

During the following weeks she came back to the subject again and again. "Will Pearl Buck really come?" she kept on inquiring. "I hope she will come. Will she talk? She must be very wonderful and very wise."

Pearl Buck had to travel for three hours by train to reach New York. She arrived for lunch with great punctuality, wearing a trim blue-grey suit and a discreet flowered calotte that would never have met the measure of Tania's exalted standard in hats. Besides the Ekstroms, only one other guest was there, Arthur Gregor, a young American poet, winner of several prizes. Pearl Buck talked to them, with great restraint, very quietly, and she was indeed very wonderful and very wise. It was plain that she had assimilated her literary triumphs and the Nobel Prize without any affectation. She had had, at one time in her life, a great sorrow and she had mastered it, and now she had the poise and the calm eyes of a person who lives with trees and fields and many children. "How many children have you adopted?" the Ekstroms had asked her one day, twenty years before. "Only six" was the rather wistful reply. "My husband says that's more than enough."

And where, where was Tania?

At long last she appeared, elaborately dressed for a later afternoon reception, and diffusing her most calculated charm. She was all in black. From under a hat bordered with quivering black ostrich plumes, her enormous eyes peered out, rimmed around with even more kohl than usual. Her long suede gloves were black, and her brittle, birdlike legs were sheathed in black silk stockings. No sooner was she settled in a chair than she launched into a series of anecdotes about her stay in New York, gesturing with a long black cigarette holder as if it were a divining rod.

At lunch she waved aside her oysters and grapes, and while the others were busy with their more pedestrian fare, she went on talking, talking, talking. Pearl Buck looked at the centerpiece of leucocoryne, glory-of-the-sun lilies, arranged in her honor in a Chinese bowl, and once or twice she attempted to say something but gave up, bowing to a force majeure. When the coffee was brought, Tania interrupted her monologue to light a cigarette, which she didn't take time to smoke, but continued telling stories until someone reminded her that it was time for her next appointment.

After Tania left with her host, who wanted to make sure she would arrive safely at her destination, there was a sort of stunned silence, and then Pearl Buck said, "The small blue lilies downstairs on the dining-room table, do you know what they are? I have never seen them before."

In the taxi there was also a silence. After a long pause Tania asked, "Tell me, was that Pearl Buck?"

"Tania, you wicked creature! You know perfectly well that it was Pearl Buck."

"Yes, yes. I suppose it was," Tania allowed. "She didn't say anything."

VI

The Daily Rose

—◊◊◊◊—

Many people met Tania at the airport when she returned to
Copenhagen—she had, at long last, become a beloved celebrity at
home—but in the crowd awaiting her it was Nils she singled out.
There he was, a boy with a dazzling smile and an armful of red
roses like the ones they had handed to her after the intoxicating
sessions at the Poetry Center. Her smiles were all for him, and the
news photographers were beside themselves trying to catch some
sentimental shots of the little Baroness in the wheelchair with the
grinning tow-headed youngster.

Back at Rungstedlund the inevitable letdown followed upon
the hectic months in New York. For the first time she felt a profound weariness at the thought of arranging all the flowers, and no
desire at all to go out into the garden. As for Ewald's Hill, she
could not muster the strength to walk up there again. Everything
seemed stale and flat. And unprofitable, she added instinctively
with a wry little smile at herself.

A few discouraging days later she called Erling Schroeder.

"Erling," she lamented, "we are so dull here! In New York everything was exciting. In New York everyone loved me. Tell me you love me. I need to hear that. I need it."

"I love you," came Erling's velvet voice over the telephone. "I love you, Karen Blixen. I love you, Isak Dinesen."

And it was true, he thought to himself, as he put down the receiver. He loved her with gratitude for being a bright flame in a grey world, for her refusal to accept mediocrity, for being brave, for being a witch. To demonstrate his love, especially now when she needed to know and be reassured by it, would take some careful planning. And his accomplices must be trusted to keep a secret because Karen (he was the only one to call her so) loved the romantic and mysterious as much now as she ever had as a young girl.

When all was arranged, a single, perfect rose was delivered at Rungstedlund for Tania. Perhaps she didn't pay much attention to it then, but the next day there was another one. And the day after that, yet another. From then on, every day for the rest of her life there was a rose, anonymous, magical. It was brought to her when she went visiting. When she went abroad it followed her. After a while she named it the "daily rose."

"Who do you think sends you the daily rose, Tania? Aren't you curious to know?"

Perhaps she guessed, perhaps not. But wasn't it always better not to probe into exquisite mysteries?

"Rungstedlund, 30 June, 1959

Dearest darling Parmenia,

. . . I left part of my heart in New York. People had told me before I went there that it was a unique and magnificent place, but that in some way it had no heart. Now as I look back on the time I spent there, although I am well aware that it is in a way an awe-inspiring, even a demonic city, the chief impression that I have brought back with me is that of a most wonderful generosity. I have always loved demons, I am yearning for the particular New York demon. I do not think that I could ever fall in love with anything demon-free. I am in love with New York and with you all there. Please give this love of mine to everybody kind enough to remember me . . . As to my own small house in Copenhagen, there are so many troubles about my getting it arranged in the way I want, that I fear I shall have to give it up after all, and to remain in my old house in the country . . . I have got two or three new stories in my mind, the one about Drude Angel . . . I am going on a trip to relations in Funen [Fyn Island] and Jutland before settling down to write . . . Now give my love to your husband—did you every realize that I am a little bit in love with him?—(but then he has got a small devil in him too). I wish he and you were in Denmark; it has been the loveliest summer I can remember, and I have had the most beautiful flowers for my bouquets, which to me are one of the greatest pleasures of summer time. So I am sending you the smile of the Danish landscape, and a kiss from the rooms of my old ramshackle inn."

May and June at Rungstedlund had worked their customary spell, and Tania was happy again. She was busy arranging her sumptuous bouquets, and she was planning new stories and a second book about Africa. When she entertained the continuing stream of guests at tea, the old lilac tree poured gusts of perfume into the drawing room, and through the opposite windows her view of the sea was framed in Nevada roses, with Hveen Island hovering like a mirage on the horizon line. "I am *really* happy here," she thought, and by degrees the memories of New York blurred into a pleasant confusion of hurry and noise, faces and parties, parties, parties.

Only one subject rankled whenever she thought of America: how angry she was with Truman Capote and Richard Avedon, how hurt she had been when they sent her *Observations*, their book of photographs and commentary. She who loathed all the sordid aspects of old age, how she had hated the caricature of herself which Avedon had exposed to the world, and his cruel rendering of her hands! The camera never lies, they said, but of course it did. And how she hated Truman Capote's mocking tone which transpired through all the compliments he had heaped on her. Sophisticated and heartless he was. "I wrote and told Truman Capote," she reiterated whenever his name was mentioned, "that I had always found Americans very kind and that I was surprised to find that he and Avedon were capable of being so ungenerous. I had previously agreed to write a preface to Truman Capote's book and felt it would be mean and vindictive not to keep my promise, but I wrote it with bitterness in my heart because of his ungallant treatment of me."

During Tania's absence on Fyn Island and in Jutland, Clara retired to her cottage to accomplish some work of her own. To her already impressive list of translations she had added *A Cure for Serpents* in 1956 and *A Grave for a Dolphin* in 1957, both by A. Denti di Pirajno. "I stayed at Dragør a couple of months this summer translating Lampedusa's *Il Gattopardo* while Tania was visiting friends," she wrote to Eugene, who had gone to Uruguay for a series of concerts. "It got a surprising amount of praise from reviewers—who usually do not notice the quality of a translation at all." For Danish Radio she also translated a story by Frank O'Connor, and then hurried back to Rungstedlund where great rebuilding plans were afoot.

Since the tiny city house which Tania had hoped to use for winter quarters could not, it turned out, be adapted to her needs, something had to be done to Rungstedlund to render it warm and comfortable. There were seldom big snowfalls along the coast between Copenhagen and Elsinore, but sometimes the Øresund froze over and the wild gales tearing across it filled the house with icy drafts. There was no central heating—how could there be in a house that had no center? Over the centuries, rooms had been added, here and there, upstairs and down; in the vast attic sprawling above them, basins stood on the floor to catch the leakage whenever it rained; there were three stairways; and the servants complained that they walked a dozen kilometers a day, fetching and carrying. If Tania resented references to her weakness and her age, she had to admit, at least to herself, that she would soon be unable to stand the winter with nothing but fires and iron stoves to stave off the dampness and cold. And she was still bathing in a portable tin tub which her American friends would have laughed at as a quaint relic of unenlightened times.

A good friend of hers, the eminent architect Steen Eiler Rasmussen, had agreed to see to the long-deferred alterations, and could be trusted to preserve the spirit of her old inn while yet making it practical. He was a good neighbor too. He often dropped in to see her and to make photographs of her flower arrangements, and Tania also went often to the beautiful house he had built nearby for his family. "The wind is blowing from Elsinore," she announced one day at their door. "I have come over because I could smell your Christmas cakes as they came out of the oven."

But it was not the aroma of spice cookies that had lured her there, it was the children. Many of Tania's friends had heard her remark, at one time or another, that she disliked children, though no one was in the least misled by what she said. The truth of the matter was that she found children irresistible, and few persons could have handled them with more imagination and tact. In Africa there had been the *totos* in and around the house—Kamante; the deaf-and-dumb Karomenya, whose horizons had suddenly widened when she had given him a whistle; and the little goat-herds who trooped into her living room at noon every day when the cuckoo in the old German clock pushed open the door of its wooden house and came out to proclaim the hour. ". . . by a quarter to twelve I could see them approaching the house from all sides, at the tail of their goats, which they dared not leave behind. The heads of the children and the goats swam through the bush and long grass of the forest like heads of frogs in a pond.

"They left their flocks on the lawn and came in noiselessly on their bare feet; the bigger ones were about ten years and the youngest two years . . . As the cuckoo rushed out on them, a great movement of ecstasy and suppressed laughter ran through the group. It also sometimes happened that a very small herdboy, who did not feel any responsibility about the goats, would come back in the early morning all by himself, stand for a long time in front of the clock, now shut up and silent, and address it in Kikuyu in a slow sing-song declaration of love, then gravely walk out again." Here in Denmark it was her little neighbor Ole Arnbak, who thought she looked like a gnome, and Nils, and all those children of her own creation: Peter and Rosa, the Dreaming Child . . .

Perhaps the aspect of children which appealed to her was that they accepted as perfectly natural the fantastic and miraculous which older critics derided and which, in her personal life as well as her writing, were as necessary to her as the air she breathed. Perhaps, too, John Becker's intuition had found her out. In the poem he wrote for Tania he commented on the fact that she had pressed him for details about his small daughter, Haidee.

> *. . . And as I told you I wondered*
> *If it was because she too, like you,*
> *Has a magic, although of a different kind,*
> *Or if because my child in some way represented*
> *The one thing you had perhaps always wanted and never had,*
> *Or, more than that, if it was simply her childhood*
> *With the vitality of the promise*
> *That you were clinging to.*

Architect Rasmussen's children were given a doll house, an exact replica of a wing of their parents' house, and when Tania came to call they dragged her away to look at it. Yes, yes, it was beautiful, she told them, but she would never spend a night in it because it had no bathroom. The children laughed: she was much too big to stay overnight in it anyway! Did they really think so? argued Tania. Hadn't they read *Alice in Wonderland,* and didn't they think that at night she might grow larger or smaller just like Alice? And the next time she went to see them she brought along all the furnishings for a miniature bathroom.

In the summer of 1959 Bent Mohn gave a party which rivaled any that had been given for her in New York or Rome. He had a brawny sailor at the door to meet her and carry her up to his apartment. "I chose him for the sake of contrast," said Bent, "big and strong, and had him waiting in the street when Karen Blixen arrived in a cab. In order, I guess, both to show his strength and because it is really easier, the sailor chose to run up the stairs.

Blixen was delighted. She always liked a surplus, an excess, the feeling that more power was hidden than was visible on the surface (a principle in her own work). 'I was sitting on his arm like a small bird on a branch,' she commented." When the sailor, whose name was Leif, set Tania down, she insisted on his staying so that she could hear about his adventures in ports all over the world. Afterwards she often described the episode. "It became, in her romantic way of experiencing things," said Bent, "one of the peaks in her later life and she used it to tease more conventional hosts at more conventional parties (such as her publishers') where they could only serve champagne and intellectual people." Bent went on to explain that on his part, he had also thought of the sailor as "a romantic homage to her feeling for and understanding of the lower classes, the wandering, rather *hors la loi* category," and that later Tania had sent Leif, the sailor, a copy of *Out of Africa* with a long, friendly dedication. In her youthful response to an occurrence which, though essentially insignificant, astonished and delighted her, Tania much resembled Colette—old, bedridden and in constant pain—who said that one could endure the lack of many things but not the need to be astonished. "Astound me, try your hardest. These last flashes of astonishment are what I cannot do without"—the words could have been Tania's.

VII

Shadows on the Grass

—〰〰〰—

Alfred Pedersen died on January 13, 1960, in his ninetieth year, and was buried in the Hørsholm Kirkegaard in a plot not far from the graves of Tania's parents. Like the faithful servant he had been for sixty-five years, he was close by even in death. One by one, thought Tania, she had watched all of the ties being severed which attached her to the past. It made her feel alone and adrift in a world where hardly anyone knew that she had once been "Tanne." Pedersen, who had come to Rungstedlund the year that Wilhelm died, was the last to remember her as a pale, unhappy child, weeping in secret over her father's death, rebellious and resentful of her mother's family. Thomas and Anders were too young at the time to take notice, but Pedersen knew, and although he would not have permitted himself to speak of such things, she had felt that in a way she shared her childhood with him. Now he was gone. And Rasmussen had not yet started rebuilding Rungstedlund, and it was bleak and cold and damp in the house. And she was depressed. Very depressed.

She sat by the drawing-room fire, wrapped in shawls, half dozing, letting her thoughts run on a long, sad track of memories. Pedersen. He had driven her in the family carriage to Katholm. That was in 1900. She remembered the date well because it was the beginning of a new life for her and the start of a new century —the two had coincided. He took her there a Westenholz and brought her back a Dinesen. He hadn't guessed that, of course, but her mother had. Her mother, somehow, always knew everything, and often, alas, was not subtle enough to hide it. Pedersen drove her to her first ball—and to the ship when she left for Africa. And under her mother's guidance, what a stickler the gauche young coachman became!

"Alfred is such a tyrant," she told the reporters from *Life* magazine last year. "When I came back from Africa I wanted to wear trousers but I could tell he didn't approve. And he doesn't like the idea of my earning money. He likes me to inherit money but I am very bad about inheriting money. I never inherit any at all." And they all laughed. She laughed too, but the truth of it was that she stood rather in awe of Pedersen. Neither had he liked her to drive a car, she recalled, althought he got used to it in the end. What would he have said, she wondered, of her driving a locomotive, as she once did in Africa, sitting gaily in the engineer's seat, braking the train when ostriches loped across the tracks? And how Alfred had hated Bjørnvig! Well, all of that was past and over now . . . and forgotten. "Dear heart," she quoted, murmuring to herself, "you will have to work hard to unlearn what you have learned from me." Bjørnvig, perhaps, had not forgotten. But she would never know.

As always when she was low in spirits, writing was the resource and cure. She might be sad, she might be old, she might be weary and ill, but she would never settle for shawls, slippers and a cozy fire. Never. But it was difficult to work. From time to time a great frightening wave of pain surged through her and forced her to stop in the middle of a sentence to catch her breath. Surely it must be visible, she thought, like the visible-invisible heat waves that rise from hot paved highways. But she glanced at Clara, and Clara was waiting, poised over the typewriter, for her to go on.

Sleep was another thing. Sleep was the newest enemy of her work. Times past, sleep had been her nocturnal friend, the bringer of dreams that were always serene yet gave her a feeling of power and release, of life enhanced and magnified. Now sleep crept up on her twenty times a day. She could hear her own voice as she dictated but it seemed to come from outside herself; she could hear it stumble, falter and stop. And in some dim corner of her consciousness she could hear Clara lay down her papers and tiptoe out of the room.

"Rungstedlund is having central heating and bathrooms installed," Clara wrote to Eugene in March, "and after holding out for some months in the ruins, with the whole house surrounded by moats and mounds and a huge excavator roaring away just outside the windows all day, Tania and I are now evacuated and staying at Bellevue Strandhotel."

In the midst of all the confusion and moving and illness, Tania was putting together the book which she called *Shadows on the Grass*. It was to include "Farah," which had first been published by Ole Wivel in the days of the Heretica movement, and "Barua a Soldani" (Letter from a King), and it would take up the threads of Kamante, Old Knudsen, Abdullahi, Ali—characters dear to the readers of *Out of Africa*. Some of her people on the farm had died, but of those who remained many wrote to her faithfully and she followed their lives with passionate interest, always impatient and sad when the letters were slow in arriving.

As soon as the occupation had ended and Denmark was able to communicate with the outside world again, she had sent an inquiry to Kenya. Farah, she learned, had died, and without his help it would be next to impossible to locate the others. "The news of Farah's death to me was hard to take into my mind and very hard to keep there. How could it be that he had gone away? He had always been the first to answer a call. Then after a while I recognized the situation: more than once before now I had sent him ahead to some unknown place, to pitch camp for me there."

Then Sir Philip Mitchell, the Governor of Kenya, had written to her at the repeated request, he said, of his boy, Ali Hassan. Ali, he told her, "was the best servant he had ever had, but from the beginning he had made it clear to his master that he looked upon himself as still being in my service, and that if I ever came back to Africa he would feel free to leave Government House without notice.

"Here Ali at least had come forth, then, in great state, accompanied by the Lion and the Unicorn. He would order the others back as well, and we would all be gathered together once more. I started on a correspondence with Ali. From the style of his letters I gathered that for these years he had—in contrast to earlier days—been living in a household with no financial worries. But he was faithful to the past, naming the horses and dogs and bringing back things that I myself had forgotten."

It was not Ali but a Danish journalist, Helge Christensen, who succeeded in finding Kamante for Tania, in the outskirts of Nairobi "in the midst of the maze of *shambas* with hemp, corn and sweet potatoes, and of grassland." Kamante had been temporarily blind but an operation had given him back at least partial sight; he had also, he confided to Mr. Christensen, spent a year in prison for taking the Mau Mau oath; and finally he had fetched a letter out of his pocket. " 'Look,' he says, 'msabu writes to me: "My good and faithful servant Kamante." ' As again he folds up the letter and sticks it into his pocket, he adds: 'And so I am.' "

As they grow old—and Tania was now in her seventy-sixth year— people enjoy letting their thoughts slip back to what made them happiest in the past. When she first returned from Kenya and passed through the difficult period of homesickness and grief, Tania had early fallen into the habit of daydreaming about Africa, Denys, Farah and the farm. Age exaggerated the tendency and the new book was a reason for indulging the habit even more. The problem, she complained, was the concentration and work involved in organizing these memories into the sort of book that might be an adequate sequel to *Out of Africa*.

The Bellevue Strandhotel, where Tania first settled during the rebuilding of Rungstedlund, was one of the most attractive hotels in Denmark, with its garden, private beach and wide view over the Øresund, and its excellent cuisine. For Tania, it was very conveniently situated midway on the road from Copenhagen to Rungsted. Unfortunately every room had been booked for Easter, so the next move was to the Hotel Angleterre in the city. There too her residence had to be curtailed because of previous reservations. There was always Dragør, suggested Clara. After Eugene's visit, Sandy Campbell, the actor, had stayed there and Donald Windham, the writer, and they had all found it conducive to work as well as relaxation.

Tania took over the cottage like visiting royalty, sleeping in Clara's bedroom, installing her maid in the guest chamber, while

Clara was reduced to camping on a couch in the study downstairs. Clothes, medicines, notes and manuscripts were unpacked; and as infallible as the rise and setting of the sun, the "daily rose" appeared each day.

Exhausted by the move, Tania was nevertheless ecstatic. What painter's eye would not be captivated by the picturesque character of this place? And she listened with rapt attention to every detail of Clara's account of the local history and lore. There, at the left of the port, Clara pointed out, as she had for Eugene, was the huge pier her great-grandfather built for sailing ships and fishing boats. And beyond the harbor, out in the channel, was Saltholm—Salt Island. Since time out of mind the people of Dragør had sent their geese to the island to fatten them for the holidays. Each spring the geese departed by boat—single geese, the treasured possessions of poor widows and laborers, whole flocks belonging to wealthier folk, cackling tourists off for a country holiday; and each winter the geese came home and were handed back to the waiting crowd at the pier to grace their tables for St. Martin's Eve and Christmas Eve. Except for the geese and their keeper and an astonishing variety of sea birds, the island was uninhabited—a bleak stretch of salt grass, bracken and scrub.

Tania wanted to see Salt Island. Clara, looking at Tania's pallor and pathetic, wasted physique, said no, but Tania argued. Clara reasoned. Tania insisted, and off they went in a little boat that belonged to the son of Clara's house painter. Clara literally feared for Tania's life, so she appealed to Thomas' daughter Anne Kopp, and she and her husband and Nils joined the expedition. As there were neither cars nor roads, Tania rode around Salt Island all day perched next to the gooseherd on the high seat of a farm tractor, bumping and rattling across the moors and meadows, pleased as a small child on a roller coaster.

.   .   .

From Centralsygehuset, Hillerød, 10 October, 1960, Tania to Denys Finch-Hatton's niece, Diana, and her husband, Peter: "I ought to have written to you long ago to thank you for the charming picture of my Tania and for Diana's sweet letter. But I have for the last three months had one foot in the boat of Charon. It is only these last days that I have begun to believe that I shall ever really get back into human existence. I was taken into this hospital from Dragør in an ambulance, the doctor and my own people convinced that I should last only a week or two, and with the most terrible pains—I had let things go from bad to worse too long. I am still terribly weak and I cannot get my weight above 30 kilos [66 pounds], but I have got rid of some of my complaints, amongst others a most distressing inflammation of the eye. I am generally quick to pick up once I have started, and I do think I shall be all right again . . . Thanks be to God I got my book finished a few days before I got in here! It was for the last few weeks a race against death. It will be published in Scandinavia and England on 31 October, somewhat later in America because it has there been made Book-of-the-Month for January. It is named *Shadows on the Grass* and is a collection of memories from Africa. There are a few pictures in it, reproductions of portraits I painted out there, of the Natives . . . With all my love and a kiss to each of you."

Racing against time, against death, as she felt herself to be, Tania gave in to despair as she lay confined in the hospital for three long months. It was not only the postponement, perhaps even the end of her work that distressed her, but other dashed hopes as well. As for physical suffering, she was quite enured to it by now. Pain was her *cavaliere servente* who had trod on her heels for forty-five years.

In March, from the Bellevue Strandhotel, she had written to

Diana to say how much she looked forward to attending the wedding of "Little Tania" in April. A note of doubt and caution crept into the letter: "Now unfortunately I have not been well for some time. At the same time as I shall be looking forward to the 30 of April, I feel that I may possibly have to give up going at the last moment, but I hope that this would not cause you too much inconvenience. I shall most certainly do my best to come, and I have for some time been planning to go to England in April or May, so I do trust I may collect the strength to appear at St. Mary's Church." She would bring Clara with her because she had great difficulty in walking and "altogether I shall come hobbling to the wedding with one foot in the grave."

When it turned out that she was, in fact, not well enough to travel, it had been a great disappointment. She had imagined the trip as a sort of "sentimental journey," a renewal of contact with all of Denys' family: Diana, whom she had grown to love for herself, not merely because she was Denys' niece; her exquisite sister, Daphne (Antony Tudor, himself the creator of so much beauty, had said of her, "When she walked into my studio she was the most beautiful creature I had ever seen"); and her own "Little Tania." How touching it would have been to see this child married!

She had written to Diana again in June, this time from Dragør: "Beloved friends, Diana & Peter! What more delightful news could I possibly receive than that you two would come to Denmark! I can hardly believe it to be true, it is so filled with happy possibilities. Welcome! Welcome! . . ." But neither did this hoped-for visit materialize.

In the hospital, between bouts of pain and that no man's land of being, brought on by drugs to annul the pain, regrets, impatience and confused dreams gave her no rest. Her mind, for a while, strayed to the wedding guests and from them quite naturally to Denys. Soon, she thought, soon . . . In the meanwhile, she would have to resign herself to this dreary hospital bed, feeling too weary to read, and with no distractions except the afternoon visitors with their oddly subdued voices. Thomas would stop in, since his house was near the hospital, and he would talk to her quietly and calmly. It had not always been so in the past. Though he had been very good to her, they had often quarreled. She couldn't quite remember now what it was that had caused the arguments—the farm, her painting, their inheritance—none of it mattered any more. She had even quarreled with him about whom his daughters should marry, and she had been arbitrary and wrong. Now she felt only gratitude and affection for Anne's husband Erik Kopp, who had been like a devoted, attentive son to her. How curious that she had once thought of Bjørnvig as an ideal son!

Her thoughts drifted to Clara. What would become of her? As soon as she left the hospital she would arrange— But would she leave the hospital?

The image of Clara slithered away from her, and Clara herself came into the room and stood next to the bed.

"Clara," murmured Tania. "You have shared so much of my life, Clara, and I am very grateful to you. But tell me, Clara, one day when I shall have died, one day are you going to write 'Karen Blixen *en pantoufles*'?"

Clara recognized the tone and her tears welled over suddenly with relief. Tania was teasing again. The old wicked spark was back in Tania's eye and she would get well once more.

She would get well—as well, considering her seventy-five years and chronic ills, as could be hoped for. In the spring she had complained of the difficulty of working, but the real difficulty, the one she refused to face, was the problem of merely living from one day to the next—in a manner compatible with her age and condition. And this last collapse had not been an object lesson, not at all. As soon as she found she was able to stand on her feet, she would begin again the depleting round of work, crowds of callers, travel and parties.

Eugene, kept up to date on events at Rungstedlund by letters from Clara, sent roses for Tania's homecoming—it had been six months —and she wrote to thank him, adding: "The house is much the same to look at, thank God, but more fit for human beings to live in than it was before, warm all through and practical."

Leaning on Clara's arm, she had made a slow tour of the house when she came home. Nothing, in fact, seemed very changed. The old iron stoves still stood in their accustomed places: the elegant slender stove in the study, the rather comical one with buckled shoes on its splayed feet in the drawing room, where a fire also continued to blaze on the hearth. But heat, welcome heat, poured out of the radiators that Rasmussen had installed, enough to hold off the worst winter weather. She was tired, dreadfully tired, but she would not be cold again. Not cold again, she thought wearily, until the grave had claimed her.

Before she said good night, she called as usual for something to read. Years afterwards Monica Stirling said she could hear a voice "still very much alive: Karen Blixen's asking for a book on her way to bed, 'Where's my Andersen?'" The Andersen, like Shakespeare, had traveled a long journey with Tania. When she was a little girl her old nurse would read one of the tales aloud each night after she had been put to bed, and when she grew up and married Bror, the same nurse had given her a nice bright-red copy of the fairy tales with both their names inscribed in it. She would tell this to a new group of young readers, for the publishers, Macmillan, had asked her to write an introduction to an American children's edition of Andersen.

With her book tucked under her arm, she went for a few minutes to the study for the nightly ritual of Africa and Denys. And then to bed, to her own bed, at last.

Part Five

—⁓⁓—

The Legend

I

A Talent for Friendship

—◌◌◌◌—

In *Out of Africa* there is a chapter entitled "Visitors to the Farm" which includes sketches of British and Scandinavian friends in Kenya and some of the most memorable descriptions of the Somali, Masai and Kikuyu. After Bror had left and the farm became Tania's, most of the visitors were men; and since she also preferred them that way, they were nearly always misfits or outcasts, men of pronounced but unusual or unusable talents. Old Mr. Bulpett had made a name for himself as a sportsman, climbing the Matterhorn and mountains in Mexico, swimming the Hellespont and the Thames—in evening clothes and high hat—and he had been one of the lovers of the great Parisian courtesan La Belle Otéro. Berkeley Cole, sophisticated and brilliant, demanded his bottle of champagne in the jungle every morning at eleven; but he was also a friend of the ferocious Masai and spoke their language, and he spurned the society of normal folk. Denys himself was a rebel and a lone wolf. At the farm all of them felt at ease, free to come and go as they wished, confident that their various gifts and idiosyncrasies would be savored with humor and understanding, and never measured by conventional standards.

Knudsen, the derelict and woman-hater, sensed that he had an ally in Tania. And the quixotic "Emmanuelson," who had been an actor, a waiter in a Paris café and a *maître d'hotel* in Kenya, also knew that she would listen to him. In the tale "The Deluge at Norderney," he was the model for Kasparson, which was actually his real name, but when Tania wrote about him again in *Out of Africa*, even under another name, the portrait was unmistakable and some of his staid relatives in Sweden protested. Shortly before the German occupation, Tania had arranged a conciliatory meeting with Kasparson at the Grand Hotel in Stockholm, and they shared a bottle of Chambertin in memory of the strange evening he had spent at the farm before walking all the way from Nairobi to Tanganyika.

"And what are you doing these days?" Tania inquired when matters had been settled between them.

He was living on a roof terrace with a Sioux Indian girl who had been traveling with a knife thrower when Kasparson met her in Egypt.

"And how did a Sioux Indian girl ever get to Egypt?" wondered Tania.

"On a bicycle," replied Kasparson as if it were the most natural thing in the world, and the answer delighted her. Here in the flesh was an Isak Dinesen character as whimsical as she might have wished.

It is a pity that Tania never wrote "Visitors to Rungstedlund," nor, in fact, anything at all about Rungstedlund except for a few brief articles to publicize and raise funds for the bird sanctuary. At the time of the Heretica movement she began her custom of receiving a great many guests for tea which, in the manner of an English high tea, was a prodigality of broiled mushrooms on toast, Danish pancakes, tarts filled with preserves, strawberries and cream, biscuits and cakes, with an equal abundance of stimulating talk. After the war, when food rationing ended and Fru Carlsen ably took over the housekeeping, it became a matter of pride and pleasure to entertain in the evening. Tania combined dinner guests imaginatively, without too much concern for convention, and she directed the conversation with skill.

Guests also came and went all during the afternoon even after she came home from the hospital. Writers of various countries made the pilgrimage to Rungstedlund, curious to see the author who belonged to "that small band of independent writers who dared to write as they please and as they must, little, early, late; the grand and lonely ones who had the courage and the genius to keep—at their cost—to their vision and eccentric disciplines (Karen Blixen even chose the language she saw fit for herself to write in, and she wrote it superbly) without regard to fashion, the mainstream and the time, not because they were dilettantes, but because they were artists."

Laurens van der Post, whose books have disclosed a new, sensitive and very personal image of Africa, was Tania's good friend. Whenever he went to Kenya he would visit Denys' grave and "give her love to it and report back on its condition to her." Aldous Huxley was an old friend too. On one of his last visits to Denmark he brought with him Dr. Timothy Leary, professor at Harvard, who in 1965–66 created a great scandal in the American press for having encouraged college youth to experiment with LSD, for smuggling marijuana across the Mexican border into the United States with his young daughter as an accomplice, and for running a sanatorium which permitted strange, unsavory practices with narcotics. Huxley and Dr. Leary had been experimenting with the now-famous Mexican mushrooms which provoke hallucinations, and they were eager for Tania to try them too. Huxley, whose eyesight was impaired, said the mushrooms gave him marvelous visions, and Dr. Leary, whose hearing was faulty, said that he heard great orchestrations of sound under the influence. But Tania was not to be persuaded. She was filled with enough fantasies, she told them, without any external stimulus.

The author of *And Quiet Flows the Don*, Mikhail Sholokhov, spoke no language except his native Russian but, said Tania, after a bit one gets on to the trick, which is to talk directly to the person and forget all about the interpreter. In spite of the language barrier they managed well, and Tania, always unmindful of illness and age, told him that she would be pleased to accept his invitation to visit him in Russia.

Barbara Howes, poet and wife of the poet William Jay Smith, who had introduced Tania when she appeared at the Poetry Center, spent only one afternoon at Rungstedlund but came away deeply impressed. She had expected Isak Dinesen to be a "grandly remote and more eccentric and Gothic" personality and was surprised to find her simple and natural, and as willing to discuss children and housekeeping problems as the loftier aspects of literature. They did, nevertheless, talk about books and Tania explained her preference among the Americans for such nineteenth-century writers as Twain, Melville and Poe.

Robert Langbaum, while preparing *The Gayety of Vision*, had more detailed, exploratory conversations with Tania than anyone except for the Danish writers who were able to see her regularly over long periods of time. Scholarly and painstaking, he won her esteem and gratitude.

Not all of the authors, however, fared as well in Tania's appraisal of them. Since she herself was struggling against a tendency to fall asleep during the day, she spoke with disdain and impatience of Tennessee Williams. He came after lunch one day and when she wanted to talk with him he was drowsy, she complained. He had even slept on the lawn! As for Hudson Strode, he had been welcomed with more than usual enthusiasm when Tania first invited him in the spring of 1939. He had letters from Dorothy Canfield, and at an authors' dinner in Stockholm he had recently met Prince Wilhelm of Sweden, who twenty-five years before had stood witness at Tania's wedding in Mombasa. Strode saw her again in 1946; but in June 1962, when she asked him to lunch with a friend of hers, Solita Solano, and Eugene Haynes, she detected elements of snobbery in him which she could not forgive.

Photographers had always found her an interesting and responsive subject, and they were all the more attracted when old age and emaciation had brought her fine bones into prominence and had etched a maze of lines and wrinkles on the parchment pallor of her face. One of those who came to Tania's house was Peter Beard, a dynamic young American, who after reading *Out of Africa* had taken the next plane for Kenya and remained there for two years. He tracked down Kamante and took the only existing photograph of this lone survivor of the farm natives. Eventually, armed with a letter of introduction, Peter arrived at Rungstedlund with all the violence of a tornado. Tania found him exhausting, but endearing too, and she made a great effort to help him, posing for pictures and supplying data which, long after her death, were incorporated into one of the most beautifully illustrated books on Kenya and its wildlife.

The last photographer to see her was Cecil Beaton. En route for Spain, he stopped for several hours at Rungstedlund a few weeks before she died, and at her suggestion, took some pictures.

His studies of her had appeared in *Harper's Bazaar*, *Réalités*, and other magazines and books. This time his impressions were recorded not only with a camera lens but in a drawing and in writing. "I shall always remember," he said in the book *Isak Dinesen: A Memorial*, "the beauty of this thin little figure with the dark eyes peering out into the sunlight, as if this world were already unfamiliar to her." Cecil Beaton was the photographer whom Tania admired the most. However, she had a sentimental preference for old snapshots of herself that had been taken in Africa; she had a quantity of them reproduced in post-card size, and often when she had short notes to write, instead of using letter paper, she would dash messages off on the backs of these old pictures.

A guest for tea one afternoon was Wamboi, a Kikuyu girl who was finishing her student year in Denmark. Tania was moved to learn that she was the daughter of the chief who had replaced Kinanjui. Memories rushed upon her of the old chief, who had always helped her to settle the native disputes with wisdom and dignity, who had never failed to journey to the farm when she called for him to add the weight of his word to her decisions, and whose death had been a confused and sorry event. *"Na-taka kufa"* he wants to die, his son had said when he came to conduct Tania and Farah across country on a strange night of moonlight and mist, to his father's hut. Kinanjui had sent for her because he wanted to die in her house, not in the dreaded hospital; and she had had to refuse for fear of trouble with the officials and the mission people. In *Out of Africa* she told how, after the funeral, "Farah and I drove home by ourselves. Farah was as silent as the grave we had left. It had been hard to Farah to swallow the fact that I would not take Kinanjui back to my house with me, for two days he had been like a lost soul, and in the clutch of great doubts and depressions.

Now, as we drove up before the door he said: 'Never mind, memsahib.' " And here in Rungstedlund, after the passage of more than thirty years, was Kinanjui's grandniece! "I only regret I had not met her earlier . . ." Tania said, "she was, to me, very beautiful . . . There was a dignity about her, an aura of virtue not to be found among us. You know, their young ladies are brought up in this tradition. For me she demonstrated so vividly that virtue is a very positive quality."

"Has Clara shown you my grave?" was the question most frequently asked of the visitors who came from far away. Preoccupied with the idea of her burial place since she was a young woman, Tania was all the more absorbed in the thought of it now that she sensed the approach of death. So patient Clara would set out on an almost daily guided tour across the lawn and up to the top of Ewald's Hill. And countless were the times Tania drove to Elsinore and waited stoically in the car while her guests climbed the steep road to inspect Hamlet's castle.

In his portrait sketch of Tania, Truman Capote reported her as saying: " 'I have a talent for friendship, friends are what I have enjoyed most, to stir, to get about, to meet new people and attach them.' " She did indeed attach them, and not always consciously.

There was, to be sure, one last young man who fell in love and remained to console and encourage Tania at the very end of her life. But surely Viggo didn't mean that he was really in love with Tania? She was seventy-three years old the very first time he saw her. Oh, but he was, he insisted. He could only say that he had been obsessed with her even before he met her, and after he saw her his feeling ran deeper yet. Entirely apart from what she meant as a writer, to him she was beautiful.

And he was right; for although most women are at their loveliest in the first blush of girlhood or sometimes when knowledge and poise enhance the maturer charms of middle age, nevertheless there are always a rare few who achieve their moment of greatest beauty when they are no longer young at all. Such, no doubt, was Madame Récamier, who lived to be seventy-three with her allure quite undiminished. Chateaubriand could not resist going to see her every day during her last fifteen years. Eleonora Duse, too, as she grew old, acquired an aura of beauty that she had never had before. With Tania it was the same. Sorrow and success had combined to give her a sort of radiance, and she had gradually learned all the feminine wiles of being an enchantress. After a moment, she was able to make people forget her age, her myriad wrinkles and all her infirmities, and what remained was the spell of her ageless eyes and voice and spirit, and her ability to distill magic out of the most humdrum anecdotes.

Tania could not understand why Viggo hadn't come to see her sooner, before he completed the essay he had written about her books. And he explained that he had wished to avoid knowing her while the work was in preparation. He had wanted to stay outside the sphere of her personal influence until it was finished.

Tania heard him out and was undecided whether to feel flattered or annoyed. At first she feared that this was another dreadfully earnest young writer. But she was mistaken. In spite of his studious horn-rimmed glasses, his air of serious purpose, and the reserve characteristic of persons from Jutland, his sense of humor soon came rippling to the surface. He laughed with the abandon of a child, and Tania laughed with him. He had, he confessed, been tense and nervous at their first meeting merely because he had heard too much about her being exclusive and difficult. Later, when they had become good friends, he always contended that

Tania was not at all the solemn, tragic figure that most people made her out to be but, on the contrary, gay, eternally young and full of fun. It was this gaiety of hers which gradually became the leavening in the routine of his everyday life. To Robert Langbaum it was also a dominant trait in her character; he called his book on her work *The Gayety of Vision.*

As a young boy Viggo Kjær Petersen had been especially interested in Martin A. Hansen's many-faceted writing. In the 1930's Hansen had produced novels of social consciousness which dealt first with the possibilities and later with the failure of putting into practice the philosophy of agrarian communism; in the 1940's he had turned to works of fantasy and imagination; and by 1950, with the psychological *Løgneren* (The Liar), he had become Denmark's leading novelist with a constantly growing prestige. Widely read, he had also made a deep impression on many young intellectuals who hoped for literary careers of their own.

"But," said Viggo, "when I read Karen Blixen it was a sort of revelation. I felt that she named things of which I had been unconsciously aware."

In the winter of 1958–59, in his third year at Aarhus University, where he was majoring in English literature, he decided to make Karen Blixen the subject of his thesis, not only because of his admiration for her books but because he felt that her work was largely misunderstood, even by some of his professors, whose Marxist leanings prejudiced them against her. His project met with a blunt refusal—it was not acceptable to write a thesis about a living author—and when he persisted, he was grudgingly given permission to proceed on his own responsibility. In the space of twenty-one days Viggo wrote an essay one hundred and fifty pages long, resisting any temptation to call on his subject because, as he said, there was always too much reliance and emphasis on personal interviews with contemporary authors, rather than a detached view of the work itself.

His study was considered a courageous achievement, braving the dominating view as it did; it also won the highest possible marks given by the university for a literary thesis. Encouraged by this recognition, he sent a copy to the Baroness. In return, he received a long, prompt reply with an invitation to call at Rung-stedlund to discuss the essay and the comments in her letter.

What could have been the feelings of an inexperienced boy of twenty-three, already profoundly involved in the author's books, who makes the discovery of a personality like Tania's, and in the romantic surroundings of a place such as Rungstedlund? Viggo said he fell in love, and we are compelled to believe him. And even if we are tempted to smile at his early contention that Karen Blixen's work constituted the greatest artistic experience of his life, it is obvious that in spite of his youth he actually knew his mind and the direction his life would take. For, as time passed, he was increasingly drawn into her work, until he became the definitive authority on the subject, lecturing, giving radio talks and devoting himself at last to a major volume of analysis and criticism.

Through Clara, Ole Wivel learned of Viggo's first visit. He asked to see the thesis, and agreeably surprised at its competence and maturity, recommended that Gyldendal bring it out in book form. It was felt that publication of the essay would draw new attention to Tania's writing and give added weight to her can-didacy for the Nobel Prize, which was still a much-discussed pos-sibility. For a beginning young author the honor was great indeed. Viggo, however, more sensibly preferred to wait until he had given further thought to the thesis, which he feared had been far too hurriedly composed.

When Tania came home from the Hillerød hospital in 1960, Viggo had known her for more than two years and could claim a share of her affections previously accorded only to Eugene. How gratifying it was for her to know that she was adored, almost idolized, at an age when no woman could reasonably expect ever again to inspire such feelings! It was an even greater satisfaction to know that someone had a true insight into the intentions of her books. From the start Viggo had had an almost intuitive understanding of her aims, and sometimes, she realized, a grasp of certain elements in her work of which she herself had been only subconsciously cognizant. He was one of the first to perceive not only an aesthetic unity in the whole range of her writing but also a significant, quasi-organic unity in the work as it related to her personal life or destiny. Too great a distinction had always been made between the imaginative tales and the more factual *Out of Africa,* and too much emphasis had always been placed on the fantastic or weird aspect of her tales and the fact that she had not wished to set them in the twentieth century. "The fairy tale should be a serious statement about our existence," and in her own *Tales* it had been Tania's object to achieve this.

Viggo came often to see Tania. He made the journey from Jutland not by driving across Sjælland and taking the channel ferry as she did when she went to Leerbæk or Frijsenborg, but by taking the night ferry to Copenhagen and then the little toy train that ran from the city to Rungsted. On the return voyage to Aarhus, where he was now a teacher, the ferry sailed up the Øresund and he would stay on deck for a last landward glimpse of Tania's house, a sombre spreading shape in the night, with a lone light in the window of the room where she lay in bed reading. He had left her only a few hours before and already his thoughts would be racing ahead to the moment of their next meeting. Tania, he knew, was also impatient to have him come back. She had made it clear that she trusted him and felt increasingly that after her death, her name and reputation would rest more securely in his hands than in any others'.

In their many conversations she frequently spoke to him of the young Heretica writers. "They have all left me," she said sadly, fixing her eyes on him as if a vague doubt sometimes crossed her mind that he might do the same. She need not have worried. Questions of personal vanity did not enter into Viggo's attitude toward her, so he would never feel compelled to leave her.

Before the end of the year, Clara handed Tania several additions to the Isak Dinesen-Karen Blixen shelf. That shelf had grown and grown and was still growing. Soon it would take over an entire section of the library. By now there were twenty-six editions of *Out of Africa* and her American publisher had brought out an inexpensive hardcover edition, the Modern Library, which was pleasant proof of a continually widening circle of readers. The English edition had a very un-African jacket, rather like tapestry, and the Germans had used a painting by Rousseau. Tania disliked them both, but was proud of the fact that *Seven Gothic Tales*, brought out by Putnam's, London, had a frontispiece by Rex Whistler. The new items for the shelf were the Danish and British first printings of *Shadows on the Grass;* the December issue of *Esquire* magazine, containing the oft-told story "Letter from a King"; and the marionette comedy, *Sandhedens Hævn*, which was now, after a varied career of half a century, from children's performances to a presentation at the Royal Theatre, in a permanent, slim little volume published by Gyldendal.

II

Last Fling

—⌇⌇⌇—

In announcing *Shadows on the Grass* for January 1961, the Book-of-the-Month Club News, in addition to the usual review, contained a touching tribute from Robert Haas of Random House. "In one of her stories," concludes his article, "there is a lady who says, very simply, that a hostess wants only to be thanked. Well, Isak Dinesen has set before us feast after feast. So we should, I think, from deep down in our hearts, thank her for her elegant and sumptuous hospitality."

Generally speaking, the reviews of the new book about Africa were good—a few tinged with the accustomed sneers at her "florid" style, but many betraying an almost romantic enthusiasm for the author. Perhaps the most perceptive remark came, rather surprisingly, from *Time* magazine, January 6, 1961: "Many writers affect to understand Africa; Author Dinesen accepts and respects its opacities." William Jay Smith, in *The New Republic,* for January 23 also made the comparison with *Tourist in Africa,* by Evelyn Waugh, who had gone on from Kenya to Tanganyika,

Rhodesia and South Africa: "Mr. Waugh goes further and sees less, while the Baroness, distant, old, and ill, is always infinitely closer to her subject."

With the new book in print, Tania was all impatience to start another, in spite of the summer's long months of hospital treatment and the fact that she still was the victim of pain, nausea and all the old symptoms of exhaustion. Elizabeth Barrett Browning, for many years an invalid, had perhaps arrived at the best kind of acceptance when she suggested that physical suffering led to increased awareness: "If illness suppresses in us a few sources of pleasure, it leaves the real *ich* open to influences and keen-sighted to facts which are surely as natural as the fly's wing, though we are apt to consider them vaguely as supernatural." Other writers had made the same discovery. In *Freud and the Future*, Thomas Mann says that Nietzsche "on every page seems to instruct us that there is no deeper knowledge without experience of disease, and that all heightened healthiness must be achieved by the route of illness. This attitude too may be referred to his experience; but it is bound up with the nature of the intellectual man in general, of the creative artist in particular, yes, with the nature of humanity and the human being, of which last of course the creative artist is an extreme expression. '*L'Humanité,*' says Victor Hugo, '*s'affirme par l'infirmité,*' a saying which frankly and proudly admits the delicate constitution of all higher humanity and culture and their connoisseurship in the realm of disease. Man has been called '*das kranke Tier*' because of the burden of strain and explicit difficulties laid upon him by his position between nature and spirit, between angel and brute. What wonder, then, that by the approach through abnormality we have succeeded in penetrating most deeply into the darkness of human nature; that the study of disease—that is to

Tania in the bearskin coat, 1956/Aage Henriksen (left); Eugene Walter (right)

Tania with Anders at Øregaard/Leerbæk

Countess Wedell with Betsey/Wedellsborg

Tania with Edith Hamilton/Tania with Marilyn Monroe at Carson McCullers' house

Viggo Kjær Petersen/Tania with Clara and Pepper

Tania at the footbridge

The mayflowers/Last portrait

The grave on Ewald's Hill

say, neurosis—has revealed itself as a first-class technique of anthropological research?"

Much, however, as Tania may have agreed that ill-health and consequent neurosis might contribute to a heightened perception, she nevertheless wished these factors to remain a sort of mystique. She had a distinct aversion to Freudian probing as such, and as it manifested itself in modern literature. In an unpublished fragment of one of her newspaper interviews with Bent Mohn, she explained her position.

MOHN: You spoke of the unconscious. What do you think of Freud?

TANIA: I don't really know enough about Freud to pronounce myself about him. I have always had beautiful, happy dreams myself, and have felt free and serene. I have never experienced what is called a nightmare, but my dreams have seldom had any real connection with my daily life. I believe that Freud did his time a great service by acknowledging "complexes" or facing up to them and thereby freeing people of much worry and anxiety. But I believe also that those who came after him frequently carried his searchings too far, or that they misunderstood them. The roots of a tree, a plant, may be deep down in soil or darkness; when we don't pull them up to examine or study them this does not mean that we are unaware of them or that we want to underestimate or deny them. We know very well that they are the life conditions of the tree, perhaps the most important part of it. There are in the nature and being of people many things, perhaps the most significant among them, that demand darkness and that need to go unobserved in order to grow soundly.

The work which Tania now began was a new collection of stories to include a tale about Drude Angel entitled "Thirty Years After," "Ehrengard," "The Bear and the Kiss," "The Last Day," and others. She decided to get into her writing stride by revising "Ehrengard," a first version of which she had composed in 1950. At that time Clara had not felt that Tania was bringing any sort of "heightened perception" to this tale. All her devotion to Tania had never in the slightest impaired Clara's critical faculties, and as the work progressed she was filled with dismay. Again and again she interrupted her typing to look at Tania, trusting that she would alter this or that passage or even the general course of the story. But Tania was not going to allow herself to be overruled. She tolerated Clara's silent or spoken comments until she began to find them exasperating. Then she simply packed her off on a tour of northern Italy and southern France.

She finished the new version of "Ehrengard" and had it duplicated at considerable cost, but she felt unsure of the results. She then rewrote it a second time, had it duplicated again, and then was sufficiently satisfied to let the *Ladies' Home Journal* have it for publication, in 1962. In its final version it expounded some of Tania's favorite ideas, especially on the subject of women. One of the main characters in the book, the painter Cazotte, says: "However admirable she be, the woman who does not awaken in man the instinct of seducer is like the horse of the Chevalier de Kerguelen, which had all the good qualities in the world, but which was dead."

But such fragments were not enough to satisfy Clara, "You can imagine my sadness," she said later, "at the fact that this 'warming up' was the only part of the new book which was finished and declared ready for printing by Tania herself. Since she had insisted on acknowledging this story and taking it up again to rewrite, I felt it would be the only loyal thing to let it be published as she had wished. [It appeared in Denmark, England and the United States after her death, in 1963.] But, of course, I felt it was really too slight to stand alone in a volume by itself—in the Memorial Edition [Karen Blixen's complete works, which are being published by Gyldendal] we incorporated it in *Anecdotes of Destiny,* where Tania had had the plan of putting it originally." Clara's opinion of *Ehrengard* proved justified when the book appeared for, by any standards, it is a minor work, comparable only to *The Angelic Avengers.* The latter, however, was admittedly written merely as a pastime during the war, almost as a joke, and Tania disowned it by publishing it under a new pseudonym.

The moment had perhaps arrived when Tania's life was of greater importance than her writing. It is a sad juncture to which many creative artists come if they reach an advanced age, and it is fortunate for their self-esteem that few of them ever realize it.

In the spring of 1961 *Ehrengard* was temporarily laid aside, partly because of recurring periods of illness but mainly because once more Tania had the urge to travel, and when this mood was upon her she acquired a mysterious energy from no one knew where.

In June, Clara wrote to Eugene: ". . . Tania had to spend two days in bed having an awful time. Today she had to go to Copenhagen for a fitting of a suit, a fitting of several dresses somewhere else, a hairdo—so I feared the worst. But she managed it all; shopped for flowers on Højbroplads; after climbing the awful stairs at her tailor's (almost like Bent's) she walked all the way from Gammelstrand 46 round by the canal to Thorvaldsen's Museum to look at his best work including the marble bust of Byron; gave autographs to a girl in the street and to the Museum's special guest book; after the hairdo continued to Charlottenborg, climbed the stairs and went twice through the exhibition 'The Danish Landscape'; and back home after dinner she graciously invited a crowd of literary pilgrims to pass through the drawing room and out by the verandah where she was sitting herself; went into the garden to collect flowers for bouquets, made one and stored the rest for tomorrow! Would you not call that a day, for an invalid?

"As for Paris, what it will be like is totally unpredictable. It may be wonderful, but if Tania is sick and has to cancel engagements, it will be a strain for me apart from being a cruel disappointment for her. So I do not know at all what to advise you to do. Personally I should be delighted to know you were in Paris and to see as much of you as possible. But if you do not go I shall also be glad to know that you are at Dragør while I can spare the house . . ."

Tania also wrote to Eugene. She would be very happy, said her letter, to see him between June 15 and 20, before she left for Paris, and he could have Clara's cottage while they were abroad. But she had such a good time with him during his five days at Rungstedlund that at the last minute she couldn't bear to leave him behind. "1961 was the fabulous year," gloated Eugene. "I stayed at Rungstedlund, Dragør, and went to Paris to be with Tania there, at her request."

For weeks in advance, Tania was tense with anticipation over the trip. As with that perpetual traveler, Hans Christian Andersen, a change of scene renewed her inspiration whenever it became dulled by ennui. Perhaps, too, she sensed that this was to be a last fling. It was the prospect of more parties, more people, more outings at the theatre that had given her the strength to go through with the tedious fittings.

Clothes were very important, and in Paris, of all places, she must be properly dressed. Afterwards Clara wrote to Solita Solano: "You cannot imagine the rounds of fashion shows, inspection of what they have in the best shops, fittings, etc., etc., etc., that precede any additions to her wardrobe! Even if she can hardly stand on her legs! And when it is all over, I myself feel like joining a nudists' camp."

It was not that Tania wanted to be elaborately or extravagantly dressed or even that what she finally chose to wear was in any way extraordinary. She was simply a perfectionist, in this as in her prose, her flower arrangements, the hospitality she offered. When she put on things that other people wore, they immediately took on a curious personality of their own and in turn imparted to Tania an air which they couldn't have given to anyone else. The most banal knitted scarf tied around her head acquired the look of a medieval coif or wimple, and trousers which might have made other women seem masculine gave Tania the graceful aspect of a marsh bird on delicate, reedlike legs.

Like any other woman she was humanly pleased when her appearance met with success. A connoisseur's word of approval was flattering, but she had been just as delighted when the Kikuyu chiefs made long, admiring speeches to her about the silver brocade gown she was wearing when the Prince of Wales came out to dine at the farm. "Wait a little, Farah," she had pleaded. "I am talking with the old people, they are talking with me." "No, memsahib," said Farah. "No. Now these Kikuyus have said enough about this frock."

Tania felt, besides, that the garments one wore had an almost mystic significance and that they did much toward creating the true femininity, which she frequently observed was disappearing from the modern world. She would have applauded the wistful backward glance of Romain Gary when he said that "woman, pride and jewel of our civilization, no longer exists. She has become a human being."

It was a very feminine Tania who set out for Paris in the summer of 1961, filled with romantic verve in spite of her age, as pleased as any young girl with her new clothes, and happy to share the excitement with the persons she loved the most. The little group which escorted her was an incongruous, almost comical mixture of individuals: Clara, in her most Sancho Panza mood; Eugene Haynes, vivacious young Negro pianist; and Erling Schroeder, handsome, distinguished theatre director. Schroeder, having also had a premonition that this might be Tania's last trip abroad, had decided he must accompany her.

"I have been here nine days and have been to the theatre every evening," she told the reporters who came on July 4 for an interview at the Hotel France et Choiseul. "On the twenty-fourth of this month I have to be back in Denmark, but I shall continue going to the theatre every night until I leave." Though Shakespeare was her first and most enduring love, she said, she had always greatly admired the French theatre and the French tradition of acting. When she was twelve years old she had written her earliest essays on Racine and Corneille, and fifty-one years ago, when she had made her first visit to Paris, she had seen Sarah Bernhardt—*la divine Sarah!*—playing the role of Hamlet. The newspaper that printed the interview also reported that Hemingway had just finished his best novel, and Tania was pleased that they were once more in the news together.

She had, it was true, always been much impressed by the theatre in Paris and especially by the highly perfected performances of the Comédie Française, but she had, besides, what amounted to a passion for theatre of every kind—the puppet shows at Tivoli, ballet, Shakespeare in any language, and contemporary plays as well. It was for her an escape from everyday life into the fantastic but quite believable atmosphere which in her own writing she created for other people. She only drew the line at plays that aroused painful memories. Once during an earlier stay in Paris she had been invited to dinner and a performance of *The Diary of Anne Frank*. Recalling the wartime horror in Denmark of Jews concealed and ferried to Sweden, Jews betrayed and shipped to concentration camps, she begged to be excused immediately after dinner. Her hosts graciously changed the tickets and she found herself instead at a dramatized version of *The Castle*, by Franz Kafka. "And that was a real nightmare," she said afterwards, "worse even than Anne Frank's Diary."

To see plays this time in the company of Erling Schroeder, who brought to the subject a lifetime's experience of acting and directing, was a great pleasure for Tania. Sometimes Schroeder paid a price, however, for sitting next to her and hardly saw more of a play than the first act. On one such evening Tania leaned toward him and whispered, "Erling, I think I shall die if I do not have a biscuit right away." Schroeder rose and headed for the street. Where and how, at ten o'clock at night, in the neighborhood of the Place de l'Opéra, would he find the kind of biscuits that Tania was able to eat? He did succeed, slipped back into his seat, and handed the biscuits to Tania, who without a word and without averting her eyes for a moment from the stage, nibbled away at what was actually the only food she had had since morning. It never occurred to Schroeder that Tania might be considered capricious or wayward in her demands. He felt with Balzac that *"on ne doit jamais juger les gens qu'on aime. L'Affection qui n'est pas aveugle n'est pas."*

Several sojourns in Paris and an enthusiastic following of readers there had brought Tania a large and varied circle of acquaintances among the Faubourg Saint Germain, café society and intellectuals, including Princess de Polignac, the legendary Violet Trefusis, Edmée de la Rochefoucauld, Ghislain de Diesbach, Princess Dolly Radziwill (the wife of the Danish artist Mogens Tvede), Philippe de Rothschild, Philippe Jullian, Janet Flanner (the Paris correspondent known to *New Yorker* magazine readers as Genêt), Monica Stirling, and Solita Solano, who, with her almost naïve warmth and generosity, had especially endeared herself to both Tania and Clara. Tania crowded all of these people, at parties or singly, into her four-week stay and for good measure spent any spare daytime hours at art exhibitions or shopping.

"She appears to be hovering, elegant and unconcerned, on the very brink of death," commented one of her Paris friends, "and hastening the inevitable end by the exhausting life she leads."

"Ah, but wasn't it Tennyson who wrote: 'More and more life is what we want. Indifference to life is disease and therefore not strength,'" said someone else. "The Baroness derives strength and renews herself precisely because indifference to anyone or anything is totally alien to her nature."

"Just the same, human endurance has a limit. And what will become of Clara? Her life seems to be utterly submerged in the life of the Baroness. She's to be pitied, I suppose."

"Clara is in no way to be pitied," emphatically put in Janet Flanner, who had joined the group. "She has had two great romantic loves in her life—Byron and Isak Dinesen."

Had Janet Flanner known Clara better, decided the person who had first spoken, she could have added a third love—the Church; as Tania, too, had had her great loves which had given direction and meaning to her entire existence—her father, Denys Finch-Hatton and Africa, and her writing.

The engagement at the end of the month which lured Tania

back from Paris was the grand celebration on July 26 of Count Wedell's eightieth birthday. It had been assumed by the doctor and by Clara that Tania ought to rest after the strenuous exertions of her Parisian escapade, but she herself thought otherwise. Count Wedell was one of her oldest and closest friends and she refused to miss this occasion. No sooner had she and Clara arrived and unpacked at Rungstedlund than they packed up once again and were on their way to Wedellsborg.

The birthday banquet did not take place in the state dining room but in the great hall of the castle, with its high beamed ceilings, its Renaissance mantel and furnishings, and its atmosphere of cinquecento festivity. A long table had been set up, laden with Wedellsborg's unique silver and crystal, and a double row of candles. Tania, in a beaded white gown with an elaborately pleated skirt and a capelet to hide her painfully thin arms, sat next to Tido Wedell, who because of a tragic accident was to inherit his father's title in less than a month.

At the end of the dinner Tania rose and made a speech which ended with a long poem about friendship:

> "... *On s'approche, on sourit, la main touche la main*
> *Et nous nous souvenons que nous marchons ensemble*
> *Que l'âme est immortelle—et qu'hier c'est demain.*"

Three years after Tania's death Clara came across the poem at Rungstedlund and was moved to find that it and the after-dinner speech had been typed by Tania herself on the old portable Corona which she had brought back from Africa, and on which she had also typed every line of her first three books.

After Wedellsborg, Clara went to her cottage for two days of rest and relaxation. Young and sturdy as she was, even she felt wilted after the excesses of Paris and the birthday celebration. Dragør, she found, was all caught up in the revelries of the *Havnefest*, the harbor festival which had been held there traditionally for many long years. She rode on the merry-go-round, disported herself with the townsfolk, and for forty-eight hours put cares and worries out of her mind.

As for Tania, it became increasingly clear that she could no longer overdo with impunity. Each time she paid a heavier price for having been tempted by too much work or too much gaiety. On September 10 she was obliged to write to Solita Solano canceling a promised invitation for a weekend at Rungstedlund: "I have no strength at all and I cannot stand up or take two steps from one room to another. I think that my miserable state of health now comes from a long time of undernourishment; the doctor tells me that all my symptoms, such as the really terrible swelling of my feet, legs and hands are typical concentration camp prisoners' worries. Also my sight and hearing have grown suddenly much worse." The doctor was urging her to come at once to the hospital for blood transfusions and serum but Tania had been there too many times with only negative or temporary results, and she had little faith in any cure or treatment. Perhaps she ought to try American doctors? They couldn't do any worse. "I am not good at resigning myself" was her conclusion. "I have never before felt so low in spirit." Solita was in despair when she read the letter. Her feeling for Tania from the first moment she met her had been a tender, almost possessive affection and a respect that bordered on reverence. When Tania gave in and went to the hospital, she sent letters, roses and a book. What more could she do?

A timely gift also awaited Tania at home, a grey Dandie Dinmont brought by Baroness Bille-Brahe Selby. Nothing could have done more to revive Tania's spirits. Having always kept and loved dogs, she felt somehow incomplete without one, and Pasop's death had left a great void. The new little terrier was given the name of Pepper, from Walter Scott's *Guy Mannering*, a most prophetic choice. Shy at first, cowering under the drawing-room stove when guests arrived, he gradually grew bolder and developed a peppery temper. When Clara fell heir to him after Tania's death, he became an absolute tyrant and had tantrums of jealousy if anyone so much as spoke to her. Clara, too, became a jealous guardian of Pepper's status, both as a favored dog who had once belonged to Tania and as a true aristocrat of his breed, lean, high-strung, intelligent and courageous, and she was truly indignant when he was described in *Vogue* magazine as "low-slung and fat."

Pepper never succeeded in filling Pasop's place in Tania's heart, but he amused her and he helped her resign herself to being a semi-invalid. She now was unable to walk at all without assistance and she spent her days in an armchair with Pepper keeping her company during the rare moments when she was without callers. Nothing would induce her to give up the fatiguing stream of people that kept coming to see her; only now, instead of giving them tea in the drawing room as before, she began to receive on the verandah overlooking the Sound. It was as if she could not see enough of the ships and sailboats, the gulls, and the sky and sea in all their varying moods.

III

"My Life, I Will Not Let You Go..."

—⁓⁓⁓—

Already the days had grown short. By midafternoon the setting sun aimed its last luminous darts at the trees on Ewald's Hill and then the long night closed in, engulfing woods, house, gardens, and a grey sea where sailboats no longer shuttled back and forth providing a passing show for Tania. Sails furled, the little boats were safely laid up in port for the winter. "And here am I," mourned Tania, "sails furled too—wings clipped, one might say—moored for the winter in my old ramshackle inn. No, not so ramshackle any more, but a warm snug harbor." And when spring returned and boats put out into the Sound again, would she still have the strength to sally forth once more? *"Navigare necesse est . . ."* but perhaps her old motto would have to be reversed. Perhaps now she would have to resign herself to a new necessity—merely to live, and to put sailing out of her mind for good.

Architect Rasmussen stopped in to see her and she remembered to tell him how very pleased she was with the house. He was to be chairman of the Rungstedlund Foundation and had many details to settle with her. While he was there, or other good friends and neighbors, Clara felt free to slip away to her room. In October she had agreed to translate Carson McCullers' *Clock Without Hands* and somehow or other she would get it finished, though she was more and more reluctant to leave Tania alone or with strangers for even an hour.

Tania sat in her chair and talked and dozed, talked and dozed, while the neighbors and friends came and went. Loath to believe it, they nevertheless saw her growing paler and frailer day by day. The sinister collection of vials and goblets at her end of the dining-room table contained the only nourishment she seemed willing or able to take, though Clara pleaded and Fru Carlsen tried everything. She was withdrawing from them all, little by little, inevitably, divesting herself of flesh and blood and any material needs, and only her eyes in their deepening sockets retained a semblance of life and fire. "Time," Truman Capote had said, "has reduced her to an essence, as a grape can become a raisin, roses an attar."

As she became more remote and insubstantial, those who watched over her became increasingly conscious of what she had meant to them in the past. Rasmussen assembled his recollections in an article that appeared in *Berlingske Tidende* on April 17, 1965, which would have been her eightieth birthday, and it was reprinted afterwards in a little pamphlet. He payed tribute to Tania as painter, writer and friend. In particular, he spoke of the time when she had gone every day to visit a blind and crippled neighbor—not to commiserate with him, since she herself would have repudiated pity, but to be of encouragement. The man had been an avid reader all his life and had an extraordinary memory for history and literature. He longed now for something new, so Tania had set herself the task of inventing a tale to tell him every afternoon, preparing as carefully for these sessions as for her audience at the Poetry Center.

Birthe Arnbak, always touched by Tania's devotion to little Ole, cherished a memory of the day when Tania had found her very depressed by bad reviews of her book of poems. Immediately after she returned home Tania sent off a letter lending wings to Birthe's efforts. "My advanced age permits me to write you this," she said, following it up with sound advice and enclosing all the unfavorable Danish reviews of *Seven Gothic Tales* to show that they had no bearing at all on one's eventual success. And on another occasion she had further proven her interest by reciting the younger author's poems from memory.

As for Viggo, he refused to envisage a future without Tania. His encounter with her had been the turning point in all his aims and ambitions. Every hour he spent with her seemed to reveal new possibilities, new subjects for consideration, new ideas to explore. She had become, he said, the real inspiration of his life. It was a privilege he wanted to share, and knowing the pleasure Tania took in a circle of listeners, he brought many young writers to meet her, and finally Jens Kruuse, who had for so many years admired her from a distance and championed her in his column in *Jyllands-Posten.*

Convinced that she could not live much longer and that she had written her last book, some of her devotees were tempted to try to assess Tania's total achievement as an author. What would her place be, they wondered, in the history of permanent literature? They were not so naïve as to give importance to the fact that she had always been a best seller; nor did it matter that she had not received the ultimate mark of distinction conferred by the Nobel Prize. Fashions in writing come and go, and the respected authors of one generation may sink into obscurity during the next, some to remain forgotten, others to be rediscovered and to acquire a second fame. Today there are few who can read such once-admired novels as those of Zola or the Goncourt brothers; Henry James, on the contrary, has emerged from neglect as one of the idols of the contemporary intelligentsia. France has her Académie of "Immortals," but even the relative immortality of a writer would seem to be a question which only the passage of time could resolve.

While the pros and cons were being debated and people anxiously hovered around her, Tania herself appeared quite unconcerned. She no longer spoke of finishing *Albondocani,* and her main preoccupation was with death itself rather than posterity. "Death is my oldest flirt," she remarked more than once, and with a certain coyness. She had faced death in the shape of a charging lion or rhinoceros; she had courted death after Denys died; and furiously she had fought off death with each successive illness. Now death was like an old familiar lover with whom one achieves an easy, semiplatonic relationship.

To people who did not know her well, Tania also often appeared to be on casual, even frivolous terms with God. In conversation and in writing she attributed to the Deity a whimsicality which expressed itself in weird beasts and flowers, thunder and lightning and other extravagances of nature, as well as the quirks and coincidences that marked human events. "God loves a joke," she would say. But she also attributed to God the all-seeing wisdom that laid out an ineludible destiny for every individual; and it was her submission to this which enabled her to accept the idea of her own death. Her acceptance of God's will was positive rather than negative, a fulfillment rather than the puritan's abnegation of life. Her beliefs did not intrude on the closed world of nonbelievers but instead offered new horizons to adherents of any creed. "If I discussed my religious beliefs with Isak Dinesen," said the ardently Roman Catholic Clara, "there was always an insurmountable barrier. But as she wrote her stories it happened time after time that they came to contain ideas about these matters which I could never have formulated myself, which I felt very doubtful about and even protested against—and then to my surprise found to be shared by such particularly deep-digging pioneer theologians as I had the good luck to meet with."

In *Out of Africa* she had already set down some thoughts about life and death:

"An old lady sat in a party and talked of her life. She declared that she would like to live it all over again and held this fact to prove that she had lived wisely. I thought: Yes, her life has been the sort of life that should really be taken twice before you can say that you have had it. An arietta you can take *da capo*, but not a whole piece of music—not a symphony and not a five-act tragedy either. If it is to be taken over again it is because it has not gone as it ought to have gone.

"My life, I will not let you go except you bless me, but then I will let you go."

In the last years of her life Tania was fond of quoting from a poem by Walter Savage Landor:

> ". . . *Nature I loved; and next to Nature, Art.*
> *I warm'd both hands before the fire of life;*
> *It sinks, and I am ready to depart.*"

She was not, however, in this winter of 1961–62, in spite of the forebodings of the friends who surrounded her, she was not at all ready to depart.

IV
Partings

—⁓⁓—

During that last interminable winter Tania sat in her chair and
longed for spring. A pale sun doled out its stingy quota of daylight
hours, and from every window wherever she looked the view was
bleak. A thicket of twigs and thorns was all that was left of her
hedge of Nevada roses, and out beyond it the sky was grey, the
Sound was leaden. Cowering under the dripping fog, Hveen Island
was slowly dissolving into the sea.

Seeing the tangle of gnarled bare boughs at the back door, one
could hardly imagine that it could ever come round again to its
spring profusion of lilac and green. As who could believe that
Tania would rise from her wearisome chair and walk out into the
garden once more? Numbed and withdrawn into herself like an
animal that hibernates, she sat out the winter, drowsing, dreaming
and waiting for May. Somehow the manuscript of *Ehrengard* was
being completed, and many letters went off to distant friends. And
sometimes when Viggo was with her she seemed to recapture her
old *élan,* her *joie de vivre*. Eyes kindling, she would launch into a

story, a story perhaps too often told with the propensity of the very old to repeat themselves again and again, a story which nevertheless always retained the special savor that Tania alone could bring to it. Viggo listened enthralled. Once when the conversation turned to matters relating to him, he spoke of the doctor's thesis which he would soon have to prepare. "Will you write another thesis about my books?" Tania wanted to know, and was not in the least put off when he reminded her of the traditional objection to papers on living authors. "I think we should do it," she urged, "I think we should try." The "we" was encouraging—a happy conspiracy—and their talks became a collaboration as a result of which Viggo became the only person, apart from Clara, with a detailed, firsthand understanding of her aims.

And then at long last spring arrived. Not when the calendar indicated its arrival, but when the skies suddenly cleared and turned blue and the Sound mirrored the blue of the sky and sea gulls were wheeling overhead and sailboats went scudding by on the sea, and beeches unfurled their pale new leaves and mayflowers spilled their white stars down the slopes . . . and Tania began to live again.

Nils, albino-pale from the long winter, was out in the sun in the backyard. He had become Nils the boatbuilder. The hull of his boat, begun in his basement workshop under the south wing of the house, was hauled up into the light, the half-finished boat of one of his friends was racked up alongside, and Tania listened contentedly to the clamor of sawing and hammering and boys' voices.

Fru Carlsen came in with the first violets clutched in her hand, and Clara found Tania herself ready and impatient to go out for a walk.

"Why," Tania kept asking herself during those days, "why does not the heart grow old along with an aging body? Why does one have to put up with the torment of a perpetually young, yearning heart entrapped in shabby, worn-out flesh that cannot keep pace with it?" How sad it was to long to be part of the spring, part of the world of flying, flowering, growing things, and to be good for nothing more than to totter a few steps beyond the house, leaning on Clara's arm like a broken reed!

But as it had happened many times before when she was coping with illness, laying plans for a trip abroad or trying to finish writing a book, strength came with her need and desire for strength, forces surged up within her because she willed it so. In the spring she walked a few steps across the lawn, then she walked out to the pond to feed the ducks; and before spring became summer she was talking of new work, travel and dinner parties.

Solita Solano was still hoping to visit Tania and in the meanwhile letters sped back and forth between Rungstedlund and Paris. Any subject was grist for this correspondence and Solita collected a cross-section of many of Tania's opinions and whims. "There are a few things in life which in themselves, notwithstanding the quantity, give you the feeling of unlimited wealth," said one of Tania's letters. "One such thing to my mind is linen, bed or table linen or underwear, in really fine quality. I have still got a few chemises, made in Paris for my trousseau, in real, fine batiste, and am keeping one to be buried in."

Only Tania would have thought of keeping part of her trousseau to be buried in. Always and always her thoughts reverted to death and the grave. But now at last death could no longer be far away, she was convinced, and it led her thoughts on to the question of her biography. No doubt, it was more than time for further interviews—last interviews, perhaps.

She who had always done the writing, how was she now to convey without written words all she had cherished most in her life, her love for Rungstedlund and Folehave, scenes of so many childhood sorrows, scenes too of joys she had only later learned to value. Some of the places could be visited but she could not be sure that they would speak for themselves. Or that another person would feel what she had seen and felt, and say it for her. Others might go to Elsinore, but would it be the Elsinore of her de Coninck sisters? "The palace [at Hirschholm] that had housed such blasphemy was itself left and finally pulled down, partly because the royal family did not like to see it, partly because it was said to be sinking, of itself, into the lake. The whole splendour disappeared, and a church, in the classical style of the dawning nineteenth century, was erected where the palace had stood, like a cross upon its grave." Others might visit the lake at Hirschholm and look across to the church on its grassy island, but would anyone ever sense what her thoughts about it had been when, as a little girl in her grandmother's house, her fingers were busy embroidering and her dreams went flying out of the window toward the lake, its sunken castle and unhappy queen?

"My life, I will not let you go except you bless me." My life, I will not let you go until I have given you, shared you, poured you out in all the stories that can be told.

Rungstedlund showed itself forth that May in all its most radiant moods. Sometimes it seemed like a display of what Tania described as "charlatanry" and "divine swank." A blue-eyed boy, bareback upon a white horse, rode up the beach, splashing along in the white surf of a blue sea where white boats with blue sails drifted under a blue sky with white gulls winging and soaring. After the boy and his horse were out of sight, one could only ask what painter would have dared such a blue and white palette. Night descended, the strange, luminous dark of Nordic nights, and a hundred candles flickered and gleamed in the windows. It was May 4, and there the old house was, exactly as it had been on a night seventeen years before when Tania and all of Denmark wept and exulted over the Liberation. "Has Clara shown you my grave?" asked Tania, as she had asked countless times before. And Clara again led the way to the top of Ewald's Hill, following the path where many years ago Wilhelm had walked hand in hand with little Tanne. Clara knew all the ins and outs of the promenade. She lingered so that the ancient lilac tree could be admired, she waited a moment at the bridge, and she loitered along the uphill path to allow guests to exclaim over the mayflowers. "The woods," said Clara appreciatively, "are beautiful this year." So they were. So they had been in Ewald's and Wilhelm's day, and so they would be when time had eroded the stone on Tania's grave.

Thomas and Jonna came; Inger Wedell and another dear friend, Fritze Ahlefeldt-Laurvig, came for tea; Anders came down from the lonely heights of Leerbæk to spend a few days. People. That was what Tania liked, and her spirits soared. Anders, solitary and sparing of words as ever, went alone to the garden to cut the flowers that Tania wanted. She was decorating the house for his birthday—the sixty-eighth—elated at the pretext for making bouquets, for giving a festive dinner party, for bringing out a seldom-worn frock and jewel.

While the guests devoted themselves to the chefs-d'œuvre which Fru Carlsen sent in from the kitchen (they were visual works of art as well as delectable), Tania held forth from her end of the table. Anders abstractedly opened the birthday presents piled next to his plate, listening to his sister with the gentle, remote smile of someone who has just emerged from the wilds and has not yet made his peace with society. Tania talked on and on, interrupting herself from time to time to toss out a challenging question. "Who," she finally demanded, as intransigently as Castiglione's Emilia Pia, "who were the most representative geniuses of each of the great nations, the ones who have made the most important contributions to civilization?"

To the suggestion that music—Bach—was Germany's contribution she countered that Goethe ranked before Bach—before Mozart even, since she personally disliked Bach. For Italy she chose Michelangelo in preference to Leonardo, which touched off a heated argument. As for the Danes, a Hans Christian Andersen tale, perhaps "The Ugly Duckling." And after debating the virtues of Lincoln's and Jefferson's writings, she concluded that *Huckleberry Finn* might be the choice for the United States. France she merely dismissed with a Gallic shrug of the shoulders, and everyone laughed. It was a game, of course—a parlor game, the beguiling game of the Court of Urbino, but Tania was very arbitrary. Who else would have dared to link the splendors of Michelangelo with the homelier merits of *Huckleberry Finn*? The game, in her hands, gradually turned into a dissertation. She was entertaining her guests, to be sure; but she was also thinking aloud, sifting and summing up for herself a lifetime of reading and meditation.

By the end of the week Clara had cause for alarm again as she saw Tania completely caught up in the momentum of too much activity. Not content with visitors and the birthday party, Tania wanted "to stir, to get about, to meet new people" and had commandeered Thomas to drive them all to Elsinore, to the King's summer palace of Fredensborg, and to Frederiksborg Castle and its park, on the outskirts of which stood Thomas' own house. The following day it had been an excursion to Knud W. Jensen's new Louisiana museum, where "5000 Years of Egyptian Art" was on view. This time Anders had taken them there in his little car, driving at top speed with his mind on the sky and the gulls, the cows in the fields, the sea, on anything except the road. At one point he hurtled up onto a sidewalk rather than slowing down for an elderly pedestrian who took too long in crossing. Tania, merely exhilarated by a ride which had left the other passengers stunned, chatted with the visiting curator from the Cairo Museum, and during tea at Louisiana's cafeteria laid plans for the next afternoon's adventure. And the next. To Hørsholm to see the lake of "The Poet" and the church on the site of the sunken Hirschholm palace; to the museum and gardens at Øregaard; to Folehave to call on her niece, Anne Kopp; to a forest to listen to nightingales singing. And with all the new-found energy, she walked as far as the edge of Rungstedlund's woods.

Nor was Solita deprived of her visit. She arrived from Paris and enjoyed at firsthand all the details of Tania's life which hitherto she had only known through letters: the routine of free mornings for the guest while Tania stayed in her bedroom to dictate or rest; afternoon drives and excellent dinners; coffee and liqueurs in the drawing room while Tania and Clara played their nightly game of bezique. She was shown the Masai spears in Tania's study, the painting of young Abdullahi in his bright turban, the shelf that held Denys' books and Denys' photograph. She saw portraits of Tania's father and mother, and all the things, large and small, that make up the character of a house long lived in and much loved. It didn't seem possible that Tania would go to Elsinore again. But she did, and from there to a restaurant in the town where "with both of us before her and tea ordered, she set herself out to enchant . . . This inanimate invalid who had crept forth from a deathbed (she had been very ill and in great pain the previous night) now became from the shoulders up a true siren with electric lamps for eyes, a restored face of high beauty and a speech that flowed on without stopping for an hour."

Eugene Haynes had returned to Denmark too and on June 12

Tania gave a dinner, the main purpose of which was to bring him together with Viggo, whom he had never met. Several years later he wrote about it at length: "I remember that dinner party very well. Tania and Clara were radiant. Anders was to send a goose, but sent a turkey instead. For the first time in my long association with Rungstedlund, the conversation was all in Danish, Tania's charming way of emphasizing my complete acceptance. I always regarded the lack of a piano as a nice symbol of my being just a good friend. As you know, conversation *chez* Tania always sparkled, and she seemed to enjoy talking with me. When a piano is present an artist is not always certain which is wanted, him or his music. She *never* asked me to entertain the guests. Once she brought several close relatives in to see Clara's spinet, and I played a Debussy 'Arabesque'—on my own initiative."

Birthe Andrup and Bent Mohn had also been asked to attend the party for Eugene. It was a touching aspect of Tania's many generosities that she gave her friends to each other, wanting them to be mutually helpful and stimulating, and encouraging a true rapport among many of them which endured after her death. In the summer months following their first meeting Eugene and Viggo became really close friends, and much of Tania's last letter to Viggo, written a few days before her death, dealt with their friendship and her happiness at having brought them together.

It was Viggo who escorted Tania to a dazzling last evening at the theatre shortly before the close of the ballet season, a gala performance of Lander's *Les Victoires de l'Amour* and *Etudes* at the Royal Theatre. Bent and another friend joined them. "Tania came in alone in the car, all in black, more beautiful than ever. The King was there and the usual crowd of Copenhagen diplomatic society, but everybody was looking at *her*. When the King came into the royal box, of course everyone rose—except Tania, who said: 'I am really afraid I cannot get up this time.'. . . When *Etudes* was over it was over almost impossible to get her out. She kept saying: 'Oh, it cannot be over. It was beautiful, so very beautiful! How I wish it would go on!' "

Tania had first seen ballet as a young girl in Copenhagen, she had been among the fortunate ones to attend a Paris performance of Diaghilev's troupe in 1910, and she shared the possessive pride that Danes have in the Royal Danish Ballet. Viggo, with all his unwillingness to think of life without Tania, must have sensed nevertheless that she was now seeing her last ballet. Her eyes glowed, her voice throbbed with excitement, but it was a wraith who sat in the theatre with him.

On August 2, Clara wrote: "Tania's health has deteriorated. More and more she needs someone at hand constantly."

Four days later Eugene came out for the afternoon. He recorded the conversation in his diary and later wrote several pages about it for the Isak Dinesen Memorial Book. "When I arrived at Rungstedlund at about three-thirty P.M. on August sixth, the Baroness was sitting on the enclosed veranda that looks out on the soft green lawn. The Swedish coast seemed close enough to touch. She embraced me as though I were a son, gave me strawberries to eat (red ones and pink ones from her gardens) and as I had just returned from Greece—having succumbed along with so many other people in Denmark this year to the lure of Hellenism—she asked me questions about Mycenae, Corinth, Olympia, the Acropolis and Aegina.

"It was an afternoon I would never forget. Ten years ago Bent Mohn had brought me out for my first visit to Rungstedlund. We had often said, in jest, that I was a bit of Africa sent out to comfort the 'Honorable Lioness' in her last years. She had offered her friendship and I had prized it. She had shared beautiful hours with me at Rungstedlund, in Paris, in New York—and now, as though we had come full circle, we were having our last dialogue. Is it possible to know such things? I would have to insist that we both felt that this was to be a great parting."

There were, during that summer, many partings. Perhaps a fatidical intuition is what grows out of the heightened perception induced by illness. Perhaps, simply, she knew her own weariness. She forewarned Cecil Beaton, "If you do not come now you will never see me again," and she had said the same to others. When they left her house she insisted on seeing each one as far as the courtyard door, and they carried away a last image of her, a pathetically dwindled figure leaning on Clara's arm for support, her eyes filled with tears, waving kisses and farewells.

V

The World Withdraws

—ᘠᘠᘠ—

Tania falls asleep by the fire. Yes, there is a fire constantly blazing on the hearth though it is summer and the central heating is on. It is so hot in the drawing room that the daily rose nods and scatters its petals on the table long before its day is done. But Tania is cold all the time. The blood in her veins is pulsing feebly and she has complained lately that her fingers feel numb.

When she opens her eyes she will find Erling Schroeder sitting beside her. How handsome he is, she thinks. Small wonder everyone falls in love with him. She is a bit in love with him too. She smiles at him encouragingly because she sees he is somehow on the defensive. He has not yet learned to accept what he considers the fall and decline of his youthful good looks; he has not yet sensed a transition to something far more alluring and valid, so she smiles at him reassuringly. She would like to— But she doesn't say it because she knows that he would not like to hear it. Instead they talk of other things. For years she has hated any allusion to weakness or old age, but with Erling she has always felt free to complain. She cannot walk . . . she is in pain . . . Clara does this or does not do that . . . "they" have never appreciated her . . . so-and-so has not come to see her . . . She knows she can grumble like this to Erling and he still will think her brave, wise, witty, unique—a witch, in fact. He will still love her, and that is consoling. But the effort of talking to him has tired her, and now she will sleep again.

On another day Thomas' daughter Bitter comes to have tea with her, and seeing the strength that radiates from this beautiful lithe young creature, Tania decides that she will get up and walk. So they walk out to the garden, Tania biting her lip to hold back the pain, leaning on Bitter's arm, a frail sick bird with a broken wing, a reed that cannot stand alone, gossamer which the wind will dishevel and blow away. When they come back to the house she is too tired to drink the tea that Fru Carlsen brings, but she listens to Bitter with interest and feeling. Bitter has difficulties in her life and doesn't know how to solve them. They are all traveling somewhere in search of something, alone and in darkness, thinks Tania. *Ibant obscuri per umbram sub sola nocte.* They have not yet learned to be, like her natives, "on friendly terms with destiny." What shall she tell this child? What *can* she tell her?

Clara comes to sit with her too but Tania is now too tired to tell more tales. *Albondocani* will not be finished. Just the same, she would like to tell Clara . . . but this too will be left unsaid.

The weather is fine and Tania lies in a deck chair on the lawn, swathed in blankets and shawls, with Pepper asleep at her feet. In the backyard, on the other side of the trellis fence, sedate Ping Pong is drowsing in the sun with a sleepy eye on the people who visit the bird sanctuary and straggle uphill and down, hushing their voices as they approach the house. Never has there been a calmer, more golden afternoon. It is still, almost breathless on the lawn, but high overhead a wind is propelling huge white clouds across the sky, islands of vapor afloat on a sea of blue ether. A cloud drifts in front of the sun; its wide dark shadow runs over the grass and Tania's thoughts are running with it: . . . "a shadow hastened over the grass and over my feet, and looking up I could distinguish, high in the light-blue sky, the circling of vultures. My heart was as light as if I had been flying it, there, on a string, as you fly a kite. I made a poem:

> *'The eagle's shadow runs across the plain,*
> *Towards the distant, nameless air-blue mountains . . .'* "

. . . the air-blue mountains, the Ngong Hills, where Denys now lies alone in the grave they chose together.

September 6: Clara to Solita Solano.

Dearest Solita,

Tania is terribly ill. Please thank Elizabeth for her letter, and thank her from Tania for the record player. It came yesterday, and she spent the evening listening to Mozart and a Handel aria that Denys Finch-Hatton used to sing. Now if the doctor is right in what he says she will never hear it again. I cannot yet believe it is true, but perhaps it is . . .

Thomas and Jonna had come, and Fru Carlsen and Clara were there. They stood at the door of her bedroom, and to Tania it was as it had been when she left her farm in Kenya: "As I . . . looked at

them a fancy came back to me that had taken hold of me before:
It was not I who was going away, I did not have it in my power to
leave Africa, but it was the country that was slowly and gravely
withdrawing from me, like the sea in ebb tide."

The world was withdrawing from her, and she fell asleep.

Notes

Bibliography

Index

Notes

PART ONE

I Wilhelm

4   *Note 1*   "Fair one . . ."   Johannes Ewald, "Til Jomfrue Anna Hedevig Jacobsen" (1773), translation by Clara Svendsen. Ewald (1743–81) was Denmark's greatest lyrical poet, later acclaimed for reforming the pompous rhetoric of his day and for arousing interest in the ancient Danish myths.

8   *Note 2*   Tycho Brahe (1546–1601), the great Danish astronomer. His observatory was on Hveen Island in the Sound, opposite Rungsted.

10   *Note 3*   Boganis, pseudonym of A. Wilhelm Dinesen. His book *Jagtbreve* (Letters from the Hunt), 1890 and 1892, is considered a classic of its kind in Denmark and has been reprinted many times.

II Katholm

19   *Note 4*   "Copenhagen Season" in *Last Tales*, 1957, p. 260.

III First Stories

27   *Note 5*   Georg Brandes (1842–1927), one of Denmark's greatest literary critics and essayists. P.M. Mitchell says: "The deep and

lasting impression Brandes made upon his time is recorded not only in literary history but in literature itself . . ."

PAGE

31 *Note 6* These and several other poems, the Norwegian Saga frag-ment, "The Ploughman," "The Hermits" and "The de Cats Family" were published after Isak Dinesen's death in *Osceola*, 1962. They have not appeared in English translation.

IV Bror

37 *Note 7* "We rode in the . . ." Eugene Walter, "Isak Dinesen," *Paris Review* (Autumn 1956), pp. 43–59.

41 *Note 8* "The human imagination . . ." Bror von Blixen-Finecke, *African Hunter* [*Nyama*], 1938, p. 5.

42 *Note 9* ". . . if you commission . . ." *Out of Africa*, 1938, p. 244.

PART TWO

I Tycho Brahe Days

46 *Note 10* "No one had . . ." *African Hunter*, p. 279.

47 *Note 11* ". . . one figure . . ." *Shadows on the Grass*, 1961, p. 3.

49 *Note 12* "wrote and instructed . . ." *Out of Africa*, p. 266.

50 *Note 13* "The introduction into . . ." *Shadows on the Grass*, p. 15.

50 *Note 14* "On the third evening . . ." *African Hunter*, pp. 91–2.

53 *Note 15* "Out on the safaris . . ." *Out of Africa*, p. 15.

59 *Note 16* "The Star," poem quoted in *No Man's Land*, by Thomas Dinesen (1929), and published posthumously in *Osceola*.

II *Happiness in Africa*

PAGE
62   *Note 17*   "was a great figure . . ."   *Eton College Chronicle*, obituary of Denys Finch-Hatton, May 21, 1931.

63   *Note 18*   "Denys could indeed . . ."   *Out of Africa*, p. 215.

64   *Note 19*   "had no other home . . ."   *Ibid.*, p. 225.

65   *Note 20*   "We sat over . . ."   *Ibid.*, p. 157.

65   *Note 21*   "I knew very little . . ."   *Ibid.*, p. 24.

66   *Note 22*   "Letter from a King" in *Shadows on the Grass*, pp. 51 ff.

IV *Thomas in Kenya*

78   *Note 23*   ". . . in contrast with . . ."   Letter from Thomas Dinesen to the author, July 3, 1963.

80   *Note 24*   "It was very lonely . . ."   *Out of Africa*, p. 20.

80   *Note 25*   "In Africa when . . ."   *Ibid.*, p. 90.

V *Farewell*

83   *Note 26*   "It was a large ugly . . ."   Letter from Lady Diana Tiarks to the author, July 3, 1963. It is curious that both the estate of Denys Finch-Hatton's family and Tania's farm in Kenya should have become girls' schools. Karen College, named after Tania, is a group of modern buildings constructed by the Danish government in co-operation with Kenya, but the old farmhouse and its garden are still a feature of the college.

84   *Note 27*   "Farah came . . ."   *Out of Africa*, pp. 323–4.

PART THREE

I Seven Gothic Tales

PAGE

94   *Note 28*   "what was most profound . . ."   Marcel Brion, *Schumann and the Romantic Age* (The Macmillan Company, New York, 1965), p. 83.

96   *Note 29*   "I am so much under its spell . . ."   Dorothy Canfield, *Book-of-the-Month Club News* (March 1934).

96   *Note 30*   "Some five years . . ."   Robert Haas, *ibid.* (February 1938).

97   *Note 31*   "Over a quarter . . ."   *Ibid.* (December 1960).

99   *Note 32*   ". . . there is a great deal . . ."   Dorothy Canfield, *ibid.* (March 1934).

100 *Note 33*   Frederick Schyberg, *Berlingske Tidende* (Copenhagen, September 25, 1935).

101 *Note 34*   "There was much disease . . ."   *Shadows on the Grass*, pp. 115 ff.

II Geneva Interlude

103 *Note 35*   Baroness Budberg was Moura Benckendorff by her first marriage. According to Harold Nicolson's *Diaries & Letters*, H.G. Wells intended to marry her. She also had been an intimate friend of Maxim Gorki.

III Out of Africa

107 *Note 36*   "I cannot say . . ."   *African Hunter*, p. 3.

113 *Note 37*   ". . . and herons stand . . ."   R. Ellsworth Larsson, *O City, Cities!* (Payson and Clark, New York, 1929), p. 98.

IV More Tycho Brahe Days

PAGE
116 Note 38 "travel grant . . ." It has long been a custom for the King of Denmark to bestow travel grants on distinguished authors and artists for purposes of research and inspiration. Hans Christian Andersen spent most of his adult life traveling thanks to such grants.

117 Note 39 ". . . all the young men . . ." "The Monkey" in *Seven Gothic Tales*, 1934, p. 122.

118 Note 40 "She was the woman . . ." *Out of Africa*, p. 190.

119 Note 41 The Berlin articles appeared as they were written. Eight years later they were published in *Heretica* magazine, and were then included in an anthology of Danish literary essays published by Erling Nielson, Norway.

V Winter's Tales

121 Note 42 "There is nothing . . ." "The Monkey" in *Seven Gothic Tales*, p. 145.

122 Note 43 "I felt, in a way . . ." *Isak Dinesen: A Memorial*, 1965, p. 12.

123 Note 44 "I can sign . . ." *Shadows on the Grass*, p. 134.

123 Note 45 ". . . the very same fatality . . ." "Sorrow-acre" in *Winter's Tales*, 1942, p. 51.

124 Note 46 "who behaved as . . ." *Shadows on the Grass*, p. 18.

125 Note 47 Robert Langbaum, *The Gayety of Vision*, 1965, p. 74.

125 Note 48 " 'Madame,' said the Cardinal . . ." *Seven Gothic Tales*, p. 14.

VI The Angelic Avengers

128 Note 49 "It was on that Sunday . . ." Letter from Birthe Andrup to the author, June 17, 1963.

132 Note 50 "Since I looked upon it . . ." *Shadows on the Grass*, p. 132.

VII Clara

136 Note 51 "felt, as with no other . . ." *Isak Dinesen: A Memorial*, p. 204.

143 Note 52 "I have been trying . . ." *Seven Gothic Tales*, p. 355.

143 Note 53 "The real difference . . ." *Ibid.*, pp. 121–2.

VIII The Heretica Movement

154 Note 54 "The story suggests . . ." *The Gayety of Vision*, p. 225.

IX Of Birds and Boys

162 Note 55 "I want to tell you . . ." *Seven Gothic Tales*, p. 79.

164 Note 56 "I would like Beethoven . . ." *Out of Africa*, p. 227.

X Essayist and Plagiarist

170 Note 57 "Everybody will remember . . ." *Seven Gothic Tales*, pp. 198–9.

171 Note 58 "Pride is the faith . . ." *Out of Africa*, p. 261.

172 Note 59 "Each puppet has . . ." Heinrich von Kleist, "Über das Marionettentheater," *Berliner Abendblätter* (December 12, 13, 14 and 15, 1810). Translation from *Five Essays on Klee* (published by Merle Armitage and distributed by Duell, Sloan & Pearce, New York, 1960).

172 Note 60 "All of life becomes . . ." Eric O. Johannesson, *The World of Isak Dinesen*, 1961, p. 89.

173 *Note 61*   "Kierkegaard . . ."   Tania especially enjoyed her many discussions about Kierkegaard with William Kennedy in 1953. They also went together to examine the Kierkegaard manuscripts. William Kennedy first met Tania in 1946; in 1953 he recorded her reading of "Letter from a King" and many hours of conversation were also put on tape.

173 *Note 62*   ". . . it was far better . . ."   *Seven Gothic Tales*, p. 17.

175 *Note 63*   "Heretica is, I feel . . ."   Letter from Karen Blixen to Bent Mohn, Rungstedlund, October 21, 1952.

176 *Note 64*   ". . . an insignificant prank."   Poul Sørensen using the pseudonym Joachim Stenzelius in *Gys og Genfærd, Danske Spøgelseshistorier* (Borgen, Copenhagen, 1952); "Enkelegen" in *All Världens Berättare* magazine (March 3, 1953).

176 *Note 65*   "But there was another book . . ."   Eugene Walter, "Isak Dinesen Conquers Rome," *Harper's Magazine* (February 1965).

178 *Note 66*   "It was about 7:40 . . ."   *Ibid.*

PART FOUR

I "Queen of the Northern Monkeys"

184 *Note 67*   "At times he simultaneously . . ."   James Thrall Soby, *Tchelitchew* (Museum of Modern Art, New York, 1942).

188 *Note 68*   "In my last ten years . . ."   *Shadows on the Grass*, p. 58.

189 *Note 69*   "Am I a gentleman . . ."   Ernest Hemingway, *A Moveable Feast* (Charles Scribner's Sons, New York, 1964), p. 87.

192 *Note 70*   "I ought not to undertake . . ."   Eugene Walter, "Isak Dinesen Conquers Rome."

II "A Magnificent Spectre"

PAGE
195   *Note 71*   " 'Children,' he later remarked . . ."   *Isak Dinesen: A Memorial,* p. 199.

196   *Note 72*   "Under the pseudonym . . ."   The American Academy of Arts and Letters and The National Institute of Arts and Letters, May 22, 1957.

197   *Note 73*   "Dear Monkey Prime Minister . . ."   Eugene Walter, "Isak Dinesen Conquers Rome."

198   *Note 74*   "Dear Parmenia . . ."   Letter from Isak Dinesen to the author, October 16, 1957.

198   *Note 75*   "Tania literally made . . ."   Letter from Eugene Haynes to the author, no date.

III Work and Repose

205   *Note 76*   "You will see here in Denmark . . ."   *Isak Dinesen: A Memorial,* p. 102.

205   *Note 77*   *Politiken* (November 29 and December 13, 1952).

206   *Note 78*   Frydenlund. All efforts to locate this township failed, and it was only in 1963, a year after Isak Dinesen's death, that the author discovered the community of Frydenlund, which had its own post office from February 25, 1878, until December 26, 1888, with Ludvig Motzfeldt as first postmaster.

IV Anecdotes of Destiny

213   *Note 79*   "I have been terribly ill . . ."   Letter from Isak Dinesen to the author, April 25, 1958.

215   *Note 80*   "Will each of you . . ."   Reprinted as "Tale of Rungstedlund," *Vogue* (November 1962).

215   *Note 81*   "As I was one day . . ."   *Ibid.*

PAGE

216   *Note 82*   "I discovered . . ."   Isak Dinesen interview, *Politiken* (October 10, 1958).

216   *Note 83*   "It is with this book . . ."   *Ibid.*

217   *Note 84*   "The novel will be . . ."   *Ibid.*

217   *Note 85*   "It is a monumental . . ."   Curtis Cate, "Isak Dinesen: The Scheherazade of Our Times," *Cornhill* (Winter 1959–60).

219   *Note 86*   "We had three . . ."   Letter from Thomas Dinesen to the author, November 12, 1966.

V *New York*

222   *Note 87*   *Publishers' Weekly* (January 12, 1959).

222   *Note 88*   "She was very, very frail . . ." *Isak Dinesen: A Memorial*, p. 37.

223   *Note 89*   "the chief platform . . ." Glenway Wescott, "Isak Dinesen Tells a Tale," *Harper's Magazine* (March 1960); reprinted in *Images of Truth*, 1962.

224   *Note 90*   "One must imagine . . ."   *Out of Africa*, p. 47.

228   *Note 91*   "Although I had seen . . ."   *Isak Dinesen: A Memorial*, pp. 40 ff.

229   *Note 92*   "Unfair clubwomen . . ."   *Images of Truth*, p. 150.

VI *The Daily Rose*

234   *Note 93*   Drude Angel appears in "Copenhagen Season" (*Last Tales*) and was modeled on Tania's aunt and godmother, Christentze Dinesen.

235   *Note 94*   Richard Avedon and Truman Capote, *Observations* (Simon and Schuster, New York, 1959).

PAGE

235 *Note 95* "Truman Capote's book . . ." *Holly [Breakfast at Tiffany's]* (Gyldendal, Copenhagen, 1960).

237 *Note 96* ". . . by a quarter to twelve . . ." *Out of Africa*, p. 47.

238 *Note 97* ". . . And as I told you . . ." *Isak Dinesen: A Memorial*, p. 159.

238 *Note 98* "I chose him . . ." Letter from Bent Mohn to the author, April 4, 1966.

VII Shadows on the Grass

241 *Note 99* "Dear heart . . ." *Last Tales*, p. 189.

243 *Note 100* "The news of Farah's . . ." *Shadows on the Grass*, p. 135.

243 *Note 101* "was the best servant . . ." *Ibid.*, pp. 136–7.

243 *Note 102* "in the midst of the maze . . ." *Ibid.*, pp. 144 ff.

249 *Note 103* "Where's my Andersen?" Monica Stirling, *The Wild Swan* (Collins, London, 1965), p. 19.

PART FIVE

I A Talent for Friendship

255 *Note 104* "that small band . . ." Sybille Bedford in *Isak Dinesen: A Memorial*, pp. 21–2.

255 *Note 105* "give her love to it . . ." Letter from Laurens van der Post to the author, July 22, 1963.

258 *Note 106* "Farah and I drove home . . ." *Out of Africa*, p. 342.

259 *Note 107* "I only regret . . ." *Isak Dinesen: A Memorial*, p. 196.

PAGE
259 *Note 108* "I have a talent . . ." *Observations,* p. 143.

263 *Note 109* "The fairy tale should . . ." Marianne Thalmann, *The Romantic Fairy Tale* (The University of Michigan Press, Ann Arbor, 1964), p. 34.

II *Last Fling*

266 *Note 110* "on every page . . ." Thomas Mann, *Freud, Goethe, Wagner* (Alfred A. Knopf, New York, 1937), pp. 10–11.

271 *Note 111* "Wait a little . . ." *Shadows on the Grass,* pp. 45–6.

271 *Note 112* "woman, pride and jewel . . ." Romain Gary, "Twilight of the Goddess," *Ladies' Home Journal* (March 1965).

III *"My Life, I Will Not Let You Go . . ."*

279 *Note 113* "Time has reduced her . . ." *Observations,* p. 142.

281 *Note 114* "If I discussed . . ." *Isak Dinesen: A Memorial,* p. 204.

282 *Note 115* "An old lady . . ." *Out of Africa,* p. 276.

IV *Partings*

286 *Note 116* "The palace [at Hirschholm] . . ." *Seven Gothic Tales,* pp. 446–7.

289 *Note 117* Øregaard, the beautiful house and park of Tania's maternal great-grandfather A. N. Hansen, halfway between Copenhagen and Rungsted, which is now a museum.

289 *Note 118* "with both of us before her . . ." Solita Solano, notes on her visit at Rungstedlund, June 1962.

290 *Note 119* "I remember that dinner . . ." Letter from Eugene Haynes to the author, undated.

PAGE

290 *Note 120* "Tania came in alone . . ."   Letter from Viggo Kjær Petersen
to the author, August 9, 1964.

V *The World Withdraws*

295 *Note 121* ". . . a shadow hastened . . ."   *Out of Africa,* p. 231.

295 *Note 122* "Please thank Elizabeth . . ."   Elizabeth Jenks Clark, who
shares a house with Solita Solano at Orgeval on the outskirts
of Paris.

295 *Note 123* "As I looked . . ."   *Out of Africa,* p. 381.

Bibliography

BOOKS BY ISAK DINESEN

(*in English and Danish*)

1934   ISAK DINESEN, *Seven Gothic Tales* (Harrison Smith and Robert Haas, New York; Putnam, London).

1935   ——, *Syv Fantastiske Fortællinger* (Reitzels, Copenhagen).

1937   KAREN BLIXEN, *Den Afrikanske Farm* (Gyldendal, Copenhagen).

      ISAK DINESEN, *Out of Africa* (Putnam, London).

1938   ——, *Out of Africa* (Random House, New York).

1942   ——, *Winter's Tales* (Random House, New York; Putnam, London).

      KAREN BLIXEN, *Vinter-Eventyr* (Gyldendal, Copenhagen).

1944   PIERRE ANDRÉZEL, *Gengældelsens Veje*, "translated into Danish by Clara Svendsen" (Gyldendal, Copenhagen).

1946   ——, *The Angelic Avengers* (Putnam, London).

1947   ——, *The Angelic Avengers* (Random House, New York).

1957   ISAK DINESEN, *Last Tales* (Random House, New York; Putnam, London).

      KAREN BLIXEN, *Sidste Fortællinger* (Gyldendal, Copenhagen).

1958   ISAK DINESEN, *Anecdotes of Destiny* (Random House, New York; Michael Joseph, London).

      KAREN BLIXEN, *Skæbne-Anekdoter* (Gyldendal, Copenhagen).

1960   ——, *Skygger paa Græsset* (Gyldendal, Copenhagen).

1961   ISAK DINESEN, *Shadows on the Grass* (Random House, New York; Michael Joseph, London).

1962   OSCEOLA (posthumous), collected early stories and poems (Gyldendal, Copenhagen).

1963   ISAK DINESEN, *Ehrengard* (posthumous) (Random House, New York; Michael Joseph, London).

      KAREN BLIXEN, *Ehrengard,* translated into Danish by Clara Svendsen (Gyldendal, Copenhagen).

1964   ————, memorial edition of collected works (Gyldendal, Copenhagen).

1965   ————, *Essays* (Gyldendal, Copenhagen).

OTHER PUBLISHED WORKS BY ISAK DINESEN

1907   OSCEOLA, "Eneboerne," *Tilskueren* (August), pp. 609–35.

      OSCEOLA, "Pløjeren," *Gads Danske Magasin* (October), pp. 50–59. Reprinted in *Osceola.*

      OSCEOLA, "Familien de Cats," *Tilskueren* (January), pp. 1–19.

1925   K. BLIXEN-FINECKE, "Ex-Africa" [poem], *Tilskueren* (April), pp. 244–46; also in *Berlingske Søndags Magasin* (December 6, 1942), pp. 1–2. Reprinted in *Osceola.*

1926   KAREN BLIXEN-FINECKE, "Sandhedens Hævn: En Marionetkomedie," *Tilskueren* (May), pp. 329–44. Reprinted Karen Blixen, Gyldendal, Copenhagen, 1960.

1929   "En Stjerne" [poem], in Thomas Dinesen, *No Man's Land* (Reitzels, Copenhagen). Reprinted in *Osceola.*

1938   ISAK DINESEN, "Karyatiderne: En Ufuldendt Fantastisk Fortælling," *Tilskueren* (April), pp. 269–308.

      KAREN BLIXEN, "Om Retskrivning," *Politiken* (March 23–24). Reprinted Gyldendal, Copenhagen, 1949, and in *Essays,* 1965.

1943   ISAK DINESEN, "Sorrow-acre," *Ladies' Home Journal* (May), pp. 22 ff. From *Winter's Tales.*

1948   KAREN BLIXEN, "Breve fra et Land i Krig," *Heretica,* Vol. I, No. 4, pp. 264–87; No. 5, pp. 332–55; also in *Essays,* 1965.

1949   ISAK DINESEN, "The Uncertain Heiress," *Saturday Evening Post* (December 10), pp. 35 ff.

1950   KAREN BLIXEN, *Farah* (Wivel, Copenhagen). Reprinted in *Shadows on the Grass.*

      ISAK DINESEN, "Babette's Feast," *Ladies' Home Journal* (July), pp. 34 ff. Reprinted in *Anecdotes of Destiny.*

      ————, "The Ring," *Ladies' Home Journal* (July), pp. 36 ff.; *Harper's*

Bazaar (October 1958), pp. 159 ff. Reprinted in *Anecdotes of Destiny.*

KAREN BLIXEN, "Hartvig Frisch som Nabo," in *Hartvig Frisch* (Fremad, Copenhagen).

1951 ———, *Daguerreotypier* (Gyldendal); also in *Essays,* 1965.

ISAK DINESEN, "The Ghost Horses," *Ladies' Home Journal* (October), pp. 56 ff.

1952 KAREN BLIXEN, *Kardinalens Tredie Historie,* illus. Erik Clemmsen (Gyldendal, Copenhagen). Reprinted in *Last Tales.*

1952 ———, *Babette's Gæstebud* (Fremad, Copenhagen).

———, *Omkring den Nye Lov om Dyreforsøg* (Politikens Forlag, Copenhagen).

1953 ———, "Samtale om Natten i København," *Heretica,* Vol. VI, No. 5, pp. 465–94. Reprinted in *Last Tales.*

ISAK DINESEN, "The Immortal Story," *Ladies' Home Journal* (February), pp. 34 ff. Reprinted in *Anecdotes of Destiny.*

KAREN BLIXEN, *En Baaltale med 14 Aars Forsinkelse* (Berlingske Forlag, Copenhagen); *Det Danske Magasin,* Vol. I, No. 2, pp. 65 ff.; also in *Essays,* 1965.

1954 ———, "Dykkeren," *Vindrosen,* Vol. I (November), pp. 400–14. Reprinted in *Anecdotes of Destiny.*

1955 ISAK DINESEN, "The Cloak," *Ladies' Home Journal* (May), pp. 52 ff. Reprinted in *Last Tales* as "The Cloak," "Night Walk," "Of Secret Thoughts and of Heaven."

KAREN BLIXEN, *Spøgelseshestene* (Fremad, Copenhagen).

1956 ———, review of Sacheverell Sitwell, *Denmark,* in *Sunday Times of London* (May 6), p. 5.

1957 ISAK DINESEN, "The Caryatids: An Unfinished Gothic Tale," *Ladies' Home Journal* (November), pp. 64 ff. Reprinted in *Last Tales.*

———, "A Country Tale," *Botteghe Oscure,* Vol. XIX (Rome), pp. 367–417; and *Ladies' Home Journal* (March 1960), pp. 52 ff. Reprinted in *Last Tales.*

———, "Echoes," *Atlantic Monthly* (November), pp. 96–100. Reprinted in *Last Tales.*

———, "The Nobleman's Wife," *Harper's Bazaar* (November), pp. 139 ff. From "Tales of Two Old Gentlemen," *Last Tales.*

KAREN BLIXEN, "Den Store Gestus," *Alt for Damerne,* No. 51, pp. 10–14. Reprinted in *Anecdotes of Destiny.*

1958 ———, "H.C. Branner: Rytteren," *Bazar* (April), pp. 50–63; (May), pp. 71–94; also in *Essays,* 1965.

KAREN BLIXEN, "Rungstedlund: En Radiotale," in *Hilsen til Otto Gelsted* (Aarhus: Sirius).

1959   ISAK DINESEN, "The Wine of the Tetrarch," *Atlantic Monthly* (December), pp. 125–30. From "The Deluge at Norderney," *Seven Gothic Tales;* version used in American recitals.

1960   ———, "The Blue Eyes," *Ladies' Home Journal* (January), p. 38. From "Peter and Rosa," *Winter's Tales;* version used in American recital.

———, "Alexander and the Sybil," from Glenway Wescott, "Isak Dinesen Tells a Tale," *Harper's* (March), pp. 69–70. From "Tales of Two Old Gentlemen," *Last Tales.*

———, "On Mottoes of My Life," in *Proceedings of The American Academy of Arts and Letters and The National Institute of Arts and Letters,* Second Series, No. 10, pp. 345–58. Reprinted Karen Blixen, *On Mottoes of My Life* (Ministry of Foreign Affairs, Copenhagen, 1962), and in *Essays,* 1965.

KAREN BLIXEN, Introduction to Truman Capote, *Holly* [*Breakfast at Tiffany's*] (Gyldendal, Copenhagen).

1961   ISAK DINESEN, Introduction to Olive Schreiner, *The Story of an African Farm* (Limited Editions Club, New York).

1962   KAREN BLIXEN, Introduction to Basil Davidson, *Det Genfundne Afrika* (Gyldendal, Copenhagen).

ISAK DINESEN, Introduction to Hans Christian Andersen, *Thumbelina and Other Fairy Tales* (Macmillan, New York and London).

———, "Tale of Rungstedlund," *Vogue* (November), pp. 132 ff. Condensed from "Rungstedlund: En Radiotale."

———, "The Secret of Rosenbad,". *Ladies' Home Journal* (December), pp. 51 ff. Condensation of *Ehrengard.*

SOME BOOKS AND ARTICLES
RELATING TO ISAK DINESEN

BROR VON BLIXEN-FINECKE, *African Hunter* [*Nyama*, Holger Schildt, Stockholm, 1936] (Cassell, London, 1937; Alfred A. Knopf, New York, 1938).

MARK VAN DOREN, "The Eighth Gothic Tale," *The Private Reader* (Holt, New York, 1942), pp. 277–81.

TOM KRISTENSSEN, "Syv Fantastiske Fortællinger," *Mellem Krigene* (Gyldendal, Copenhagen, 1946), pp. 134–40.

HANS BRIX, *Karen Blixens Eventyr* (Gyldendal, Copenhagen, 1949).

HANS BRIX, "*Sandhedens Hævn* til Isak Dinesen: 'Vejene omkring Pisa," "Et Eventyr af Karen Blixen," *Analyser og Problemer*, Vol. VI (Gyldendal, Copenhagen, 1950), pp. 286-306.

CHRISTIAN ELLING, "Karen Blixen," in *Danske Digtere i det Tyvende Aarhundrede* (Gads, Copenhagen, 1951), pp. 521–55.

ERNST FRANDSEN, "Udsigt over et Halvt Aarhundrede," in the above, pp. 5–32.

AAGE HENRIKSEN, *Karen Blixen og Marionetterne* (Wivel, Copenhagen, 1952).

VAGN RIISAGER, *Karen Blixen* (Gyldendal, Copenhagen, 1952).

JØRGEN CLAUDI, *Contemporary Danish Authors* (Det Danske Selskab, Copenhagen, 1952), pp. 109–14.

BØRGE G. MADSEN, "Isak Dinesen, a Modern Aristocrat," *American-Scandinavian Review* (Winter 1953), pp. 328–32.

JØRGEN GUSTAVA BRANDT, "Et Essay om Karen Blixen," *Heretica*, Vol. VI, No. 2 (1953), pp. 200–23; No. 3, pp. 300–20.

LOUISE BOGAN, "Isak Dinesen," *Selected Criticism* (Noonday, New York, 1955), pp. 231–34.

AAGE HENRIKSEN, *Guder og Galgefugle* (N.S.K., Oslo, 1956).

HARALD NIELSEN, *Karen Blixen: Studie i Litterær Mystik* (Borgens, Copenhagen, 1956).

JOHN DAVENPORT, "A Noble Pride: The Art of Karen Blixen," *The Twentieth Century* (March 1956), pp. 264–74.

EUGENE WALTER, "Isak Dinesen," *Paris Review* (Autumn 1956), pp. 43–59.

JOHANNES ROSENDAHL, *Karen Blixen: Fire Foredrag* (Gyldendal, Copenhagen, 1957).

LOUIS E. GRANDJEAN, *Blixens Animus* (Grandjeans Publications Fond, Copenhagen, 1957).

P. M. MITCHELL, *A History of Danish Literature* (Gyldendal, Copenhagen, 1957), pp. 275–78.

JEAN STAFFORD, "Isak Dinesen: Master Teller of Tales," *Horizon* (September 1959), pp. 111–12.

CURTIS CATE, "Isak Dinesen: The Scheherazade of Our Times," *Cornhill*, (Winter 1959–60), pp. 120–37.

———, "Isak Dinesen," *Atlantic Monthly* (December 1959), pp. 151–55.

ERIC O. JOHANNESSON, *The World of Isak Dinesen* (University of Washington Press, Seattle, 1961).

GLENWAY WESCOTT, "Isak Dinesen Tells a Tale," *Harper's Magazine* (March 1960); reprinted in Wescott, *Images of Truth*, as "Isak Dinesen, the Storyteller" (Harper & Row, New York, 1962), Ch. 6, p. 151.

Karen Blixen, memorial anthology, with prose and verse by European, American and African contributors, translated into Danish and edited by

Clara Svendsen and Ole Wivel (Gyldendal, Copenhagen, 1962).

KUNO POULSEN, "Karen Blixens Gamle og Nye Testamente," *Vindrosen*, Vol. X, No. 5 (1963), pp. 364–80.

Isak Dinesen, memorial anthology (Random House, New York, 1964).

HANNE MARIE and WERNER SVENDSEN, *Geschichte der dänischen Literatur* (Gyldendal, Copenhagen, 1964), pp. 478–80.

HOWARD GREEN, "Isak Dinesen," *The Hudson Review* (Winter 1964–65).

ROBERT LANGBAUM, *The Gayety of Vision* (Random House, New York, 1965).

AAGE HENRIKSEN, *Det Guddommelige Barn—og Andre Essays om Karen Blixen* (Gyldendal, Copenhagen, 1965).

PETER HILL BEARD, *The End of the Game* (The Viking Press, New York, 1965).

VIGGO KJÆR PETERSEN, *Danske Digtere i det Tyvende Aarhundrede* (Gads, Copenhagen, 1966), pp. 699–734.

TORBEN BROSTRØM, *Dansk Litteraturhistorie*, Vol. 4 (Politikens Forlag, Copenhagen), pp. 195–210.

CLARA SVENDSEN, "Karen Blixen som Maler." *Almanak*, Vol. I, No. 6 (1967).

HANS ANDERSEN, "Om Karen Blixen." *Almanak*, Vol. I, No. 6 (1967).

Index